Mail @ the Millennium

Mail @ the Millennium

Will the Postal Service Go Private?

edited by Edward L. Hudgins

CATO INSTITUTE

Washington, D.C.

Library of Congress Cataloging-in-Publication Data

Mail @ the millennium : Will the postal service go private? / edited by Edward L. Hudgins.
    p. cm.
  Includes bibliographical references and index.
  ISBN 1-930865-01-5 — ISBN 1-930865-02-3
  1. United States Postal Service. 2. Postal service—Deregulation—United States. 3.
Privatization—United States. I. Title: Mail at the millennium. II. Hudgins, Edward Lee,
1952- III. Cato Institute.

HE6731 .M22 2000
354.75'9'0973—dc21

                                                 00-060110

Printed in the United States of America

CATO INSTITUTE
1000 Massachusetts Ave., N.W.
Washington, D.C. 20001

Contents

Acknowledgments

The papers in this volume are from the Cato Institute conference on "Mail @ the Millennium: The Future of Private Postal Service," which was held on December 2, 1998. I wish to acknowledge the generous support for this conference from R.R. Donnelley & Sons Company and Fingerhut Companies, Inc.

I also wish to acknowledge and thank those who chaired panels at the conference. James C. Miller III is counselor at Citizens for a Sound Economy. Among his many positions, he served as chairman of the Federal Trade Commission from 1981 to 1985, and director of the Office of Management and Budget from 1985 to 1988.

Alan Reynolds is a senior fellow and director of economic research at the Hudson Institute's Washington, D.C., office, as well as senior editor of that institute's quarterly, *American Outlook*. He also has served as chief economist at the First National Bank of Chicago, and at Polyconomics Inc.

Thomas Lenard is the Vice President for Research at the Progressive Policy Institute. Before coming to PPI he was with the consulting firm of Heiden Associates. In the 1980s he served as an economic advisor to the Office of Management and Budget, and also was a senior economist at the Council on Wage and Price Stability.

All of these individuals have written on postal matters. Their knowledge of that subject and of economics in general allowed them to lead their conference in lively and intellectually stimulating discussions.

PART I

THE STATE OF THE POSTAL SERVICE

1. The Coming Revolution in Mail Delivery

Edward L. Hudgins

In the past, periodic calls for the privatization of the U.S. Postal Service usually focused on that government monopoly's inefficiencies, and the potential cost savings and better service that would result if there were market competition in mail delivery. But recently other issues have come to the surface that make the adverse effects of preserving the status quo even more onerous and the benefits of privatization even greater.

The Postal Service is seeing its most profitable business, such as first-class correspondence and bill paying, being taken up by e-mails, faxes, online communications, and private carriers. Further, the regime governing the nearly 900,000 mostly unionized postal workers has kept labor costs high and been too inflexible to allow for needed efficiency changes. Those facts mean that the Postal Service is desperate to find new sources of revenue in new sectors to make up for projected future losses. The USPS thus is entering electronic commerce and other sectors far removed from delivering first- and third-class mail.

But the expansion of USPS product lines poses a serious threat to private-sector providers because the Postal Service enjoys important, government-established unfair advantages. First, the USPS, as opposed to its private competitors, pays no federal, state, or local taxes, and it can borrow from the U.S. Treasury. Second, it is exempt from most government regulations to which private businesses are subject. Third, even though it is a government entity, it is exempt from

Edward L. Hudgins is the director of regulatory studies at the Cato Institute and the editor of the 1996 book *The Last Monopoly: Privatizing the Postal Service for the Information Age.*

many of the constraints to which all other government agencies are subject.

Fourth, and perhaps worst of all, the Postal Service has regulatory authority that it can use against competitors or to favor one enterprise over another.

An October 21, 1999, General Accounting Office (GAO) report was correct in saying that "The Postal Service may be nearing the end of an era." Postal agencies in other countries have recognized that the communications and information revolution, with e-mails, the Internet, and private delivery companies, is making monopoly mail carriers obsolete. New Zealand and Sweden have lifted their mail monopolies. The largest mail carrier in Europe, Germany's Deutsche Post, has been reorganized as a joint-stock company under private management, with its competitive services subject to taxes and regulations like any private enterprise. In 2000 it will begin selling stock to the public, and on January 1, 2003, its monopoly will be repealed.

In the 21st century the U.S. Postal Service will need to change if it is to remain economically useful and fiscally viable. But with its monopoly and regulatory authority, the USPS will be the bull in the information economy's china shop, smashing firms and markets. To ensure quality delivery to meet customer demands at appropriate prices, the government Postal Service should be sold off to the American public and the postal workers themselves and have its monopoly and regulatory powers removed.

The Information Revolution

The last decade of the 20th century has seen the communications and information revolution burst into the economy and society much faster than the industrial revolution two centuries ago. Morgan Stanley analysts estimate that the number of Americans using personal computers was 144 million in 1995 and will be 225 million in the year 2000. The percentage using e-mail will rise during that period from 24.31 percent to 89.90 percent and the portion using the World Wide Web will grow from 6.25 percent to 67.56 percent. The power and storage capacity of PCs also continue to increase.

Those tools have changed the way business is done. E-mails and faxes now are a common means for routine business communications as well as messages between friends and family members. Online retail sales continue to grow, led by enterprises like Amazon.com, which distributes books at significant discounts. Retailing is one part of emerging e-commerce, with its supporting infrastructure. Businesses now can process and coordinate ordering, billing, shipments, inventory, accounting, and the like. The largest part of e-commerce is not direct business-to-customer sales but, rather, business-to-business transactions.[1]

The communications and information economy has been facilitated by and has helped promote the integration of functions that once were thought of as separate. Cable and satellite dishes compete with broadcasting to bring television programs into the home and also are capable of providing access to the Internet. Telecommunications companies compete to offer wire and cell-phone service as well as Internet access. Internet companies offer e-mail, links to one's bank accounts, and even telephone service. Public events that once could be viewed only live on television or later on videotape are now netcast in real time, thus allowing individuals access to hundreds or even thousands of events from all over the country and the world. Many of the netcast events are archived by the organizations staging them so they can be viewed anytime after the event.

Integrated and alternative forms of communications, however, have not done away with physical materials. Paperless offices are far in the future. Nor has the communications and information revolution done away with the need for delivery services. Although individuals can now read all the works of Shakespeare and Cicero online, more seem to be purchasing such books and every other imaginable consumer product over the Internet. Those products must be delivered to their homes by quick, reliable, and cost-effective transportation providers, whether the USPS or private competitors like Federal Express (FedEx), Guaranteed Overnight Delivery, and United Parcel Service (UPS).

The Postal Service faces severe problems in the new cyber era. Package delivery, a likely growth market in the future, will continue to be dominated by private companies. The Postal Service in its current form is unlikely to cash in on that market. Also, the USPS has seen a decline in international delivery services in the face of private competition.

---

[1]See James P. Lucier, "Dangers in Cyberspace," in this volume, p. 45.

Further, an October 21, 1999, GAO report found that although overall mail volume will continue to increase over the next decade, first-class mail volume will decline on average .8 percent annually between 1999 and 2008.[2] Users of first-class mail currently pay premium rates. That mail is a principal source of revenue for the Postal Service and covers two-thirds of USPS institutional costs. A chief reason for the drop is that in the future more bills will be paid through means other than first-class mail. Already customers can have monthly payments for everything from automobiles to satellite television either taken out of a checking account or charged to a credit card. Banking reform will offer more nonmail bill-paying options. Most important will be electronic bill-paying via the Internet. Currently such payments in the mail stream account for some $17 billion in annual USPS revenue of total annual revenues of close to $65 billion. That is bill-paying revenue that could be lost in the next decade. In addition, the Postal Service could see more revenue losses as advertisers that use mail begin to rely more on their postings on the Internet.

Unfair Competition

In the face of declining first-class mail and heavy competition in overnight and package services, the Postal Service has two options: cut costs or seek new sources of revenue (or both). Cost-cutting presents a chronic problem with which the Postal Service has been burdened since the 1970 reorganization: a labor regime that keeps many costs high and restricts the flexibility of the Postal Service to employ labor in the most efficient manner. In spite of billions of dollars invested in new equipment and other labor-saving plans over the years, labor still accounts for about 80 percent of Postal Service costs. Increasing productivity is another way to bring costs in line. And although the Postal Service has made some productivity improvements,[3] in the future such progress is unlikely to make up for lost revenue.

Thus it is not surprising to find the Postal Service seeking new sources of revenue outside of first- and third-class mail delivery. The

[2]Bernard Ungar, "U.S. Postal Service: Challenges to Sustaining Performance Improvements Remain Formidable on the Brink of the 21st Century" (Washington: General Accounting Office Report GAO/T-GGD-00-2, October 21, 1999), pp. 3–4.
[3]Ibid, p. 18.

Postal Service, for example, is offering a check-processing operation, REMITCO, out of a facility it recently purchased on Long Island, New York.[4] It is considering other e-commerce ventures that are proving lucrative for postal services in other countries. They include offering business-to-business infrastructure and other services to facilitate purchasing, shipping, inventory, billing, and the like. The Postal Service wants to be the principal provider of secure, online communications—for example, electronic signatures and encrypted messages. It wants to match all physical addresses to e-mail addresses to produce a national database that will place it at an advantage against other shippers. Postmaster General William Henderson has been quite open about his plans to make the Postal Service a leading player in online commerce.[5]

But the Postal Service has many unfair advantages over private-sector competitors. Most obviously, it does not pay federal, state, or local taxes. Supporters might argue that the Postal Service should not pay taxes because part of its mandated mission as a government monopoly is to provide delivery of first-class mail to every address in the country at a uniform price, even if it takes a loss on certain routes. But that argument collapses when made about services with which the private sector is allowed to compete, and especially new services that have little to do with mail delivery.

The Postal Service also is exempt from most regulations to which private businesses are subject. Unlike FedEx or UPS, it need not even pay parking tickets. Postal officials sometimes like to take both sides on the question of whether the USPS should be treated like a government agency, which in fact it is, or a business like any other, albeit one with a special mission. But when it comes to such regulations, the Postal Service proudly wears its government-agency identity, and claims regulatory exemptions. Recently, however, Congress did make the Postal Service subject to Occupational Safety and Health Administration regulations. But for the most part USPS operates in an unregulated world of its own.

Not only is the Postal Service not subject to the same regulations as the private sector, it is exempt from many of the constraints that safeguard the public from abuses of power by other government

[4]Lucier.
[5]Stephan Barr, "Sorting Out Mail's Place in Internet Age," *Washington Post,* January 24, 2000, p. A1.

agencies. That is a serious problem because the Postal Service has regulatory power that it can use against its competitors or simply in an arbitrary manner. For example, it is not subject to Title 5, Chapter 7 of the U.S. Code, which affords citizens an appeals process for government actions that are "arbitrary and capricious." It is exempt from the Paperwork Regulation Act, which requires government agencies promulgating regulations to adopt the regulations that have the least costly impact on small businesses. It is also exempt from the Regulatory Flexibility Act, which requires government agencies to conduct cost-benefit analyses of proposed regulations.

The dangers of leaving the Postal Service unrestrained by such normal safeguards, and a taste of what is to come if it is allowed to offer nonmail services in the future, can be seen in several recent cases.

Mailbox Regulations

Commercial mail-receiving agencies (CMRAs) such as Mail Boxes, Etc. have emerged in the past decade to meet the demands of small businesses that otherwise might rent post office (P.O.) boxes. CMRAs, unlike post offices, have more convenient business hours, sometimes 24 hours a day, and they accept deliveries from private carriers such as FedEx as well as from the Postal Service. They also give small enterprises a professional aura, allowing those businesses to list an address as a number or suite, such as "123 Main St. #401."

In late 1997 the Postal Service announced its intention to introduce new regulations to prevent the use of private mail boxes to commit mail fraud, certainly a legitimate concern. But of 8,107 public comments lodged, all but 10 were opposed to the proposed regulations.[6] The Postal Service went ahead anyway, declaring in the *Federal Register* on March 25, 1999, that if they wanted the USPS to continue to deliver their mail, CMRA customers were required to fill out a new Form 1583 and produce two forms of identification, including a photo ID. Copies of each ID were to be kept by the CMRA and the Postal Service. Customers using their boxes for business were to provide home addresses and phone numbers. Most frightening to many

---

[6]For a full discussion of this issue see Rick Merritt, "The U.S. Postal Service War on Private Mailboxes and Privacy Rights," Cato Institute Briefing Paper no. 48, July 30, 1999.

customers, according to Form 1583, that information would be made available to anyone for the asking.[7]

All private box holders also were required to contact every person or entity that might send them mail in the future and advise them that the acronym "PMB" (Private Mail Box) must precede the renter's box number on a separate line in the address. Use of "suite" or "apartment" in the address was banned. The Postal Service stated that after a certain date it would not deliver mail to CMRAs without the PMB code.

The Postal Service made no attempt to determine how serious a problem mail fraud using CMRAs really was. Inspector General numbers show that over the most recent one-year period for which there are figures, only 1,588 or 14.8 percent of convictions for mail-related crimes involved fraud. But neither the IG nor Postal Service could say how many cases involved private versus P.O. or home boxes.

The plan to release confidential information to anyone interested seemed to violate the USPS's own privacy regulations listed in the *Code of Federal Regulations*.[8] Thus on June 9, 1999, in the *Federal Register*, the USPS posted its intention to change Title 39, U.S. Code, Part 265, the prohibition "against disclosure of information in PS Form 1583." The *Federal Register* entry read that

> Under the rule change, the recorded business name, address, and telephone number of the addressee using a . . . CMRA private mail box . . . for purposes of soliciting business with the public will be furnished to any person upon request without charge.[9]

The Postal Service did not consider the adverse effects of such a policy. By making business box holders' personal information available to anyone, these regulations, a breach of the Postal Service's own privacy rules, aid "identity thieves": criminals who steal other people's credit card numbers, charge bills to others, steal from bank accounts, and the like.

Women who use private boxes for business purposes could find unstable ex-husbands or stalkers acquiring home addresses courtesy of the post office. A June 15, 1999, National Coalition Against Domestic Violence "Action Alert" stated, "These unnecessary regula-

---

[7]*Federal Register*, Vol. 64, no. 57, March 25, 1999, pp. 14,385–14,391.
[8]39 *Code of Federal Regulations*, § 266.4 (1998) at 130.
[9]*Federal Register*, Vol. 64, no. 110, June 9, 1999, pp. 30,929.

tions make it more difficult for a battered woman to effectively use a commercial postal box to keep her location confidential . . . The impact for domestic violence victims is potentially fatal."

As a result of protests about this regulation the Postal Service again changed its new rules to make confidential information available only to law enforcement officials. Making regulations on the fly illustrates the danger of leaving regulatory power unchecked in the hands of an arbitrary and capricious government agency.

The Postal Service did not shy away from using the excuse of preventing mail fraud to expand its powers. Owners of executive office suites that provide tenants with an operator to take phone calls, a location for mail and package delivery, and perhaps a small office, were surprised when the USPS declared in an April 29 memo that their operations, which had never been regulated by the Postal Service, now will be covered by the new regulations. Enterprises that forward mail to individuals who travel the country in recreational vehicles also will fall victim to the new rules. None of those businesses nor their tenants or clients had a chance to comment two years ago on the regulations to which they will now be subject.

The Postal Service made no attempt to determine the costs of the new regulations or whether less intrusive alternatives were available. CMRA customers will incur costs for new stationery, change-of-address notices, and the time spent processing and mailing out those notices. CMRAs will incur processing costs and will lose business. Rick Merritt, the head of Postal Watch, places the direct costs alone at between $619 million and $994 million. Add more for the time it will take recipients to enter those millions of changes of addresses.

If the Postal Service had been subject to the safeguards under which other government regulatory agencies operate, this ongoing costly, sloppy, and dangerous drama might have been avoided.[10] Such episodes give a preview of what will happen if the Postal Service offers nonmail services, backed by its regulatory powers.

Two lessons can be drawn. First, enterprises that offer services in competition with post office boxes are being harmed. Many CMRAs

---

[10]For a detailed discussion of the deficiencies of the Postal Service's rulemaking process, see Edward Hudgins, "Regulating Private Mail Boxes," testimony before the U.S. House of Representatives, Small Business Committee, Subcommittee on Regulatory Reform and Paperwork Reduction, October 19, 1999.

report a loss of business because of new regulations. Take the case of Sabiha Zubair, who operates a Mail Boxes, Etc. franchise in Fairfax, Virginia.[11] She tried diligently to abide by the new regulations. She collected the two forms of identification from her customers, including a photo ID, usually a driver's license. But that was not good enough for local postmaster Gerea Hayman. That postmaster insisted that Ms. Zubair verify that addresses given by customers were home addresses. In one case, for example, a police officer listed the address on his driver's license as a P.O. box. The postmaster insisted on calling many of Ms. Zubair's customers to find out home addresses. Further, in a letter dated September 20, 1999, that postmaster threatened to refuse mail delivery to Ms. Zubair's CMRA. Ms. Zubair spent countless hours trying to abide by unclear rules and undergoing harassment by the local postmaster, confirming Rick Merritt's estimates of the costs in time and effort incurred by CMRA operators. In the end, Ms. Zubair went from having 221 box renters down to 159, a 30 percent decline in business, principally because renters resented having to turn over personal information and being harassed about their addresses.

A second lesson that can be drawn from the current dispute is that in the future the Postal Service likely will form more partnerships with private-sector service providers, co-opting some firms or siding with them against their competitors. We find the corporate spokepersons from Mail Boxes, Etc. remarkably conciliatory toward the USPS with regard to the new mailbox regulations, much more so than many of its franchisees or box holders. This attitude might result from the fact that that private company also is in partnership with the Postal Service. Specifically, the USPS allowed Mail Boxes, Etc. to offer postal services in Mail Box Etc. facilities in a number of locations in the country where the quality of postal service has been low. And recently Postmaster General William Henderson announced that he wants to open operations in all Mail Boxes, Etc. outlets. Because this is an experimental service, the Postal Service can keep the arrangement exclusively with Mail Boxes, Etc. for the next year or so, to the exclusion of other competitors. Thus Mail Boxes,

---

[11]Information from author's talks with Ms. Zubair and from a letter of September 20, 1999, from Gerea Hayman, a local postmaster, to Ms. Zubair.

Etc. now has a vested interest in being not too critical of the Postal Service lest it destroy the arrangement.

Playing Favorites with Online Stamp Sales

An indication of the imperial aims of the Postal Service was witnessed in November 1997 when it tried to sneak into legislation a provision that would have granted it authority to purchase "such other obligations or securities as it deems appropriate, if such investment is closely related to Postal Service operations as determined by . . . [its] Board of Governors." Fortunately, the provision did not pass, but the attempt made clear several of the problems with the postal monopoly.

To begin, allowing government monopolies to purchase shares in private companies is a direct threat to the free market. The USPS, exempt from taxes and most regulations, is a $65 billion per year operation, compared with around $22.5 billion for UPS, $16 billion for FedEx, and $4 billion for Pitney Bowes, the largest supplier of postal meter equipment. The Postal Service's size advantage could allow it to absorb or snuff out competitors.

Speculation in 1997 was that the USPS wanted to use its new authority to acquire shares in E-Stamp, a start-up company that was developing software to allow customers to purchase postage and postmark mail online and through a personal computer. Normally customers purchase postage from the manufacturer of their metering equipment. The value of the postage purchased at any given time must be encoded into the metering machine. The customer sends a check to the manufacturer. The customer can then call the manufacturer, who gives the customer the information needed to encode into the metering machine the amount of postage desired.

The Postal Service regulates sales of postage, usually in the name of protecting against those who might "steal" postage by encoding more than they pay for into metering machines. But such regulation is unnecessary. If someone breaks the security of a metering machine and is able to postmark a greater dollar value of mail than has been paid for, the machine's manufacturer is liable for the loss and must pay the USPS the value of the postage used. Thus metering equipment manufacturers have a strong incentive to make their systems as secure as possible, even without USPS regulation. Acquiring E-Stamp would have allowed the USPS to favor that company at the expense of other competitors, since it could use its regulatory authority to hinder those competitors.

But failure of the provision in 1997, regarding purchasing companies, did not stop the Postal Service from exercising favoritism. It recently used its regulatory authority to allow E-Stamp to put into experimental use the E-Stamp version of an electronic postmarking system. One of E-Stamp's competitors, Pitney Bowes, had also developed a system that incorporated encryption software used by MasterCard to ensure secure transactions. One would think that a system safe enough for a major credit card company to use would be safe enough for the Postal Service.

Finally, in late 1998 Postal Service officials participated in the rollout of online stamp purchasing systems by E-Stamp and Stamps.com. A board member of the latter was none other than former Postmaster General Marvin Runyon. The favoritism by the Postal Service seemed clear. USPS was trying to promote more "diversity" in the market for metering mail by favoring those firms over the more established Pitney Bowes. The current Postmaster General, discussing e-commerce, admitted that the Postal Service pursues such strategies. He said, "If one private-sector company owned the platform for e-payments 10 years from now, you would have a monopoly model. You would have a model where you are forced to use one service."[12]

But for that government monopoly to set itself up as an antitrust enforcer not only is ironic but misses the point that customers in the market, not government agencies with regulatory powers, should decide from which online systems to purchase postage and postmarks.

Privatization Overseas

It is not a radical and unrealistic notion to expect that government postal monopolies can be privatized. Other countries in fact have done just that. New Zealand has eliminated monopoly restrictions on mail delivery and sold shares to the public. So has Sweden.

---

[12]Remarks by Postmaster General William Henderson at the National Postal Forum, San Antonio, Tex., May 17, 1999, http://www.usps.gov/news/speeches/99/051799sp.htm.

The most notable recent privatization project has been in Germany. The Germans are in the process of privatizing their postal service, the Deutsche Post.[13] Reunification and the need for a more efficient system were motivating factors.

The process began with the breakup of the old Post Office. In addition to the mail monopoly the government postal service included Deutsche Telekom, that country's monopoly provider of telecommunications services, and the Deutsche Postbank. (Two public offerings have already been made of shares in the commercialized Deutsche Telekom.)

Next the DP was put under private management. Although those who were employed before the privatization process began remained civil servants, new employees were treated as private employees. The workforce was reduced over a period of years from 379,000 to 250,000, through attrition and offering workers early retirement deals. DP also has been using more part-time workers than it could in the past. The handling of the labor situation is particularly significant since labor markets in Germany are much more rigid and union influence is much stronger in that country than in the United States.

Also, DP's nonmonopoly operations (e.g., parcel services) are now subject to corporate and other taxes and the regulations under which other businesses operate. DP has sold a lot of assets and shut down many of its inefficient processing and transport centers. It has used the proceeds to open fewer but more efficient processing centers and to offset pension costs.

By October 2000 DP is scheduled to make its first initial public offering of shares in the company. The amount will probably be between 26 percent and 49 percent, with other tranches to follow.

Germany already has less of a monopoly on mail delivery than does the United States. The weight limit above which competition is allowed is low, and delivery of magazines and other publications is exempt from monopoly restrictions. On January 1, 2003, the monopoly limits will be eliminated entirely.

Several aspects of the German effort are particularly relevant to America's situation. First, DP sees its future as a private company of-

---

[13]Figures in this section from *Growth in Global Markets: 1998 Annual Report*, Deutsche Post, Bonn, 1998, and from discussions by the author with Deutsche Post officials.

fering a variety of integrated services. It is a major parcel carrier and sees such business as a profitable wave of the future. (DP wants to be a major European carrier. It has stiff competition from UPS in Europe.) DP is becoming heavily involved in e-commerce. It sees the Internet as a way to generate profitable delivery volume. Also, DP has been purchasing shares in related enterprises and forming partnerships of various sorts. For example, in 1998 it purchased Danzas, a Swiss forwarding company, for $970 million. In November 1999, it purchased Air Express International, America's largest air cargo forwarding company, for $1.4 billion. DP has repurchased the Postbank that was spun off earlier in the 1990s.

A private USPS, even subject to taxes and regulations, would probably follow a similar strategy of forming partnerships, contracting out certain services, and so on. Although there might be initial downsizing, there also could be more jobs created in the future as the Postal Service took on new tasks. And even if there were no net gain in jobs for the private USPS, a lot of employment could be generated in firms that contract with the Postal Service offering related services in a fairer, more competitive environment. That is what happened with the growth of competitive telecommunications companies in the United States. Some older, established companies like AT&T experienced some downsizing, but those job losses were more than offset by increases in employment in companies like Sprint and MCI, and in industries like cable TV and Internet access that provided related services. Although increased efficiency, productivity and, thus, wealth are the principal outcomes of deregulation and privatization, more and better-compensating employment opportunities usually are generated as a result.

A second aspect of the planned German postal privatization that is relevant to the postal situation in the United States is the universal service mandate that requires delivery to every address at a uniform price. That requirement will be retained after privatization and poses potential problems. If no carrier can provide a service to an area at least at cost, an independent German government postal regulator will put the area out for bids. The company, whether DP or another, that can provide service at the lowest cost (though still above the break-even level) will get the routes. It will receive the difference between its costs and the break-even level from a fund into which all service providers fitting a certain definition will be required to pay.

One problem with the proposal is that companies will be required to pay into the fund based on their share of the mail market. Thus if DP has 90 percent of the market, not an unlikely situation, it will, in effect, be required to cover most of the cost differential. The Germans still have to think through the problems of a mandate. (Such mandates have caused serious problems in the American telecommunications market.) Although Germany has what could be a more efficient way of meeting the mandate, chances are it will still cause problems.

A third aspect of the planned German postal privatization of relevance to the United States is the use of an initial public offering. That approach is being used to privatize Deutsche Telekom. So far the Germans have sold 33 percent to private and institutional investors, with another small percentage sold to company employees. Total receipts from the two public offerings to date have been 20.8 billion euros (around $19.2 billion). Other offerings will follow. Currently the Germans plan to offer shares in DP by October 2000. That IPO could bring in perhaps $11 to 12 billion. (The company's annual receipts stand now at about $16 billion.) Future tranches will bring in more.

Conclusion

Attempts in the U.S. Congress to deal with current Postal Service problems have garnered interest but so far not enough support to become law. A perennial proposal supported by Rep. Phil Crane (R-Ill.) and Rep. Dana Rohrabacher (R-Calif.) would sell the Postal Service to its employees and remove the monopoly. The approach of Rep. John McHugh (R-N.Y.), H.R. 22, would separate the USPS into divisions to provide noncompetitive services that are restricted by the postal monopoly (i.e., first- and third-class mail) and competitive services. Competitive services would be subject to the same taxes and most of the same regulations as are private firms. The Postal Service also would be allowed to provide new services. Another approach to reform would simply restrict the Postal Service to its monopoly mail functions and to services such as package delivery for which there is competition but which the Postal Service has traditionally provided. Further, in light of the new mailbox regulations fiasco, there have been calls in Congress to subject the Postal Service to all the regulatory safeguards to which other government agencies are subject.

That last call seems to be a minimum step to restrain abuses by the Postal Service. After all, such a move simply would put the USPS under the same regime as other government agencies. If the USPS were subject to the Paperwork Reduction Act it would have to show that any new regulations foist the least burden on small businesses. If the USPS were under the Regulatory Flexibility Act it would have to show that the benefits of a regulation outweigh the costs. And if it were subject to Title 5, Chapter 7 of the U.S. Code, citizens would have recourse if its regulations were "arbitrary and capricious."

Of the major reform proposals, H.R. 22 has the best chance of being approved and it would try to address the problems currently caused by unfair USPS competition with private companies. But if that approach faces political opposition, it might be better for policymakers to marry it with the privatization approach. The result could be something along the lines of the German approach. The U.S. Postal Service could first be reorganized as a commercial joint-stock company under private managers, with competitive and noncompetitive services in separate divisions. The competitive activities could be subject to taxes and regulations as with other firms. But those activities would be steps toward an initial public offering of stock to the public and Postal Service employees. A date would be set after which the postal monopoly would be abolished.

Just such a suggestion has been made by Ruth Y. Goldway, a self-proclaimed consumer advocate and liberal Democrat, and a member of the Postal Rate Commission.[14] She observes that the initial public offering for UPS showed its market value to be over $80 billion. She estimates that if the Postal Service is privatized, it will bring in some $100 billion in revenue. She points to the many benefits to consumers of such a privatization.

The United States should not move into the 21st century with a Postal Service born in the 18th, operating on a monopoly model established in the 19th, and found to be wanting in the 20th. It is impossible to predict exactly what kind of integrated communications

[14]Ruth Y. Goldway, "The Postal Service: One Hot Property," *Washington Post*, January 19, 2000, p. A23.

and delivery system will evolve in the future to meet the needs of consumers. It is certain that a government monopoly with nearly 900,000 workers will be a lead weight chained to any system. The way to ensure an efficient system in the future is clear. The U.S. Postal Service should be privatized and its regulatory authority and monopoly repealed to create an efficient and cost-effective system for the new century.

2. A View from the Postal Service

William J. Henderson

This is the third time in the past decade that we have participated in a Cato public policy forum like this one. Usually, our role is like Daniel's in the lion's den. We come to put the lions at ease, to talk about what is right with the U.S. Postal Service and why privatization of the Postal Service is unsound public policy.

Well, it might come as a surprise to you, but I am *not* going to discuss that topic again. I am actually going to tell a story in which black will seem white, and white will seem black—although there will be plenty of gray in between. This story is about

- The rapidly—and radically—changing postal environment in the world;
- The Postal Service's attempts to measure and respond to those changes;
- Some powerful private-sector competitors who are actually trying to reduce competition in the marketplace; and
- At least for now, an unwritten ending.

The World Is Being Transformed, So Must We

Let us consider first the changing landscape in the postal world and our perspective of how it will affect the Postal Service over the next 10 to 15 years.

I heard *our* perspective expressed best two weeks ago by—of all people—George Will. George was asked by a postal executive what his views are about privatizing the Postal Service. He replied, "I'm in favor of privatizing *everything*."

William J. Henderson is the U.S. Postmaster General.

17

He quickly added, however, that our nation will always need a Postal Service—that we provide a vital universal service to the American people and to the economy. But he said that does not mean that we have to do that the same way that we did in 1855, 1955, or even 1985.

I could not agree more!

The Postal Service has a critical role to play in serving its customers in the competitive environment of the future.

We recognize that in spite of record financial results and dramatic improvements in operating performance, there still are considerable challenges ahead to move from what the Postal Service is today to what it needs to be to meet our customers' needs in tomorrow's marketplace.

Today, the United States Postal Service is a government institution, a legislated public interest monopoly. We have a universal service mandate. We have been granted a limited public interest monopoly and are regulated in introducing and pricing all domestic products and services. We will continue to fulfill universal service obligations in the future, and this belief is central to our assumptions about our transformation.

But, as George said, that does not mean we have to do it the same way we have always done it.

The posts of the world are changing. They are privatizing or commercializing or deregulating their monopolies. And, in a nation where the trend in other industries—transportation, utilities, telecommunications—has been toward deregulation, it would be naïve to assume that the Postal Service will remain immune to some form of deregulation. No one else is standing still, and neither can we.

The dramatic revolution in electronic communications also is going to drive major changes. It is becoming for us what Japan was to the auto industry. Depending on the adoption curve, there is a time at which paying bills and sending mail electronically will cut heavily into our correspondence and transactions business.

So, oddly enough, I do not think our limited legislated public interest monopoly is that big a deal. We have it, but it is becoming increasingly irrelevant. Someday—whether by legislative action or market changes—it probably will fade away.

That is one way of saying that breaking our legislated public interest monopoly and privatization are not the same thing. Privatization, after all, merely defines *ownership*—whether that means some form of joint government—private-sector venture, employee stock plan, or fully private venture.

It is hard to argue that any of those approaches would not change the Postal Service's incentives for performance, if for no other reason than they would change our objectives—from break-even to profit-making, from universal service as a first priority to some lower priority, from institution to business. But that is not really the point.

The point is that the frenetic pace of change in electronics and the rising tide of deregulation make it clear that we will change. I am not advocating that we wantonly repeal the protections of law that have helped create the strongest, most secure communications network in the world. But I do feel strongly that the clock is ticking on the postal monopoly. The Postal Service, its employees, its business customers, Congress, the American people—and even the Cato Institute—need to think carefully about the consequences of that fact.

The Postal Service is the last legislatively sanctioned monopoly in the United States for the most fundamental of reasons. It guarantees the right of every citizen to affordable, accessible mail services. And no matter what form the Postal Service of the future takes, I firmly believe that the American people will not sacrifice the advantages of universal service.

True universal service is specifically defined by the statutes that govern the Postal Service. It means the following:

- Providing daily, regularly scheduled collection and delivery to secure and protected mailboxes;
- Receiving, transmitting, and delivering written and printed materials and parcels throughout the United States and to and from the rest of the world;
- Closing no post office solely for operating at a deficit;
- Maintaining postal facilities that provide ready access;
- Showing no unreasonable discrimination or preference to users of mail; and
- Carrying a stamped letter anywhere in the United States for a uniform rate.

Make no mistake about it, we are the only entity in the United States that does this. Others close down retail offices that do not pay.

We keep open some 26,000 unprofitable post offices so that every American has access. Others surcharge the less profitable residential deliveries. We take a stamped letter anywhere in America and its territories for just 33 cents. Others redline for safety and profit. We leave no one out of the fold, making sure that whether you live at the bottom of the Grand Canyon or at the top of the tallest skyscraper, you have a link to the rest of the world and access to food, clothing, and other necessities of life.

Simply put, I do not see a future in which we will be sacrificing universal service, and we believe that we have proved we can do it profitably and effectively, as long as we are allowed to compete fairly.

Postal Service Delivering Record Results

That leads me to the second part of the story—what the Postal Service is doing to respond to its changing environment and to compete.

The last four years have proved once and for all that the nation's postal system is far from broken. It can and does perform remarkably well.

Service quality for overnight mail has now improved for 15 straight quarters, with on-time scores reaching well above 90 percent. Dramatic progress is being made in other categories of mail as well. Financially, we have netted more than $5 billion in surpluses since 1995, cutting in half the losses accumulated over the past quarter century. Our rate change in January 1999 came after four years, and it averages just 2.9 percent, less than one-third of the rate of inflation in the United States and our lowest since the days of massive taxpayer subsidies. In fact, since 1971, the real price of a postage stamp has gone down by 7 percent.

Today's Postal Service is enjoying levels of customer satisfaction among both consumers and businesses which rival that of any organization, public or private. In essence, the Postal Service has done what many believed was impossible for a legally protected monopoly: *We have become competitive.*

Now, I realize that not everyone will agree, but I think that is great news! *We are competitive!* And that is good, because the nation needs a Postal Service in the future that is a service it *chooses to use,* not one it *has to use.* We need to be a supplier of choice for 21st century postal communications. We need to be so operationally excellent that it simply will not matter whether or not we have a monopoly.

That is where we are heading!

We will achieve *operational excellence* by using private-sector quality tools to ensure that our systems and processes are as well managed and quality focused as those of any organization in the United States.

We will continue to be financially sound. Part of that soundness will come from higher productivity, as we become more and more *performance driven* by tapping our employees' ideas and dedication and providing performance-based incentives that reward excellence. Part of it also must come from being more *technology driven* and *customer driven*. We will constantly reshape our products and services to meet customer needs—even if the trial and error of introducing new services means that we do not always achieve revenue contribution.

In short, we will deliver on the promise of our brand. We will live up to our customers' expectations for high-quality, low-cost postal services that touch our lives in an important way and help to bind us into a single nation.

Reregulation Is Not the Answer

The third part of the story is a bit ironic. The irony is that, despite our recent record achievements, it is the leadership of the Postal Service that has embraced the need for change in its legislative and regulatory framework, while some of the 800-pound gorillas in the private sector are actually seeking to increase regulation of the Postal Service.

That does not make our competitors bad people, of course. Just business people. I think competitors like Federal Express and United Parcel Service can look at the changes going on in the world and conclude as we have that large parts of their businesses and ours are at risk as people change the way they are communicating.

If electronics, for example, do reduce our first-class mail volume, our competitors are smart enough to understand where we will have to go to get the volume to support our universal infrastructure. They also understand that the more excellent we become and the longer we are able to keep our prices stable, the less frequently they can raise their rates.

So, another irony is that the private-sector champions are actually arguing for more regulation of the Postal Service to drive up our costs and keep us from holding down prices. And, of course, they point out how anti-competitive we are along the way.

I have never seen a time when their lobbying machines in Washington, D.C., have operated for so long in full gear. Their mantra seems to be "tickets, tags, and taxes," which is meant to point out our *strong* competitive advantages of not paying parking tickets, license plate fees, or taxes.

The truth, of course, is that both they and we have advantages and disadvantages. For example, they do have a lot of influence over our rate, and they do argue for—and get—competitive protection in every rate case that goes before the Postal Rate Commission. With that track record in their pockets, it is not hard to understand why they would prefer reregulation—in which the Postal Rate Commission has more power over the Postal Service—to deregulation, whereby the regulation of all industry members would be equal and the playing field really *would* be level.

Reregulation is just a ruse for hemming in the Postal Service, and despite claims to the contrary, it is *not* going to level any playing field or create a more efficient marketplace. In fact, it will do quite the opposite.

So, we are going to prepare for deregulation—again, by being so operationally excellent that it will not matter whether we do or do not have a monopoly. That is the right thing to do.

My Prediction for the Future

Let me close by offering my prediction for the Postal Service over the next 10 years.

Deregulation of the postal monopoly is likely to occur and the competitive environment will be more oligopolistic. Fragmentation will increase as more companies compete for small niches of the market. Those competitors, by the way, will include many of the foreign posts.

In response, the Postal Service will be

- A high-performing enterprise able to compete with agile competitors;
- Responsive to more sophisticated customer demands; and

- An organization that provides employees with appropriate incentives and tools, not only to serve their customers but also to meet or exceed competitors' offerings.

The Postal Service will be regarded as a model of excellence, combining the strengths of public service with private-sector efficiency. In short, it will be the world-class communications system that our nation needs and wants. We will deliver on this promise. We owe nothing less to the American people.

3. The Postal Service's Market Grab

Michael A. Schuyler

The Postal Reorganization Act of 1970 established the U.S. Postal Service (USPS) as a replacement for the old Post Office Department. Although the aim of the reorganization was to place mail delivery on a more businesslike footing, the Postal Service is a wholly government-owned enterprise that is located, officially, within the federal government's executive branch.

The USPS at its core is a vast government monopoly.[1] But for a few exceptions, the Private Express Statutes of 1845 and subsequent laws and regulatory rulings make it a federal crime for any party besides the Postal Service to deliver a first- or third-class letter, regardless of whether the private carrier could provide superior service or a lower price.[2] Further, federal legislation in 1934 awarded to the Postal Service exclusive access to home and business mailboxes, giving it a mailbox monopoly.

In return for those monopoly powers, the Postal Service must accept and deliver first-class mail throughout the nation at a single price, regardless of whether the letter goes to the next block or across the country. In 1997 postal revenue just from the first- and third-class mail service it monopolizes exceeded sales at Coca Cola, McDonald's, Wells Fargo, and Microsoft combined.

Michael A. Schuyler is a senior economist at the Institute for Research on the Economics of Taxation and the author of *Wrong Delivery: The Postal Service in Competitive Markets* (1998), and *The Anti-Competitive Edge: Government Subsidies to Government Businesses: Case Studies of the Postal Service, TVA, and Amtrak* (1999).

[1]The material in this paper is drawn primarily from a longer study that appeared in book form. See Michael A. Schuyler, *Wrong Delivery: The Postal Service in Competitive Markets* (Washington: Institute for Research on the Economics of Taxation, 1998).

[2]For a detailed explanation of the private express statutes and their implications, see J. Gregory Sidak and Daniel F. Spulber, *Protecting Competition from the Postal Monopoly* (Washington: The AEI Press, 1996), Chapter 2.

Beyond its monopoly core, the Postal Service also operates in competitive markets, facing private-sector businesses offering similar products and services. Generally the private firms—not the Postal Service—either have offered such products and services first or have made them into commercial successes first. The USPS, nevertheless, is seeking to expand into more competitive market sectors. Indeed many observers, including some within the Postal Service, claim that the government-owned entity must make money in competitive markets if it is to remain viable in its monopoly market.

Leaving aside the issue of whether the Postal Service should retain its monopoly, the question can be raised whether it should be allowed to compete in nonmonopoly markets with private-sector products and services. Should it be allowed to vie for customers with private overnight letter and package delivery companies such as Federal Express and United Parcel Service? Should it be dabbling with e-mail and other Internet-based products? Or should the Postal Service offer a packing supply and wrapping service that would compete head-on with thousands of mostly small businesses?

In addition to its monopoly powers, the Postal Service possesses many advantages that are not enjoyed by private competitors: It pays no income taxes; is exempt from most other taxes; is exempt from many federal, state, and local regulations; has federally subsidized borrowing privileges; and has no investors expecting it to earn profits. That situation creates market distortions that ultimately are not in the interest of postal customers, private-sector businesses, or taxpayers. The Postal Service should leave all competitive markets or, at the very least, should not expand into new markets.

The Monopoly Market and Competitive Markets

First- and third-class mail are the heart of the Postal Service and its statutory monopoly. In 1997, first- and third-class mail together provided the USPS with $46.3 billion in revenues, up 2.2 percent for the year, and accounted for 80 percent of total Postal Service revenues of $58.1 billion.[3]

---

[3]United States Postal Service, *1997 Annual Report* (Washington: United States Postal Service, 1998), pp. 62–63. Several special services (registered mail, certified mail, special delivery, and post office box rentals) are rarely used except in conjunction with sending or receiving first-class mail. If those special services are included in monopoly

Most other Postal Service products lie outside the statutory monopoly, and with them the government entity usually finds itself in head-to-head competition with private providers offering similar wares.[4] Generally, private-sector businesses compete directly with Postal Service products except where they are barred by law from doing so.

The Postal Service's output and revenues in competitive markets are 20 percent or less of its total revenues. Nevertheless, because of USPS' massive size, the organization's competitive-market sales would, by themselves, place it in the Fortune 500 if they were the revenues of a freestanding company. If the Postal Service has its way, its presence in competitive markets will grow rapidly.

The Postal Service has placed great emphasis on expanding in competitive markets, both by increasing sales of existing products and by introducing new ones. Former Postmaster General Marvin Runyon depicted expansion as an urgent necessity:

> The Postal Service faces a daily struggle with formidable competitors, high-tech alternatives and changing customer needs. . . . [W]e must win our customers' business to stay in business. That means picking up the pace of our performance, delivering new records for service and financial achievements, and *creating a new, wider range of communications products* for our customers.[5] [Emphasis added.]

In another forum, he declared forcefully:

> We . . . need growth. Growth that will help us cover our fixed costs. Growth that will fuel the ever-expanding national network. Growth that will allow us to reinvest in better service and higher productivity.[6]

While Runyon portrayed a broader product line almost in terms of a struggle for survival, the Postal Service's *1997 Annual Report* sug-

---

revenues, they would bring that amount to $47.6 billion, which is 82 percent of total Postal Service revenues.

[4]A gray area is delivery of magazines, newspapers, and other periodicals. Although private firms are allowed to deliver those publications door-to-door, they cannot place them in customers' mailboxes; only the Postal Service can do that. Some periodicals, notably local newspapers, are delivered door-to-door without using mailboxes, but for most publications the mailbox restriction has proven a significant barrier to private delivery. If delivery of periodicals were included in the Postal Service's monopoly market, the monopoly share of total Postal Service revenues would rise to 86 percent.

[5]USPS, *1996 Annual Report* (Washington: USPS, 1997), p. 2.

[6]Marvin Runyon, Remarks at the 1997 NAPUS National Convention, at Philadelphia, Pa., August 25, 1997, www.usps.gov/speeches/97/082597a.htm.

gested that expansion should be undertaken as a way to help the public:

> Ten years from now, the environment may be transformed by technologies that are in their infancies today. Ten years from now, the Postal Service mission may be met only by *a new understanding of universal service and access—and how best to deliver them.*[7] [Emphasis added.]

William J. Henderson, the current Postmaster General, has talked less loudly of expanding in competitive markets than did his predecessor. Nevertheless, in a recent press release announcing the Postal Service's introduction of two Internet-based products, he said:

> These [Internet-based] services represent one of several areas where the Postal Service is evolving and responding to meet the changing needs of our customers as new technology emerges. . . . In order for the Postal Service to continue fulfilling its mission to "bind the country together through the personal . . . and business correspondence of the people," we must be able to provide the most convenient, efficient and reliable services possible.[8]

These words suggest that in "evolving and responding" the Postal Service should be accorded unilateral power to reinterpret the boundaries of its activities. If so, it is a breathtakingly open-ended view of the Postal Service's role.

The Postal Service's efforts to expand into markets where private-sector firms already operate are nothing new. The Post Office, for example, sought for many years (unsuccessfully) to take over the telegraph and telephone systems. In its 1911 annual report, it declared, "The telegraph lines in the United States should be made a part of the postal system and operated in conjunction with the mail service. Such a consolidation would unquestionably result in important economies. . . ."[9] In any case, it said, that was the usual practice in other countries. In its 1913 and 1914 annual reports, the Post Office also sought control of telephone service, claiming it was looking out for "the welfare and happiness of the nation."[10]

[7] *1997 Annual Report*, p. 11.

[8] U.S. Postal Service, *Postal News*, Release no. 90, September 2, 1998, at U.S. Postal Service Internet site www.usps.gov/news/press/98/98090new.htm.

[9] U.S. Post Office Department, *Post Office Department Annual Report, 1911* (Washington: Government Printing Office, 1913), p. 14.

[10] U.S. Post Office Department, *Post Office Department Annual Report, 1914* (Washington: Government Printing Office, 1913), p. 15.

A sample of the competitive-market products the Postal Service already offers or seeks to develop suggests where unfair competition might be taking place.[11]

- One of the largest and most familiar competitive-market categories, and one in which the Postal Service is eager to grow, is overnight mail delivery. The Postal Service entered the market early. But the reorganization of the Post Office in 1970 and other subsequent changes in regulations allowed private entrepreneurs to make such a service into a commercial success. Today 90 percent of overnight mail is carried by private companies.

- The Postal Service competes with the private sector in parcel delivery. For the early part of its history, the Post Office did not deliver packages. But after private companies began offering the service, the Postal Office in 1913 started such deliveries as well.[12]

- Prepaid telephone calling cards are another of the Postal Service's competitive-market products. Perhaps in an effort to associate telephone calling cards with more traditional postal activities, the Postal Service calls them FirstClass Phonecards and urges the customer to think of them as "delivered by the United States Postal Service."[13] In the first three quarters of fiscal year 1998, the Postal Service's phone card revenues of $12 million were 50 percent below the agency's sales target and accounted for about 1 percent of the phone cards sold in the United States.[14]

[11]For more information on new products that the Postal Service has publicly announced it was marketing or developing in fiscal years 1995–1997, see U.S. General Accounting Office, "U.S. Postal Service: Development and Inventory of New Products" (Washington: GAO, November 1998). The Postal Service told the GAO that in the first three quarters of fiscal year 1998, it had 19 such products and had either discontinued or was losing money on 15 of them (ibid., p. 4).

[12]See U.S. Post Office Department, *Post Office Department Annual Report, 1912* (Washington: Government Printing Office, 1913).

[13]U.S. Postal Service, "Get Connected! With the Phone Card That Means Business," Postal Service Brochure, in take-one display in a Washington post office lobby on November 5, 1998. Also see Angela G. King, "Telecards Are Starting to Ring Up Big Numbers as Popularity Spreads," *Wall Street Journal*, February 16, 1996.

[14]U.S. General Accounting Office, pp. 28–29.

- The Postal Service now provides messaging services such as voice mailboxes and fax mailboxes. Those are accessed through its prepaid telephone calling cards. The Postal Service boasts, "Think of the FirstClass Phonecard as a valuable—yet afford-able—piece of office equipment."[15]
- For a while, many post office lobbies were selling T-shirts, mugs, stationery, key chains, greeting cards, earrings, puzzles, and, in the words of a Postal Service flyer, other "gift and souvenir ideas." After many protests, Postmaster General Henderson ordered that most of the merchandise be removed from post office lobbies, declaring it "is not . . . something that we ought to be doing."[16] But retailing was stopped once before, only to be resumed later.[17]
- Desirous of expanding into new modes of communication, the Postal Service has its eye on the Internet. One of its Internet-based offerings is a service that would verify when e-mail was sent.[18] Another, Post-ECS (Electronic Courier Service), would provide secure transmittal of electronic documents.[19] Private-

[15]U.S. Postal Service, "Get Connected!"

[16]See Bill McAllister, "Postal Merchandise Sales Put in Dead Letter Box; Postmaster General Curbs Retailing Scope," *Washington Post*, August 13, 1998, p. A13.

[17]Ibid. Former Postmaster General Anthony Frank ended the practice, but his successor, Marvin Runyon, enthusiastically returned the merchandise to post office lobbies.

[18]See U.S. Postal Service, "USPS to Offer a Variety of Electronic Services," *Delivering the Future*, Vol. 1 www.usps.gov/dtf/1dtfelectronic.html. The Postal Service's Vice President of Technology Applications, Robert Reiser, both alluded to the USPS's position within the federal government and suggested that maybe private companies should not be allowed to offer verification services with the same legal weight as those of the Postal Service when he referred to businesses sometimes needing a "time and date stamp with a federal agency standing behind it." ("U.S. Postal Service Accepts Java, Starts E-Postmark Program," *JavaWorld*, www.javaworld.com/javaworld/jw-11-1996/jw-11-post.html.)

[19]See U.S. Postal Service, "Postal Service Merges onto Information Superhighway; Introduces Internet-Based Services," *Postal News*, Release no. 90, September 2, 1998, www.usps.gov/news/press/98/98090new.htm. The Postal Service's efforts to move into cyberspace and the issues that raises are discussed in greater detail in James P. Lucier, "Dangers in Cyberspace." One troubling question, for instance, is whether letting the U.S. Postal Service control the transmission of supposedly confidential documents would jeopardize people's privacy rights if the federal government is interested in the contents of the documents.

sector companies, of course, already provide similar Internet-based services and are rapidly introducing new ones. The Postal Service has similarly floated a sweeping proposal to take over the Internet top-level domain ".us."[20] A Postal Service spokesperson claims that controlling part of the Internet would be a natural fit for the organization "because of our experience managing address systems."[21] The Postal Service says one way it could use that portion of the Internet would be to assign people e-mail addresses to go along with their street addresses. It also has the idea of charging fees to private companies that want to set up electronic Yellow Pages there.

- The Postal Service has opened a facility for processing bill payments made to private companies under contract with RE-MITCO Management. A Postal Service publication reports that the center "takes an individual consumer payment, opens the envelope, deposits the check and notifies the biller that a payment was made."[22] One account describes the facility as "the first of what postal officials hope will be a national network of bill processing centers opening the mail for credit card companies, retailers, and utilities."[23] Although the Postal Service insists this is "a logical extension of the core business of the USPS,"[24] mail delivery is not usually thought to include processing bill payments.

[20]See Lucier. See also Jeri Clausing, "Postal Service Proposes Using '.us' Domain for Individuals," *New York Times*, August 5, 1998. For the text of the proposal, see James Gleve, "Postal Service Eyes .us Domain," *Wired News*, June 19, 1998, www.wired.com/news/print_version/politics/story/13129.html?wnpg=all. Federal, state, and local government agencies are the main users of the ".us" domain today.

[21]Clausing.

[22]See U.S. Postal Service, "Bill Payment Processing Center Operates under REMITO Contract," *Delivering the Future*, Vol. 3, www.usps.gov/dtf/3 short2.html#story3.

[23]Bill McAllister, "Postal Service to Open Mail for Company," *Washington Post*, July 10, 1997, p. C3. Another newspaper story quotes Cathy Rogerson, manager of new businesses for the Postal Service: "We are working on a number of initiatives to improve bill paying. We do it as an extension of the services we provide to our customers." See "Postal Service Seeks Business of Processing Bills for Corporations," *Wall Street Journal*, June 11, 1997, p. 15.

[24]U.S. Postal Service, "Bill Payment Processing Center Operates under REMITCO Contract."

- The Pack & Send service, which has been tested in selected post offices, would allow customers to bring in items to be shipped and, for a fee, have Postal Service employees supply packaging materials and do the wrapping.[25]

Erroneous Rationales for Postal Products

Is there any justification for the Postal Service to provide those and other competitive market products and services? Assuming the Postal Service continues in its core business of delivering first- and third-class mail, are there benefits if it also operates in competitive markets?

It cannot convincingly be argued that the Postal Service is supplying competitive-market products to meet otherwise unmet customer demand. Postal Service products like overnight delivery, e-mail transmission, messaging services, and retail merchandise are similar to products already available from private firms. Indeed, private businesses usually pioneered or made commercial successes of those products and services, and the offerings of private businesses are generally rated higher in quality than those supplied by the Postal Service.

To understand why the Postal Service should not be supplying products aside from first- and third-class mail delivery, if that, it is useful to review some of the arguments offered in support of an expanded USPS role.

Economies of Scale and Scope

It is sometimes argued that the larger the Postal Service is in both size and scope, the lower it can make the unit costs of the products it delivers. Thus if the Postal Service expands its services beyond the provision of first- and third-class mail, it can bring down the costs of both such mail and the competitive-market products it provides. Of course, the Postal Service is already a giant organization, with 1997

---

[25]Although Pack & Send is not currently offered, Henderson recently said, "There is a strong likelihood we will [reinstitute it]. . . . It's something our customers are screaming at us to do." (See Steve Bates, "Postal Service Not Backing Down," *Nation's Business,* September 1998, p. 47.) Another account reports that much of the screaming concerned how badly this packaging service slowed down post office lines. (See Les Winick, "Postal Service Wants to Pack Your Teacups," *Linn's Stamp News,* December 25, 1995.)

revenues of more than $58 billion and 900,000 employees.[26] Only nine American companies had higher sales and none had more employees that year. In Postmaster General Henderson's words, "Sometimes we don't appreciate how big the Postal Service really is."[27] Thus, the issue is not whether economies of scale and scope are attained in growing from a small to a large operation but whether an already enormous enterprise continues to reduce marginal costs by growing yet larger.

That is not the pattern observed in most industries. Even in industries where economies of scale and scope are pronounced, firms that reach the multi-billion-dollar revenue level usually are large enough to capture most of the benefits of those economies. It is not clear why the business of delivering nonurgent letters should deviate from this pattern.

If economies of scale and scope really drive the evolution of particular industries, why are those economies not observed with private delivery companies? Tellingly, a number of private delivery companies—all much smaller than the Postal Service—are large enough to have achieved the cost efficiencies that enable them to compete vigorously. If size-based economies accumulated whenever firms grew, there should be only one private carrier of express letters and one company (perhaps the same one) delivering all freight. In reality, in both areas several private companies are large enough to have achieved the cost efficiencies that enable them to compete vigorously. One private express service that specializes in international deliveries and is small relative to the Postal Service says of itself: "Large enough to be efficient, small enough to be flexible."[28] The message is that bigger is not automatically better; being smaller can have advantages, too.

A possible rejoinder might be that the Postal Service is a natural monopoly like a water, gas, or electric utility. Yet such an argument is based in part on the fact that utilities often must invest considerable capital in extremely high-capacity distribution systems. The Postal Service, however, has its distribution system already waiting, paid for by others: the nation's highways, rail lines, airports, and waterways. In any case, deregulation and privatization around the

---

[26]*1997 Annual Report,* pp. 60, 64. Employees include both career and noncareer.
[27]*1996 Annual Report,* p. 11.
[28]See the Internet site of IBC Pacific, www.ibcpac.com/profile.htm.

world in the telephone and electric industries indicate that the natural monopoly argument may have been overused even in some cases where the classic conditions for such a monopoly seemed to be met.

The Postal Service's own actions also cast doubt on the economies of scale and scope argument. If such economies were at work, the huge Postal Service would want to perform as many tasks as possible in-house because it would have lower costs than smaller outside firms do. The more such tasks the USPS performs, the more it could reduce its marginal costs.[29] Instead, the Postal Service frequently contracts out work because private companies often have lower costs, notwithstanding their small size compared with the massive Postal Service. Thus, for example, the USPS offers work-sharing discounts to mailers that help with sorting and transportation. It willingly contracts out much mail transportation. The Postal Service pays Emery Air Freight, a private firm, to do much of the work involving Priority Mail on the East Coast.[30] And it hands its Global Package Link parcels bound for Canada over to Purolator Courier and does not touch them again before delivery.[31]

A modest cost economy might be present in the trip to the mailbox, provided extra items can be delivered along with the regular mail.[32] But the going-to-the-mailbox economy often does not apply to the Postal Service's competitive-market products and services. Some, like package delivery, frequently require separate trips to the mailbox, and others, like online services, do not involve mailbox deliveries at all.

The Postal Service might argue that bigger is necessarily better financially. Consider the following words from Michael J. Riley, the Postal Service's chief financial officer:

> The more people use our services, the more revenue we have, and the more revenue we have, the more we can improve our services while holding the line on prices.[33]

---

[29]See the discussion of this issue in Sidak and Spulber, Ch. 3.

[30]"Business Brief—CNF Transportation, Inc.: U.S. Postal Service Awards Emery $1.7 Billion Contract," *Wall Street Journal*, April 25, 1997.

[31]General Accounting Office, "U.S. Postal Service: Competitive Concerns about Global Package Link Service," (Washington: GAO, June 1998), p. 5.

[32]See John C. Panzar, "The Economics of Mail Delivery," in *Governing the Postal Service*, ed. J. Gregory Sidak (Washington: AEI Press, 1994).

[33]*1997 Annual Report*, p. 17.

In reality, added sales help financially only if marginal revenue exceeds marginal cost. If added sales increase costs by more than they increase revenues, they hurt financially. The fact that the Postal Service contracts out to reduce its costs suggests that new business would increase costs at the margins.

Implosion of the Postal Service's Core Market

A variation on the economies of scale argument is that the Postal Service's core market will soon shrink because of a growing array of communications alternatives. To avoid a death spiral of falling volume and rising marginal costs, the argument goes, the Postal Service needs to replace what it loses in its core market with higher volume in other product lines.

But it is not obvious that a gradual decline in volume would boost marginal costs. In any case, it can be objected that the premise of the argument is wrong: Volume and revenues in the Postal Service's monopoly market are rising, not falling. Only 3 of the 10 largest American companies in 1992 had more rapid sales growth over the period 1992 to 1997 than the Postal Service did in its core market of first- and third-class mail.[34] Whereas private businesses constantly fear that their sales will be hurt by aggressive competitors introducing similar but slightly better products, the Postal Service has the security of an immense core market with products that other suppliers are barred from offering.

Of course, there are substitutes, such as e-mail instead of a first-class letter, direct deposit instead of a check in the mail, and newspaper inserts instead of a mailed advertisement. But after taking account of possible diversions to substitutes, the Postal Service's five-year strategic plan projects that first-class volume will rise 8.7 percent over the period 1997 to 2002, and that during that period third-class volume will grow 14.4 percent.[35] The Postal Service's am-

[34]*Fortune*, April 1993; *Fortune*, April 1998; *1996 Postal Service Annual Report*, p. 70; and *1997 Postal Service Annual Report*, p. 62. This comparison modifies a table in the 1997 Postal Service Annual Report that looked at the growth of total Postal Service revenues compared with sales growth at the 10 largest private-sector companies. There, too, the Postal Service's revenue growth exceeded those of most of the largest companies.

[35]U.S. Postal Service, *USPS: Five-Year Strategic Plan*, for Fiscal Years 1998–2002, 1997, p. 27, www.usps.gov/history/five-year-plan/intro.html.

bitious plan to undertake capital expenditures of $17 billion over the years 1998 to 2002 is another sign that it foresees rising volume, not contraction.[36] As to whether postal volume will fall in the years beyond then, it is worth remembering that, in the past, postal volume has risen dramatically despite the introduction of powerful substitute technologies like the telegraph, telephone, and fax.[37]

The Sure-Fire Commercial-Success Argument

In markets where the Postal Service would like to expand, some private-sector companies have been very successful. Should the Postal Service expect to do as well in those markets? A comment by Henderson suggests he regards competitive markets as extremely inviting:

> The magnitude of the Postal Service's task dwarfs the dramatically lighter load that two of our well-known competitors [UPS and FedEx] carry. . . . It's a race where *they gladly concentrate on short sprints with big payoffs*, but we are mandated to run the unrelenting marathon of universal service at uniform prices.[38] [Emphasis added.]

If the Postal Service actually earned "big payoffs" in competitive markets, it could, if it wished, use those profits to cross-subsidize the "unrelenting marathon" run by its core business.

There are problems that can be noted in such cross-subsidization; for example, why would it not be better just to remove the mail monopoly? But there are several reasons to be skeptical that the Postal Service will realize average, let alone high, profits in competitive markets. Just as nature abhors a vacuum, investors jump in when they see a good profit opportunity and continue jumping in until they have driven the expected return down to the market average. Thus, good business opportunities are often temporary, and the advantage goes to quick-footed investors and companies. The Postal Service may perhaps be described as steady, but almost never as quick-footed. The private sector is active in all the areas in which the Postal Service wants to compete outside of its core mail functions.

---

[36]*1997 Annual Report*, p. 39.

[37]See Marvin Runyon, "Quality—The Path to Business Success," remarks at the 1997 Graduate Business Conference, Owens Graduate School of Management, Vanderbilt University, Nashville, Tenn., March 21, 1997, reported at Postal Service Internet site www.usps.gov/news/speeches/97/032197sp.htm.

[38]*1996 Annual Report*, p. 6.

There is no indication that profitable opportunities are lying about unclaimed, waiting for the USPS to pick them up.

To be sure, a business does not have to be first in a sector to do well with a product. A business can still earn high profits if it is unusually good at developing product improvements, has better production methods than its rivals do, or is better at marketing its products. The Postal Service, however, has not demonstrated an edge over private sector companies in any of those areas. Hence, it is apt to do poorly when it challenges aggressive private-sector companies in competitive markets. Thus the cross-subsidy could go in the other direction from that envisioned: from core functions to competitive-market functions.

Dangers from USPS Competitive-Market Activities

Although the Postal Service optimistically describes its range of offerings, including those in competitive markets, as "delivering products that satisfy the everyday needs of a nation of customers,"[39] its operations in competitive markets can cause economic damage.

A Less Productive Economy

Private-sector businesses seek profits. They need to, because they are accountable to their shareholders, and shareholders want to earn market rates of return (or better) on their investments. Thus the pursuit of profits is Adam Smith's invisible hand, forcing businesses to act in the public interest. Businesses must be attentive to their customers' wants so that they can sell desired products in greater quantities and at higher prices than less desired products; that means greater profits. Profits also give businesses a strong incentive to ferret out waste in production and devise new, more efficient production techniques because, other things being equal, profits rise when costs fall.

The Postal Service, in contrast, is asked only to break even. Breaking even does require some attention to costs and product desirability, but much less than if the objective were to earn a competitive rate of return. Suppose, for instance, that a private firm spends $10 to produce a product that it sells for $11, giving it a 10 percent return. Because the Postal Service is content to break even, it could use $1

[39]*1997 Annual Report*, p. 9.

more of scarce production inputs than the private firm could to produce the same output and still meet its financial objective. (Revenues and costs would both be $11.) The Postal Service would also meet its financial objective if it used the same inputs as did the private firm but produced a less desirable output that could be sold for $10, instead of $11. Either way, scarce production inputs would be wasted. The result: the economy's output of goods and services would be less because Postal Service production would be displacing more efficient private-sector production. Notwithstanding the loss of aggregate output, the Postal Service would view the displacement as a success because it would be meeting its break-even target.

Perversely, the Postal Service's break-even constraint encourages expansion into more product areas even as it provides a cushion for inefficiency. Suppliers can expand a lot farther if they only need to break even rather than if they strive for a market rate of return.

Hidden Government Subsidies

The productivity gap attributable to the difference between earning a competitive return and breaking even is greater than it might seem because, in measuring break-even, the Postal Service receives a pass on many government taxes and regulations that private-sector firms must pay and observe. The Postal Service pays no federal income tax, no state or local income tax, no state or local sales or gross receipts tax, no property tax on buildings and equipment it owns, no motor vehicle licensing and registration fees, and no parking tickets. It does not pay unemployment compensation taxes but only reimburses the government for unemployment benefits that eligible former employees draw.[40] It is exempt from local zoning regulations (although it tries to cooperate, if possible), and has the power of eminent domain (although it uses it sparingly). It can borrow more easily and at lower interest rates than private firms do because of its ability to tap into the U.S. Treasury.

The money the Postal Service saves because it is exempt from the array of government-imposed charges gives it additional leeway to use an excess of scarce inputs in production. That is, for every dollar the Postal Service saves in government charges that a private company would have to pay, it can waste an extra dollar in inefficient production and still break even.

[40]U.S. Code, Title 5, Chapter 85.

The presence of a government entity in competitive markets that is willing to accept below-market returns and that receives hidden government subsidies is obviously unfair to both the owners and the employees of the private firms against which the Postal Service competes. Less obviously, it is also unfair to states and localities. When the Postal Service, instead of a private firm, produces a product, state and local tax bases shrink because of the Postal Service's multiple exemptions. That situation deprives state and local government taxpayers, who must make do with fewer state and local government services or pay higher taxes.

The Threat to Monopoly-Market Customers

Supposedly, each type of Postal Service product is priced to cover the costs for which it is responsible and also make a reasonable contribution to institutional or common costs (the term for Postal Service overhead costs not attributable to any particular product). On the surface, such pricing would seem to safeguard users of the Postal Service's monopoly products from having to subsidize the Postal Service's competitive-market products. Cross-subsidization could still occur, however, if (1) some of the costs of a product are misidentified as attributable to another product or (2) if some of the costs of a product are miscategorized as institutional, with the products furnishing the subsidies picking up those institutional costs.

The generous share of its total costs that the Postal Service classifies as institutional is consistent with the second method of cross-subsidization. In 1996, for example, the Postal Service claimed that fully 37 percent of its costs were institutional: $20.4 billion of $55.0 billion.[41] First-class mail accounted for 57 percent of USPS revenues, but it contributed $14.2 billion to cover common costs, 70 percent of the total.[42] If it had contributed a prorated 57 percent, it would have paid only $11.6 billion. Thus first-class mail seems to have provided a $2.6 billion subsidy to other postal activities. Although the Postal Service's cost allocations are reviewed by the independent Postal Rate Commission, that body labors under the disadvantage that the Postal Service largely provides the cost data.

Provided that the Postal Service as a whole breaks even, its managers and employees actually have an incentive to expand into com-

[41]*1997 Annual Report*, pp. 21–22.
[42]Ibid.

petitive markets at a loss and to cover the losses by overcharging monopoly-market customers. The reason is that rewards for individual postal employees, as with employees of any government bureaucracy, are usually more closely tied to the size and growth of the organization than to its financial performance. An expanding Postal Service means new job openings and more opportunities for advancement. Thus, although the Postal Service usually defends its competitive-market forays as somehow lowering rates for customers within the postal monopoly, the truth is that monopoly-market customers are in danger of paying *higher* rates.

Taxpayers and Customers at Risk

Because the Postal Service confronts quick-moving, determined rivals in competitive markets, unexpectedly large Postal Service losses in those markets are a distinct possibility. One method of making up losses, of course, is demanding more subsidies from competitive-market customers. Hikes in postal rates also have been a favorite way of making up for the costs of an inefficient system.

If losses are too large, taxpayers may have to pick up the tab. As part of the federal government, the Postal Service operates under an implicit federal guarantee, with its own special credit line at the U.S. Treasury. That is why there has never been any concern that the USPS would declare bankruptcy while it was accumulating red ink during most of its history. (It has been in the black for the last several years but still has cumulative losses of $5.7 billion over the period 1971 to 1997.[43] Users of what are now competitive-market products are at risk, too, because a powerful way to strengthen the entity's finances is to enact new monopoly restrictions, if the Postal Service can persuade Congress to go along.

Legislation

Many members of Congress have become concerned about the harmful effects of the Postal Service's presence in competitive markets. Congress enacted two positive, but limited, changes in 1998. A provision placed in the Omnibus Consolidated Appropriations Act (H.R. 4328) by Rep. Anne Northup (R-Ky.) assigns to the State Department, rather than the Postal Service, the task of formulating pol-

[43]U.S. Postal Service, *1997 Annual Report*, p. 60.

icy for the U.S. delegation at meetings of the Universal Postal Union. That international body sets the rules for the movement of mail among nations. There has been growing concern that the Postal Service as the nation's representative would negotiate rules favoring its own international products at the expense of private-sector competitors.[44]

A second change is that under the terms of the Postal Employees Safety Enhancement Act (S. 2112), which was sponsored by Sen. Mike Enzi (R-Wyo.), the Postal Service is now subject to Occupational Safety and Health Administration regulations. The USPS is therefore on the same footing in that respect as private-sector companies.[45]

Two other major pieces of proposed legislation would limit Postal Service activities in the competitive market. The Postal Service Core Business Act of 1999 (H.R. 198), introduced in the House by Rep. Duncan Hunter (R-Calif.), would bar the USPS from supplying any nonpostal services that it was not already providing at the start of 1994. Although the proposal would not remove the Postal Service from all competitive markets, it would restrict the Postal Service's expansion plans and remove it from markets into which it has only recently entered. The approach also would allow the Postal Service to retain services that customers already have gotten used to, such as copier machines in post office lobbies. A containment strategy could be politically practical because it is usually easier to prevent a government agency from entering an area than trying to extricate it after it has already become entrenched.

The Postal Modernization Act of 1999 (H.R. 22), introduced by Rep. John McHugh (R-N.Y.), chairman of the House Subcommittee on the Postal Service, seeks to accommodate the Postal Service's claim that, for its core services to remain strong, the organization must be allowed to expand substantially in competitive markets and operate in those markets with little regulatory oversight. Thus, H.R. 22 would give the Postal Service much more discretion over pricing

---

[44]It appears from the legislative language, however, that the Postal Service usually also will be representing the United States at international postal meetings, meaning that the opportunity for abuse is diminished but not eliminated.

[45]OSHA has many critics. They may view this extension of OSHA's jurisdiction positively, in the hope that as more government agencies are on the receiving end of OSHA regulations and enforcement actions, pressure to reform OSHA will mount.

and expansion in those markets. The competitive side of the USPS would be allowed to do such things as buy equity in private companies, not directly but through a new "private" corporation that the Postal Service would wholly own.

Simultaneously, in response to criticisms of the Postal Service's current privileges, H.R. 22 would reduce, but not eliminate, the entity's long list of tax and regulatory exemptions. For instance, the Postal Service's new "private" corporation would be subject to income taxes, but the Postal Service would remain exempt from income taxes on its own sales of monopoly and commercial products. The bill also would attempt to erect strong firewalls between core and commercial Postal Service functions. Those firewalls are supposed to defend captive postal customers from being forced to cross-subsidize competitive-market products, protect private-sector companies from predatory activities by the Postal Service, and guard taxpayers from having to finance a government bailout if major new forays into competitive markets turn out badly.

But it is a difficult legislative challenge to design secure firewalls. Even openings that might appear minor at present could be interpreted in unexpected ways by the Postal Service and the courts. Further, there are serious problems concerning cross-subsidies in the current system. Giving the Postal Service a wider scope will only make those problems worse. Moreover, even if the firewalls hold, the overall result of H.R. 22 would be a larger USPS presence in competitive markets, and that would mean a less productive economy as the empire-building Postal Service displaces more efficient private-sector businesses.

Conclusion

From its monopoly on the delivery of nonurgent letters, the Postal Service has expanded into a wide range of other mail delivery services and nonmail services. Moreover, it seeks to continue expanding in competitive markets. But such expansion promises few benefits and many risks. The Postal Service's efforts to parlay its monopoly into a variety of commercial ventures would be analogous to the Defense Department's seeking to establish a commercial airline because it has expertise in flying aircraft. It would be like the State Department's starting a commercial travel agency because it has considerable knowledge of other countries. It would be like the IRS' setting up a private bill-collection agency on the side because it has experience collecting taxes.

There is no economic justification for treating the Postal Service's competitive-market products differently from private-sector products. At a minimum the USPS should pay income taxes, state and local sales and gross receipts taxes on such products, and state and local real and personal property taxes on properties it owns. (Those taxes could be prorated based on the share of Postal Service operations occurring within competitive markets.) The Postal Service should pay all applicable vehicle registration fees (again, that could be prorated by the share of Postal Service operations occurring within competitive markets). And it should have to obey traffic laws, just like everyone else. 'It should be subject to local zoning and land use regulations and subject to the antitrust laws regarding its behavior in competitive markets.

But the best situation for the economy's productivity, the well-being of customers within the postal monopoly, and the safety of taxpayers would be for the Postal Service to leave competitive markets.

4. Dangers in Cyberspace

James P. Lucier

The Postal Service . . . will put you and your products above its own self-interest.[1]

With little fanfare, the U.S. Postal Service (USPS) is transforming itself from the mostly postal business of the past to something more like an Internet portal of the future. The venerable agency charged with delivering mail—letters, parcels, and advertising materials—now seeks to become a logistics and information intermediary. Functions that were once peripheral to its current mail monopoly are central to its new role as the postal e-mail inspector, paymaster, address-book keeper, trusted third party, guarantor of identities, architect of online business directories, and universal intermediary of cyberspace.

All evidence suggests that the mailstream of printed materials and packages will continue to be a bloodstream for the nation's commerce. But it is also probable that the postal monopoly on delivering letter mail will one day disappear. Thus it is not surprising that the Postal Service is seeking to leverage that monopoly, while it lasts, into new forms of market power. Of course, the Postal Service is exempt from all taxes and most government regulations but itself wields considerable regulatory power. Indeed, the USPS actions of late are consistent with a bold campaign to seize what early industrial policy theorists might have called "the commanding heights and central switchboard of the Internet economy." Such a transformation poses a serious threat not only to private companies with which the Postal Service might compete but also to the information

James P. Lucier is a senior Washington analyst at Prudential Securities, Inc.
[1]Remarks by Postmaster General and CEO William Henderson at the National Postal Forum, San Antonio, Tex., May 17, 1999, http://www.usps.gov/news/speeches/99/051799sp.htm.

and communications revolution, to which the Postal Service bureaucracy could be a chain slowing its every step.

The Postal Service's Current Context

Postmaster General William Henderson concedes that the letter monopoly, granted by Congress in the 1845 Private Express Statutes, someday likely will be repealed. Thus the Postal Service's challenge in years to come should be to make structural adjustments in a heavily unionized workforce approaching some 900,000 members strong. Unfortunately, to forestall those more difficult changes, the Postal Service instead has been seeking new sources of revenue, competing with the private sector in everything from the sale of neckties, key chains, and phone cards to more serious, higher-valued, and substantive services in the communications and information sectors.

The Postal Service makes a curious argument for its foray into nonmail services, claiming that it offers a desirable public service alternative to the private-sector "monopolies" that might dominate cyberspace in its absence. Thus it attempts to use its own, real monopoly, backed by federal government power, to leverage itself into the private sector. It seems that the Postal Service wants to make other functions part of its core services so that if and when its monopoly on letter delivery is removed, it can argue that those currently peripheral functions are in fact cornerstones of its franchise. But to judge the prudence of the Postal Service's actions, it is necessary to consider the current context of mail delivery and the information revolution.

First, there is no danger that the need to carry communications on physical media, that is, mail, will disappear. Letter mail may be a mature medium, growing in volume by only a few percentage points a year. But it *is* still growing and shows no signs of imminent demise. Package delivery does seem to be entering a period of explosive growth, making the growth in mail seem small. But what is changing is the composition of the mail. Although certain categories of mail may dwindle—most notably billing mail—other categories are growing.[2]

[2]For a discussion of projected trends in mail volume, see *United States Postal Service 1998 Annual Report*, pp. 32–33. Total mail volume is projected to grow at 3 percent to 4 percent a year for the next decade. First-class mail will grow 1 percent to 2 percent per year. But bills, statements, and remittances represent $13 billion to $16 billion of

Second, the growth of the communications and information revolution and the Internet, especially in the past five years, indeed has been explosive. Many observers, including Federal Reserve Chairman Alan Greenspan, see that growth as the fundamental driving force behind the extended period of inflation-free growth and rapid productivity gains in the U.S. economy in recent years. A University of Texas study funded by Cisco Systems argues that the total volume of e-commerce—defined as business-to-business and consumer-to-business orders placed over the Internet or through Electronic Data Interchange (EDI) channels but excluding purely financial transactions—in the United States in 1998 was $102 billion, much higher than previous estimates. Estimates by Forrester Research suggest that business-to-business transactions in the United States could top $1 trillion in the year 2003 and that worldwide e-commerce, both business and consumer, might top $3 trillion by that time. That means that in only 10 years' time, starting from very low levels in 1994, up to 10 percent of America's gross domestic product and 5 percent or more of world economic output will be moving over the Internet, with no end to the rate of growth in sight.[3]

But the Postal Service has $60 billion in annual revenues, is exempt from all taxes and most government regulations, has borrowing privileges at the U.S. Treasury, and has zero-cost capitalization. Thus the Postal Service is a behemoth that could easily overwhelm the typical, more fragile Internet start-up company and create serious distortions in the information sector. The danger is seen especially when one considers the difference between regular mail and e-mail, or what Massachusetts Institute of Technology Professor Nicholas

---

revenue, with a very large contribution to covering costs and net income. See also *Five-Year Strategic Plan, USPS Fiscal Years 1998–2002*, pp. 10–13, for discussion of class mail as "a mature product." But for a more optimistic view, "Ironically, the Internet May Generate *More* Snail Mail," B. Alex Henderson, Future Shocks 1999 Annual Forecast Issue, Prudential Securities Global Equity Research, 45. See also the summary of projections for package volume growth in "Technology: Digital Commerce; Online Sellers Learn How to Get Packages to Cyberspace Consumers," Denise Caruso, *New York Times*, March 30, 1998.

[3]For a detailed discussion of trends in e-commerce, the June 22, 1999, Commerce Department Report, *The Emerging Digital Economy II*, http://www.e-commerce.gov. See also press release, "U.S. Online Business Trade Will Soar to $1.3 Trillion," Forrester Research, December 17, 1998, http://www.forrester.com. See, in addition, the University of Texas study, "The Internet Economy Indicators," Anitesh Barua, Jay Shutter, and Andrew Whinston, http://www.internetindicators.com.

Negroponte characterizes in another context as the difference between atoms and bits. Digital information can be aggregated, centralized, linked to individual persons, and, if collected on a suitably widespread scale, used for purposes of surveillance and control that were unimagined even by George Orwell. When the Postal Service proposes to provide various centralized security services, it invites abuse. In any case the Internet already has decentralized, nongovernmental methods of its own for dealing with secure communications, authenticating messages, verifying senders, executing contracts, and performing commercial transactions.

Models from Overseas

Post offices and administrations outside the United States historically have engaged in a much broader range of business lines than has the USPS. Foreign post offices often have been part of a larger state monopoly in postal and telecommunications services. Some, for example, Japan, offer postal savings accounts and thus have been major players in financial services. Additionally, unitary governments, as opposed to a U.S.-style federal system, often find it convenient to use the postal system as an all-purpose point of contact with the public for filing government paperwork and managing government benefits.

The best example of the way a state-owned postal monopoly facing privatization might develop is the TNT Post Group, the Netherlands' postal service. That enterprise was recently partially privatized. It is publicly traded but the majority of shares are still owned by the state. It has moved aggressively into areas outside the traditional postal domains and, some charge, substantially cross-subsidizes those activities from the monopoly on letter delivery that it still holds, despite legal barriers that would theoretically prevent it from doing so. TNT businesses include parcel delivery, corporate logistics, retail distribution in partnership with online sellers, bill generation for giant clients such as Citigroup, and mailing services for direct marketers. TNT Postal Group both prints and mails the European editions of *Time* and *Newsweek*.[4] Those activities generate roughly $500 million in revenue per year.

---

[4]"TNT: A Dutch Courier That Could Be Cyber Dynamite," by William Etchikson, *BusinessWeek* e.biz, June 8, 1999, http://www/ businessweek.com/ebiz/9906/

The USPS is unlikely to have ambitions as far-ranging as those of TNT, but its underlying strategic game plan could take it in the same direction. While USPS officials have been cautious about letting their future plans be known, the overall strategic posture of the agency is unmistakable. In a 1997 document, *USPS Five Year Strategic Plan for Fiscal Years 1998–2002*, then–Postmaster General Marvin Runyon explained his plan to concentrate primarily on bringing the Postal Service up to contemporary standards in business management. That document does, however, identify the lack of an integrated enterprise-wide information technology platform, the lack of package-tracking capabilities, and the inability of the Postal Service to share data with its customers as problems that keep the Postal Service out of developing markets for business logistics. The paper also specifically mentions redesign of Priority Mail, financial services, electronic services, and new "strategic business units" as focal areas for "product and service innovation."[5] More recently, Runyon spoke of his vision for the Postal Service in the year 2020, in which the agency is part of a "value chain" that spans the world and is characterized by "a seamless partnership among suppliers, producers, and consumers."[6]

More recently still, Postmaster General William Henderson described his thoughts on an "Internet Strategy" for the USPS:

> [First,] obviously, with e-commerce there is going to be a need for a residential delivery system that is cost effective, that is low price, that doesn't have a surcharge. . . .

> Secondly, we do see bill payments in the future being made electronically. That represents to the United States Postal Service somewhere in the neighborhood of $15 to $18 billion. . . . We think the Postal Service has a role in e-payments. If one private sector company owned the platform for e-payments 10 years from now, you would have a monopoly

---

ec0608.htm. According to *BusinessWeek*: "TNT is using its monopoly and old postal business 'as a cash cow to fund all sorts of electronic services,' says Steve Vroik, a research analyst for ING Barings in Amsterdam." Citing cross-subsidies, UPS has filed an antitrust complaint with the European Commission over TNT's continuing letter monopoly. From the same article: "'Right now, [TNT] has the best of both worlds—a legal monopoly and commercial freedom,' complains UPS-Netherlands Vice-President Anton van der Lande."

[5]*United States Postal Service Five-Year USPS Strategic Plan for Fiscal Years 1998–2002*, http://www.usps.gov.

[6]Marvin Runyon, luncheon address to the National Press Club, Washington, D.C., April 14, 1998.

model. You would have a model where you are forced to use one service. On the other hand, if you don't have one supplier, then everyone builds their own model, you will have cellular phone model suboptimized networks. So we think the answer is our role as a trusted third party. . . .

What if every physical address in the United States had an Internet address? We would own the physical address, and we would maintain it. That means that all that information that you our customers have developed around a physical address could now migrate through the Internet and be a part of commerce.

. . . If you had an Internet address attached to a physical address you could reach someone by way of the Internet, and if they didn't have a computer it could be converted to hard copy for delivery to the physical address. . . .[7]

Because e-commerce has emerged only in the past five years, the Washington policy community has yet to grasp the nature of its elaborate taxonomy of new business functions and mediating institutions. That situation has meant that the potential dangers of the Postal Service's move into e-commerce have not been significantly appreciated. The USPS has targeted five areas in which to expand its activities: the payment system or financial intermediation; business-to-business e-commerce including both financial and logistical intermediation; e-commerce centering on residential delivery; the many roles of a *trusted agent*; and finally, the management of Internet address space, somewhat analogous to managing addresses in physical delivery space. A review of those areas suggests the problems that the Postal Service could pose to e-commerce in the future.

Payments

Foreign post offices even today play a role in payments processing and financial services that would be unimaginable in the United States. Japan's postal service, for example, allows individuals to maintain postal savings accounts. Originally the Japanese government authorized those accounts, with 100 percent of the value of deposits guaranteed by the government, to promote savings. The accounts also allow the postal service to facilitate bill payments. Further, Japan's postal service sells life insurance. That system makes the Japanese postal service the custodian of trillions of dollars

[7]Henderson.

in assets and makes it one of the world's largest financial institutions. Yet that postal service for the most part diverts its resources into unproductive investments, mostly government slush funds that are invested in targeted, often unprofitable, enterprises. The unsoundness of that practice has contributed to Japan's ongoing financial crisis.[8]

Recently France's La Poste derived almost one-fourth of its annual revenue from payment services.[9] In Italy, Poste spa., the successor company to the Italian postal service, handles more than twice the volume of payments processed by the entire banking system in that country.[10] In Britain, Postal Counters Ltd. calls itself the largest retail organization in Europe, with more windows than all banks and building societies combined. It offers an impressive range of services, from bill payments to pension savings accounts and insurance.[11] U.S. postal money orders seem almost trifling by comparison.

However, in the United States a radical change is occurring in the delivery of certain financial services. Specialist companies such as First Data Corporation, State Street Bank, and Keycorp offer consolidation of billing, credit card and other payments, account management, custodial services for mutual funds, and other back-office functions on an outsourced basis, all of it done electronically.

The most direct threat to the Postal Service revenue stream is electronic processing of bills and transaction-related mail, for which the Postal Service currently charges premium delivery rates. At present, inefficient payment processing still largely relies on paper statements transmitted through the mail at a total cost for paper, envelopes, bills, and postage of perhaps $1.50 per bill in addition to the high costs of processing checks. Some estimates suggest that those processes might impose on the U.S. economy costs of around 1 percent of GDP, or $70 billion.[12] That sum would include the $15 billion to $17 billion that Postmaster General Henderson estimates the Postal Service could lose in postage revenues if all bills are handled through all-electronic bill presentation and payment (EBP&P). That sum also would include the costs to the bill presenter preparing bills

[8]"Japan's Debt Menace," *The Economist*, June 5, 1999. "Japan. Return to Sender," *The Economist*, October 18, 1997.

[9]Michael H. Sedge, "Can Bill Gates Save the Italian Postal System?" *Internet News*, September 8, 1998.

[10]Ibid.

[11]http://www.postoffice-counters.co.uk/WhatWeDo.htm.

[12]*BusinessWeek*, August 31, 1998, p. 101.

and processing payments. The best-known provider of such services to consumers in the United States is Checkfree, but other firms such as Pitney Bowes, Princeton Telecom, ebills.com, and the Micro-soft–First Data Corporation (MS-FDC) joint venture, known as Transpoint, are rapidly entering the field, and a host of other consumer finance companies have begun offering outsourced EBP&P services to consumers under their own nameplate.[13]

Outside the United States, both state-owned and privatized postal systems are rushing to offer payment services. In 1998, Post Canada announced a joint venture with Cebra Inc., a subsidiary of the Bank of Montreal.[14] Its electronic post office box (EPOB) service will go into operation soon.[15] The EPOB would allow customers to receive bills by e-mail and make payments from a secure Website in which customers could view their account statements and payment options. Canadian banks for the most part have been wary of EPOB, although Post Canada insists it will not compete with financial institutions but rather serve as a transactions clearinghouse in which all banks may participate. But that might simply be a verbal distinction without a difference, still allowing Post Canada to compete unfairly with the private sector. Still, it is clear that Post Canada will move from being a financial intermediary to a marketing intermediary as well. Subscribers to EPOB will be able to join affinity lists maintained by Post Canada that will allow them to receive sales literature of potential interest electronically, by fax, or in the mail.

In New Zealand, the privatized NZ Post has launched a similar service in partnership with U.S.-based Checkfree. Should the venture be successful it will be offered in Australia by the same partnership. Checkfree has indicated that it may consider similar ventures in other countries as well.

---

[13]For more information and general background, visit sites such as http://www.checkfree.com.

[14]"Online Banking: Canada Team Ahead in Web Presentment Race," Drew Clark, *American Banker*, September 10, 1998. "Canada Post and Cebra to Develop New System to Receive and Pay Bills on the Internet," Post Canada press release, http://www.mailposte.ca/ CPC2/corpc/Newsrel/cebra.html. For current status on the plan, see http://www.canadapost.ca/CPC2/eps/cebra/epofaq.html. See also unsigned, "Future Money: Canada Post Hotwires Bill Payment," *American Banker*, August 3, 1998.

[15]See Andrew Flynn, "Canada Post to Launch Electronic Post Office," *Cnews*, October 28, 1999, www.canoe.ca/techNews9910/28-post.html.

A significant foray by the USPS into bill processing started with its purchase in 1996 of a Long Island facility from American Express that it operates as REMITCO. That enterprise receives and processes checks made for bills presented to customers, on paper. In the future REMITCO hopes to purchase other facilities. Moving into EBP&P would put the USPS even more directly into competition with private financial services institutions. Under legislation currently being considered in the U.S. House of Representatives, the USPS would be allowed to purchase thrifts and compete even more directly with the private sector. An analysis prepared by the consulting firm ISD Shaw suggests: "The new [postal private law corporation that would be created in the legislation] could, for example, use its formidable operating advantages to establish itself as a 'trusted intermediary' for the handling of transactions associated with online commerce, supplanting private providers now investing billions [of dollars] to enter this business."[16]

Business-to-Business Logistics Management

Perhaps the most important impact of the Internet on existing business models has been to make outsourcing not only of billing but of many other business functions possible on a scale that was not previously imaginable. Already the existence of the Internet has allowed even small companies to aggregate a so-called "thin market" and serve as global suppliers to consumers of books, specialty chemicals, electronic parts, financial services, and the like. Now the Internet allows specialty companies to aggregate markets and achieve economies of scale for essential business services distinct from what most businesses would consider their core competences. About 80 percent of the total e-commerce by volume is business-to-business. Logistics and financial intermediation, data processing, and e-mail hosting are among the first such services to be massively outsourced over the Internet. Many more such services, including accounting and tax preparation, will follow soon. The result will be smaller but more highly valued companies that increasingly rely on specialized knowledge and unique intellectual properties for their competitive advantage. In the future, most companies will be in some way virtual

---

[16]"Bill in Congress Pushes Postal Service in Direction of Competing with Banks," Scott Barancik, *American Banker*, April 6, 1999.

companies. For example, customers purchasing clothing over the telephone from Laura Ashley may never realize that the helpful clerk on the other end of the line is an employee of Federal Express, which manages all of Laura Ashley's direct contacts with customers, inventory, and order fulfillment.

Amazon.com is a good example of a company that relies on e-commerce not only to ship books to customers but also for its very infrastructure. Amazon.com is really more a brand name than a company in the conventional sense. Internet interfacing allows consumers individually to access the benefits of a heavily computerized book distribution infrastructure. Wholesale book distribution is dominated by the Ingram Book division of Ingram Industries, Inc. In essence, Amazon.com combined access to that already existing company with previously existing delivery services from United Parcel Service, the postal service, and FedEx to make an online enterprise that allows customers to realize significant savings.

Moreover, UPS and FDX, the parent corporation of FedEx, compete to offer any entrepreneur with an idea that could make it the next Amazon ready-built e-commerce services, available from their Web sites. Those companies will accept customer orders and payments in their call centers, warehouse products, source and assemble parts if necessary, and deliver the product to the consumer. The Japanese computermaker Fujitsu, for instance, has recently embarked on a campaign to sell personal computers of its design in the United States, although it will supply little more than design and a brand name. Assembly and delivery of the computers will be managed by FDX. The Fujitsu venture follows a similar venture between Ingram; Micro, a leading distributor of personal computer components; and Selectron Inc., a leading contract manufacturer with Baldrige-award-winning quality standards that builds products for everyone from mighty Hewlett-Packard to entrepreneurs still operating from their garages.[17]

The TNT Post Group from the Netherlands has developed a powerful presence in the corporate logistics market, offering many

---

[17]"Souping up the Supply Chain," *BusinessWeek*, August 31, 1998, p. 110. For evidence of Solectron's importance to the information economy, see also press release, "Solectron ranked Number 3 behind only America Online and Dell Computer in *BusinessWeek's* 1999 World's Best Performing Information Technology 100 listing," http://www.solectron.com/webc/enter.html?url=/news/pr_6-10b_1999.html.

of the same services in just-in-time delivery and supply-chain management that UPS and FDX offer.[18] For instance, building on its experience as a logistics provider for Fiat in Europe, TNT Postal Group is also the lead logistics coordinator for four Ford automobile assembly plants in North America.[19] In other announced projects, TNT has launched an aftermarket automobile parts supply network that will coordinate orders and shipments between repair shops, distributors, and manufacturers, largely over the Internet. It will use ECXpert electronic commerce software from Netscape Communications. The launch of a similar network for hospital supplies is under way.[20]

Given the success of the TNT Post Group and the USPS's interest in following corporate models like TNT's, it is not unreasonable to expect the Postal Service to enter the field of corporate logistics as expeditiously as it can. In a sense it will simply be expanding some of the services it already offers to businesses.

But the specter of USPS expansion into electronic infrastructure raises a number of problems, many of which already dog its activities in other competitive economic sectors. First, can the Postal Service, with notably dysfunctional labor-management relations and intense internal opposition to outsourcing its own nonessential functions, truly lead in the outsourcing economy?[21] Second, can the Postal Service truly compete on an equal basis with private logistics support businesses, including other delivery and mailing services, when it still presumes to regulate its competitors in some areas while it competes with others? After all, Postmaster General Henderson's justification for providing billpaying services is, in essence, that the USPS is using its regulatory and monopoly powers to administer its own ad hoc antitrust policy against financial intermediaries that it fears could become monopolistic. And third, if private companies are already able to raise capital in the financial markets to perform advanced logistical services without government assistance, why should the Postal Service be likewise allowed to raise private capital

[18]http://www.tnt.com/logistics/mn_overview.html and http://www.tnt-logistics.com/comp_profile/value.htm.

[19]http://www.tnt-logistics.com/case_studies/ford/ford.htm.

[20]Michael Moller and John Pallatto, "TNT Logistics Blasts Bottlenecks," *Internet Business*, November 1, 1998.

[21]See, for instance, "At Postal Union, Priority Mail Outsourcing Is a Crucial Issue in Contract Negotiations," Nancy Fonti, *Wall Street Journal*, November 25, 1998.

for purposes of competing with those companies through an unregulated wholly owned subsidiary?

Business-to-Consumer Sales and Residential Delivery

Business-to-consumer sales, a kind of subset of business-to-business services exemplified by Amazon.com, is another emerging Internet phenomenon. At the moment, online sales tend to be for small, light, nonperishable items such as books, CDs, electronics, and apparel. Consumers may buy the items frequently, but the purchases are basically intermittent. The next big wave of online offerings should change that state of affairs dramatically.

For example, after a few false starts, the online grocery business is building up steam and appears poised for a market breakout.[22] Groceries are heavy and often perishable, and, unlike books, they are routine and repeat as opposed to intermittent purchases. Steady customers for online grocery services may easily require deliveries twice a week or more, contributing, in the process, to an alternative local delivery service. Companies offering online grocery ordering include WebVan (www.webvan.com), Peapod (www.peapod.com), Streamline (www.streamline.com), Shop-link (www.shoplink.com), and Netgrocer (www.netgrocer.com). Following groceries, the next wave of online sales will most likely involve "heavy goods" such as household appliances and furnishings. Those items will most likely require local warehouses and shipping operations of their own, further adding to competition in local delivery markets.[23]

But delivery to the doorstep is only one side of the residential delivery equation. Virtual concierge service, depot services, and smart mailboxes considerably extend the universe of possibilities.[24] Consider, for instance, Packagenet, a Fairfield, Iowa-based company that

---

[22]"Amazon.com Buys 35% Stake of Seattle Online Grocery Firm," by George Anders, also *Wall Street Journal*, May 18, 1999. "Co-Founder of Borders to Launch Online Megagrocer," by George Anders, *Wall Street Journal*, April 22, 1999.

[23]See Evan I. Schwartz, "Technology: An Online Grocer Bets against Bananas and Meat, Instead Pushing Low Prices and National Delivery," *New York Times*, May 4, 1998, as well as "Heavy Lifters May Win Next Retail Round," by Tim Clark, *CNET News.com*, April 20, 1999. "Online Shopping Lifts Delivery Concerns' Volume," by John Simons and Douglas A. Blackmon, *Wall Street Journal*, December 30, 1998.

[24]"Gifts: Masterminding the Mazes of Package Delivery," by Eleena de Lisser. *Wall Street Journal*, December 23, 1999, p. B1.

has long been offering consumers shipping services from counters inside some 4,000 supermarkets. Packagenet is now developing a "Depot Network" whereby from its existing drop-off counters consumers will also be able to pick up packages at convenient times from a grocery or other store they probably would be visiting anyway. (Indeed, one would expect that Packagenet might eventually develop a local delivery service of its own.) The result will be the convenience of a postal window without the need for a dedicated post office building. Private couriers without postal overhead will offer efficient two-way shipping services. And most impressive of all, dropoff points will be linked to delivery tracking systems and merchants' online databases through e-commerce software that Packagenet is developing in partnership with companies such as Microsoft, America Online, and Netscape Communications.[25]

Meanwhile, other private ventures include smart mailboxes, climate-controlled outdoor delivery cabinets that can accept shipments from authorized delivery agents, and even the "virtual doorman," a remote delivery box monitored and controlled by means of the Internet.[26]

The growth of online sales to consumers seems to be generating higher volumes of other mail. Prudential Securities analyst B. Alex Henderson estimates that each online sale results in about six to nine pieces of mail.[27] But the Postal Service is not satisfied with just delivering extra paper. Postmaster General Henderson has indicated that he wants the USPS to maintain "a residential delivery system that is cost effective, that is low price." The Postal Service argues that its large installed base of local post offices and delivery fleets makes it uniquely well suited to handle residential deliveries. But that argument does not necessarily withstand closer scrutiny.

First, studies and historical experience have shown there is no reason to believe a natural monopoly normally exists in local delivery. In fact, private couriers with less overhead and less restrictive work

---

[25]Caruso. Since the article appeared, Netscape Communications has been acquired by America Online.

[26]De Lisser.

[27]B. Alex Henderson. Driving much of the transaction mail is payment for goods by check. As of March 1999, *The Industry Standard* reports that half of all Internet purchases are still being paid for by check. Internet Economy Metrics, *The Industry Standard*, March 1, 1999, http://www.thestandard.com.

rules may have a cost advantage over the Postal Service.[28] Second, the Postal Service has optimized its delivery infrastructure to serve every address, every business day, one time only per day. That is not necessarily the best way to serve consumers who cannot be at home during normal business hours, when the Postal Service currently delivers.

A Trusted Third Party

Another important service emerging on the Internet is so-called "trusted third party," or security, functions. Those include, for example, allowing for digital signatures; authentication of documents and the identities of communicators; postmarking of e-mail; and security for payments, escrow accounts, and other transactions. Most of those services involve the use of encryption. For secure communications to be made through encryption, the sender not only must send the message but also must give the receiver access to the electronic key or code that will open the message.

The Postal Service argues that it enjoys the public's trust and thus is the ideal institution to provide such online services. After all, its supporters maintain, individual consumers every day entrust letters to the USPS, with a high degree of confidence that those letters will not be tampered with in transit—an achievement on which the Postal Service can justifiably pride itself. Thus advocates suggest that the public will transfer this "trust" to other services. The Postal Service, for example, would be able to maintain public key infrastructures (PKI) used to archive both the "public" and the "private" keys used by citizens in secure communications so that private keys to any transaction are always available on demand to authorized law enforcement officials. A Postal Service–maintained system would also be best to facilitate government-to-citizen communication through "secure" postal channels.

But such arguments fall flat. To begin with, individuals entrust letters to the Postal Service because the Postal Service is a government

---

[28]See Peter Ferrara, "Postal Service Problems: The Need to Free the Mail" in *The Last Monopoly: Privatizing the Postal Service for the Information Age,* ed. Ed Hudgins (Washington: Cato Institute, 1996), pp. 26–28. See also Tom Lenard, "Competing Carriers," in ibid., pp. 43–52.

monopoly and individuals have had limited low-cost alternatives to government mail. Indeed, e-mail is just such a private-sector alternative that threatens the Postal Service.

In any case, in the marketplace, trust is never absolute but always relative and cost sensitive. Trusting an unknown person with a mail-order catalog, for instance, may be far less demanding than trusting that person with a satchel of gold bars or a tiny parcel filled with diamonds. It is foolish to assume that the same level of high security is necessary for each transaction. Thus, in the real world, trust occurs on an actuarial basis. Merchants trust customers with shipments if they are adequately satisfied that the risks of nonpayment are acceptable in light of the cost that further security measures would entail. Additionally, very high levels of trust are possible at low levels of cost with a counterparty about which the merchants know nothing if third parties whom the merchants respect and recognize vouch for the unknown customers. Thus letters of credit have been used for centuries. Restaurants today commonly accept colored pieces of plastic (credit cards!) as tokens of payment from diners they have never seen before and may never see again. Specialized tokens or certificates—the equivalent, for instance, of a library card or parking pass—may be appropriate for certain circumstances. The result is that w.ih multiple certificates for multiple purposes and a "web of trust" developed from overlapping third-party endorsements, a high degree of security is possible in the context of a free society.

The problem with a centralized, government-directed system for establishing trustworthiness is that invariably, as in the case of a national identification card or an internal passport, such systems work on a "guaranteed identity" basis. That is to say that governments effectively require a level of identification more suited for law enforcement than for commercial purposes. The current postal business model assumes that every customer and postal employee must be cleared in advance at a level of security appropriate to a courier carrying cash, or even to a potential criminal whose malevolent tendencies must be checkmated in advance by appropriate controls.

Such a system both makes no economic sense and is a clear danger to civil liberties. A centralized system of identity certificates—linked perhaps with biometric identifiers in drivers licenses or a "hardened" Social Security card, suggested in some actual proposals from both Congress and the Clinton administration—and cross-referenced with government records, medical histories, and transactional databases of various kinds, would pose an enormous threat to personal liberty and personal privacy.[29] The idea that the same central database would be linked to a public key infrastructure that would ensure government access to the content of all supposedly private communications on public networks is even more alarming.

There are also practical problems with governments providing such services. The British government for a number of years has used the Royal Mail in an attempt to centralize such online security services at the expense of private providers. The Royal Mail offices are the access point by which citizens secure many government services, pay taxes, and deal in other matters with government. The Royal Mail operates an electronic document filing service that citizens must use for any electronic interactions with the government. The government and the Royal Mail have hoped that the system would eventually serve as a checkpoint for herding the public into a government-controlled PKI as soon as such technology became feasible on a commercial scale. Fortunately, that day has not arrived. Technical difficulties have kept the British from fully implementing that system.[30]

In the United States, the situation has always been more nuanced. The Postal Service has developed a means by which to allow customers to use their personal computers and printers to postmark mail. Its information-based indicia program (IBIP) of course must provide a secure way to distribute postage electronically and create digitally encoded "payment evidencing," which is a legiti-

---

[29]Good discussions are available in Solveig Singleton, "Encryption Policy for the 21st Century: A Future without Government-Prescribed Key Recovery," Cato Institute Policy Study no. 325, November 19, 1998 http://www.cato.org. See also "Digital Signatures: Comments of the Center for Democracy and Technology to the National Institute of Standards and Technology," July 16, 1997, http://www.cdt.org/digisig/nistcom.html. For another useful short piece, see Will Rodger, "Digital Sigs Bill Raises Concern," Inter@ctive Week, July 27, 1998, http://www.zdnet.com/intweek/print-high/72798/pol727.html.

[30]Wendy Grossman, "Rules, Britannia", Wired News, July 7, 1998, http://www.wired.com/news/politics/story/13509.html. Also "Key to a Secure Future," Computerworld, Suruchi Mohan, August 24, 1998, http://www.computerworld.com/home/emmerce.nsf/all/980824secure.

mate and useful application of PKI technology. However, the Postal Service developed its PKI with more than online postage in mind. At that time the Clinton administration, supported by private contractors and technology consultants, strongly advocated the creation of a single national PKI that would house the cryptographic keys of all U.S. residents and companies and allow American law enforcement agencies access to those keys on demand: Postal officials made clear that they saw themselves as the logical custodians of that infrastructure. In effect, had this vision panned out, the Postal Service would have become "the keeper of the keys" to all private communications on the Internet and a primary verifier of identities. Such a system would have given the USPS considerable leverage for its commercial interests while aligning itself with the political interests of law enforcement agencies that insisted on the plan. Ultimately, limitations on available technology and public reaction against excessive demands for new surveillance powers by law enforcement both scuttled this proposal—though new variations on it remain possible.

Secure document delivery is another cryptographic application whereby postal administrations feel they can carve out a market niche for themselves by facilitating public use of cryptography in a government-friendly fashion. Thus, in May 1998, the USPS announced a cooperative agreement with the French and Canadian postal services to launch a new, global electronic courier service called PostECS. That new service is being developed under the supervision of the Brussels-based International Post Corporation (IPC). It will include document encryption, password protection, and real-time tracking and tracing of documents. Eventually it may also integrate public key cryptography, digital signature, and proof of delivery and receipt. "PostECS is a logical evolution of our original charter to provide seamless communications to our customers," said Michael S. Coughlin, who represented the USPS at the IPC Board of Directors, according to a May 28, 1998, Postal Service press release. However, UPS, which has a secure document delivery service of its own, responded by filing a complaint with the Postal Rate Commission, charging that the Postal Service unlawfully offered a competitive product on a free-trial basis. Another company offering secure document delivery is Pitney Bowes, whose iSend offering incorporates secure payment features.

Managing Internet Address Space

Address space on the Internet is organized into a loose hierarchy of domain names. Foremost among these "extensions" are the familiar generic or global top-level domains of .com, .org, .net, .gov, .mil, and .edu. To those can be added the country code top-level domain names such as .us (United States), .uk (United Kingdom), .jp (Japan), and so on. Further extensions can identify states or provinces, cities, and so forth, usually resulting in awkward names that are difficult to use and remember. Such addresses are mostly used by state and local government agencies and schools that are assigned them by local government largess. A real-life example would be addressee@ st-anselms.pvt.k12.dc.us, identifying a particular teacher at a small Catholic private (pvt) secondary school (e.g., within the K through 12 category) in the District of Columbia (dc) in the United States. For ease of use, casual users uniformly prefer shorter addresses like my-name@mymailservice.com.

In 1998, the U.S. Commerce Department turned over administration of the global domain names and other questions of Internet governance to an independent, nonprofit, and still-evolving corporation created for the purpose and known as the Internet Corporation for Assigned Names and Numbers (ICANN). The U.S. government retained control only over the .us space, which currently is managed under contract by the Information Sciences Institute of the University of Southern California. That institute was headed by the late Jon Postel, one of the Internet's founding pioneers. By virtue of being "present at the creation," he was a trusted figure who enjoyed wide discretion to manage address space as he saw fit. At the time of Postel's death in October 1998 the Postal Service was already in advanced discussions with the Commerce Department and the Information Sciences Institute about its desire to assume management of the .us space. A confidential memo from the Postal Service to Postel was leaked to the press in May 1998, creating a mild stir in the Internet community. Further, at the time of Postel's death, more details of the plan became available in formal comments filed by the Postal Service with the Commerce Department's National Telecommunications and Information Administration.[31]

---

[31]"Postal Service Eyes .us Domain," James Glave, *Wired News*, June 19, 1998, http://www.wired.com/news/news/politics/story/13129.html. See also "Confi-

In essence, the Postal Service proposed to "engage the private sector in the development of a credentialed commerce-enabling space under .us [and] promote classified business addressing under .us at local, state, and national levels as an open reference for public and private delivery systems and competing directory services." Some of the commerce-enabling functions would include assigning a secure e-mail address to every U.S. resident and mapping physical addresses onto an Internet address space. That is what Postmaster General Henderson meant when he asked

> What if every physical address in the United States had an Internet address? We would own the physical address, and we would maintain it. That means that all that information that you our customers have developed around a physical address could now migrate through the Internet and be a part of commerce.[32]

The particulars of how such a system would work are still sketchy, but one scenario is that each person in the United States should be assigned a personal e-mail address that would also encode a personal mailing address through some sequence of state, city, and street designations or rather, more likely, some curious amalgam of a social security number and a block-level nine-digit zip code. Through its traditional mail-forwarding function, the Postal Service would undertake to keep the link between those Internet addresses and physical addresses current. Goods ordered from a particular e-mail address could possibly be sent automatically to the correct physical delivery address and payment somehow expedited in the process. Additionally, low-income persons might access e-mail from public terminals in post offices and even have e-mail printouts delivered to them should they prefer.

Yet such an interconnected system managed by a government agency poses clear dangers to individual privacy. Further, linking all

---

dential Draft: USPS Coordination of the .us Domain Dated May 8, 1998," http://www.wired.com/news/news/politics/story/13130.html. NTIA documents and comments filed are at http://www.ntia.doc.gov/ntiahome/domainname/domainhome.htm#2 and http://www.ntia.doc.gov/ntiahome/domainname/usrfc/dotuslistfedreg51099.htm. For reporting on a March 10, 1999, public hearing at NTIA, "The Postal Service wants .us," see Declan McCullagh, *Wired News*, March 10, 1999, http://www.wired.com/news/news/politics/story/18371.html.
[32]Henderson.

participants to an Internet transaction by geographic coordinates and linking credentialing or certificate authority functions into the same system would import into cyberspace the entire regulatory and taxation infrastructure of geographically defined political units. That would be a sure and fast way to break up the global free-trade zone that is the greatest promise of the Internet.[33]

Finally, claims by the Postal Service that the addressing system will be open equally to private delivery services should be looked on with great skepticism. The USPS has never been shy about using its regulatory authority and monopoly status to cripple competitors. Here again Postmaster General Henderson's justification for the Postal Service offering e-commerce services, that it is to prevent private companies from creating monopolies, shows that the Postal Service will engage in industrial policy—in this case with its own antitrust action—at the expense of competitors. If the experience of other postal initiatives, such as the information-based indicia program that has occasioned much off-record grumbling in the direct marketing community, is any indication, the .us-based addressing system will be run from start to finish to guarantee the Postal Service the greatest possible competitive advantage over private-sector rivals. It will give the Postal Service control of an effectively proprietary technical standard that the private companies will have no choice but to adopt themselves.

Though some have proposed giving the Federal Communications Commission rather than the Postal Service jurisdiction over the .us space, a more sensible proposal would be the creation of a nonprofit board similar to ICANN, national in scope, and limited to the question of managing delivery address space. That would make the enterprise more manageable from the start. All stakeholders and stakeholder groups would have appropriate representation on the board, but in the name of competitive equity the Postal Service should have representation as only one stakeholder—albeit a large one—among many.

In the event that Congress privatizes the Postal Service, the current physical address correction and delivery address databases main-

---

[33]For discussion, see Harvard Law School Professor Lawrence Lessig, "Digital Dog Tags," *The Industry Standard*, October 16, 1998, http://www.thestandard.com/articles/display/0,1449,2068,00.html.

tained by the Postal Service should be spun off as a separate unit or incorporated into a truly open standards-setting process. Otherwise, control of that database could inadvertently perpetuate a monopoly privilege in substance even if Congress decides to terminate the monopoly formally. Such an approach would allow advanced local addressing systems cross-referenced with Internet addresses to evolve rapidly. It would even allow for alternative delivery systems that could route around and supplant the .us-based system if technology permits and market conditions warrant. Although .com and .us are likely to be stable in the short term, no one in the Internet community seriously believes they can and should be around forever as the fundamental organizing principles for Internet address space. We cannot easily surmise what the future holds. But it is most likely that future change for the better will come much more slowly if the current souped-up vintage 1970s addressing model becomes institutionalized in a postal bureaucracy that sees maintaining the system as its one ticket to digital relevance. Where would we be, after all, if telephone numbers were still expressed in the named local exchanges such as "Murray Hill," which were beloved earlier this century?

Conclusion

The USPS is an economic organization in direct competition with private-sector alternatives. For more than 200 years, the Postal Service and its predecessor, the Post Office, have followed the rent-seeking strategies that would be economically rational for any large organization and for any privileged state corporation in particular. To tell its assembled customers and competitors—as Postmaster Henderson did recently[34]—that "the Postal Service will put you and your products . . . before its own self-interest" strains credulity and holds the Postal Service to a far higher standard of conduct than anyone could reasonably expect, not least from a Postal Service that is ultimately "freed to compete." Why make such a claim at all?

If the Postal Service were a private business, it would be entitled to make a run at cyberspace if it wished. But inasmuch as the USPS is a

[34]Henderson.

government monopoly with authority to regulate its competitors, it should be clear that the supposedly altruistic proposals it advances have a rent-seeking element as well. Any proposal that might perpetuate the archaic postal monopoly in the new medium of cyberspace should undergo close scrutiny. The continued rapid pace of technological innovation on the Internet and the privacy rights of citizens conducting their business on the network could be at stake.

5. A Mass Mailer's Perspective

Gene A. Del Polito

When I started my career in association management, one of my mentors told me to familiarize myself with what he called "the dance of legislation." He was referring to the legislative minuet that sets the tone and pace of a legislative proposal's consideration on its way toward enactment into law.

When it comes to postal legislative reform, this is a dance with which I am somewhat familiar. In fact, in reviewing some of the articles I have written over the years, I found, even to my own surprise, an article I had written for the December 1988 issue of *Direct Marketing* magazine that marked the beginning of our present dance on the way to postal legislative reform. Never in my wildest dreams had I thought this little minuet would turn into a dance marathon.

In 1999 postal legislative reform *still* is only a matter of discussion and not yet a reality. In the meantime, the predictions that have been made regarding the transformation in the way in which America communicates and does business are well on their way to becoming reality. Indeed, with each passing year, the accelerating pace of electronic technology's development and its impact on the way we communicate virtually guarantees that the U.S. Postal Service (USPS)—at least as we know it today—is an endangered species.

Within the next three years with the widespread deployment of digital subscriber line technology and two-way interactive cable systems, Internet bandwidth, one of the last serious constraints to widespread online commerce, will have been overcome. Indeed, within the next three years, a consumer-driven electronic banking

Gene A. Del Polito is the president of the Association for Postal Commerce in Arlington, Virginia.

revolution will become reality. Within the next three years, the siphoning of bills, payments, and other transactions out of first-class mail and into electronic-based alternatives finally will make real the financing crisis that has been predicted for the Postal Service.

Customers' Lament

Over the years, the Association for Postal Commerce has been at the forefront in calling for postal legislative reform. There is an old saying that you can always tell who is the pioneer by the arrows that are stuck in his back. The old saying is true. Critics alternately have characterized us as "chicken-littles," "alarmists," and "junk mailers looking for nothing more than a postal rate free ride." Postal competitors, ideologues, and social engineers have totally forgotten that the American postal system is something that is needed, used, and paid for by mailers such as our members who pay the postage that makes it possible to send and receive mail.

They say there are three stages to the dying process: denial, anger, and, finally, acceptance. We have seen our critics pass through all three in their struggle to deny a need for postal reform, their anger over the imminence of reform, and finally their acceptance of the proposition that unless something fundamental reshapes the postal reorganization compact, the USPS, as we know it today, will not be able to survive.

Those who would prefer to transform in a heartbeat from a government-run postal system into a competitive, private-sector enterprise, or those who would prefer to hamstring the Postal Service with regulatory and legislative constraints that make surviving in a changing communications environment impossible, or those who believe that the only real purpose for the Postal Service is to ensure guaranteed employment within a cocoon insulated from the changing realities of the marketplace, or those who simply believe that the call for reform is nothing more than a replay of the narrow-minded zero-sum game that has characterized postal rate-making since reorganization's enactment have forgotten that unless the legitimate needs of postage-paying mailers are met, the mail system as an integral part of the American economic infrastructure is imperiled.

My research has brought me back to an article I wrote in 1992[1] in which I noted that postal customers have been telling postal officials consistently what they need and expect from a postal system. They want a mail service that ensures the delivery of the messages they send to any business or residential address in the nation. They want mail services that are consistent, timely, and reliable, and they want services that are priced in recognition of the changing values and needs of the marketplace. Mailers also have made clear that the definition of realistic service performance standards for all classes of mail and the provision of objective and publicly available information on service performance is essential to ensuring mail's continued value as a medium for business communication and commerce.

The Current Situation

So where are we? How far have we come?

Seven years after my 1992 comments, mail service performance still is notable for its lack of timeliness and consistency. Although certain elements of first-class mail service delivery performance have shown improvement, delivery service for periodicals and the lion's share of advertising mail is still woefully below the mark.

Former Postmaster General Anthony Frank once said, "What gets measured, improves." But here we are seven years later and we still have a service performance measurement system for only one class of mail. Regrettably, over the past seven years, we have also come to discover that even that system is not immune from internal organizational tampering and abuse. As a consequence, there still is a paucity of measures to monitor performance and to ensure accountability.

Even worse, while the Postal Service has numerous tools for gathering data from various facets of its operations, it has virtually no way of transforming those data into meaningful information that can be used readily by postal managers to improve the cost-efficiency and productivity of their operations. In fact, just recently, a group working under the auspices of the Mailers Technical Advisory Committee strongly recommended that the Postal Service "build an in-

---

[1]Gene Del Polito, "USPS Needs Rational Service Performance Standards," *Business Mailers Review*, August 1992.

formation-driven operating system linked directly to better processing technology. . . [one designed to] ensure that the information is captured and reported in real-time and in parallel to the physical mail stream."[2] Such a system, they noted, not only would be able to provide the Postal Service with the operational information it needs to better administer the mail system, but also would provide mailers with the means of determining in real time where their mail is within the processing and distribution system and when it is expected to reach its delivery destination.

Mailers have made clear that if mail's value as a medium for business communication and commerce is to endure, the nature and quality of mail service must become utility-like. When an individual walks into a room and flips on the light switch, chances are there is no doubt the lights will come on. When one turns the faucet on in the kitchen sink, it is not necessary to question whether the water will come out. In a time in which it is not necessary to question when the newspaper will be delivered, when a television or radio commercial will air, or whether one's interactive catalog will appear online, there should be no tolerance for having to wonder when mail once tendered will be delivered.

The power, the reach, the convenience, and the cost of alternative ways of doing business improve with each passing year. The same cannot yet be said for the mail. Mailers understand all too well the cost their businesses suffer when mail fails the utility test. Billions of dollars are spent each year not only on the development and distribution of mail advertising and marketing programs, but also on the call centers that are staffed, waiting for orders generated by those mailings, the thousands of square feet of inventory that are prepared for shipment, and the stock and staffing that are at the ready to satisfy customers' needs during in-store sales promotions. In short, the quality and value of postal services must improve or the reality we all will have to face is that of a thinning of postal revenues.

One might tend to believe that with this as the prospect, those who are charged with making the postal system work would be driven to bring about significant change. Some are, and some are not. Those who are amaze me, as the rewards for behaving in a

[2]"Report of the Capital Spending Work Group," Mailers Technical Advisory Committee, January 13, 1999.

manner that would minimize costs and maximize gains are virtually nonexistent.

Some supporters of the Postal Service seem oblivious to some of the problems that are at the base of their peril. For instance, in 1970, the Post Office Department was characterized as an institution in which labor constituted more than 80 percent of its costs. Almost three decades after the enactment of reorganization, the Postal Service *still* can be characterized as an institution in which labor constitutes more than 80 percent of its costs. Even today, certain elements within the organized labor community seem bent on exacting their pound of flesh without evidencing even a hint of concern for the security and viability of future paychecks. What some in labor fail to recognize is that there really is no pot of gold at the end of the postal rainbow. In fact, without the business of those who *choose* to use the mail, there would not *be* a rainbow. Yet they persist in behaving in a manner that only encourages businesses to pursue alternatives.

The Promise of Reform

With the foregoing as a backdrop, consider House Postal Subcommittee Chairman John McHugh's (R-N.Y.) brainchild, the Postal Reform Act of 1999, also known as H.R. 22.

Mailers have called for an end to precipitous, business-busting postal rate increases. H.R. 22 sets forth provisions that would change significantly the regime governing most postal ratemaking to provide for an orderly, an affordable, and a more performance-driven basis for financing the postal system. H.R. 22 also sets forth more meaningful rewards for prudent management of the nation's postal resources, even if it falls short of the kind of reform that would be necessary to radically reorient the incentives that underlie our postal system.

Mailers have called for an end to a problem that has long plagued postal ratemaking, that is, the problem of the whole-cent integer. Much of the pain and rancor associated with postal rate cases generally stems from the long-standing tradition of setting the first-class mail rate by whole-cent integers. Each penny of a first-class stamp represents some $800 million to $900 million in postal revenue. Thus, when the price of a new first-class stamp is increased (or decreased) by a penny, the Postal Service and the

Postal Rate Commission are forced to determine how to shift a subsequent $800 million in revenues across all other mail classes and services. Raise the first-class stamp too much, and all other mail classes and services get off practically scot free. Raise the first-class stamp too little, and the subsequent rate increases for all other classes and services, most particularly standard mail (A), turn out to be bone-crushing.

H.R. 22 would address the problem by placing single-piece first-class mail and bulk first-class mail in different mail classification baskets. Aunt Minnie would be assured that her rates would not be raised too much, while other mailers no longer would be held hostage to her needs. For once, everyone could truly look forward to paying only his or her fair share.

H.R. 22 would grant the Postal Service a considerable measure of the regulatory flexibility it has said it desires, to enable it to operate in a more businesslike manner. That flexibility would extend not only to those services outside the scope of its letter- mail monopoly, but also to those within the largely monopoly-protected, noncompetitive arena. Flexibility also would be afforded over the conduct of experiments and the provision of new services.

H.R. 22 would empower the Postal Service to negotiate service agreements with those of its customers that are able to provide cost savings and new revenue-generating opportunities that otherwise would not be possible within the context of the regular mail classification schedule. That would enable the Postal Service to further maximize the resources, energy, and creativity of its private-sector customers to further improve the efficiency and profitability of postal operations.

Mailers have called for standards for the measurement of mail service performance. H.R. 22 would require the Postal Service to develop and publish delivery service performance standards for every class of mail within the noncompetitive mail classification basket. It also would require that the Postal Service's performance measured against those standards be made public.

H.R. 22 would require the Postal Service to provide all the necessary financial and other information needed for regulatory review and oversight. Further, it would make clear that the provision of those data and mail service performance measures would be subject to independent audit and would be made an integral part of any consideration allowing the Postal Service to enjoy freedom from more stringent rate regulation or to provide its employees with financial reward.

Indeed, many provisions within H.R. 22 take a giant step toward addressing many of the concerns that have been laid at Congress's doorstep by mailers, postal competitors, postal workers, and postal management. H.R. 22, however, is far from the perfect remedy for all that ails the USPS. In fact, it would be a mistake to consider it the be-all *and* end-all of postal legislative reform.

For instance, although H.R. 22 would require the Postal Service to develop measures against which to assess its delivery service performance, the bill does not address how its proposed rate-making regime would address the costs of developing such a system. Although H.R. 22 would require the Postal Service to report regularly and in detail to a new Postal Regulatory Commission on the costs of its services, the cost of universal service, and other such matters, it fails to address how the Postal Service will pay for the development of those new, but essential, measurement tools. Finally, although H.R. 22 would empower the Postal Service to provide competitive postal and nonpostal services through a private law corporation, the strictures placed on the capital formation of such a corporation would seem to make it nonviable.

So instead of viewing the present iteration of H.R. 22 as the miracle elixir, I believe it would be more appropriate to view the measure more like Congress's 1986 enactment of Social Security reform: not a work of perfection, but a work that, with a little more fine-tuning, just may be enough to enable the system to survive satisfactorily for at least the next decade or until we perceive more clearly what our nation's longer-term postal needs will be.

Conclusion

Postal reform is a major policy item in Congress. I can only hope that the manner in which the postal governors, postal management, postal competitors, postal labor, and postal customers address reform will have a character that goes beyond the childish squabbling that has marked the past four years.

Each of us, in turn, has threatened to hold our breath and turn blue unless legislative proposals were crafted in our own image and likeness. We would be better advised, however, to heed the words of the Biblical letter writer Paul to the ancient Corinthians that, as adults, it is time for all of us to put away our childish things and to get on with the business of ensuring that America's postal system will remain a viable part of our nation's economic and communications infrastructure.

PART II

THE CHANGING MARKET STRUCTURE

6. Labor Market Outcomes of Postal Reorganization

D. Richard Froelke

In the year 2000, 30 years will have passed since Congress enacted the Postal Reorganization Act of 1970 (PRA).[1] Periodic debate about the continued monopoly status of the Postal Service forces those interested in that institution to pause and constructively rethink its economic utility, past performance, and future role in the communications marketplace. Postal "wages, hours and other terms and conditions of employment"[2] are largely set or influenced through the interactions of the U.S. Postal Service (USPS) and its major unions under the procedures established in chapters 10 and 12 of the PRA.[3] It is worthwhile to assess what impact that unique process for wage and work rule determination has had on the efficiency of the operations of the Postal Service. We can ask whether that labor regime is "consistent with the traditional American principle of limited government, individual liberty, and peace?"[4]

The Labor Regime of 1970

Congress did not operate in a vacuum in 1970 when it crafted the PRA. That legislation was the product of a postal history uniquely

D. Richard Froelke is a counsel to the law firm of Vorys, Sater, Seymour and Pease LLP in its Washington, D.C., office. Formerly, he served for five years with the National Labor Relations Board and for 27 years as regional labor counsel in Chicago, assistant general counsel, and manager of collective bargaining for the U.S. Postal Service in Washington, D.C.

[1]Public Law. 91–375, August 12, 1970, 84 Stat. 719, 39 USC 101 *et.seq.*
[2]National Labor Relations Act, 29 USC 158 (d) (Section 8 (d).)
[3]Specifically, 39 USC 1001, 1003, 1203, 1206, 1207, and Section 10 of Public Law 91–375 effective August 12, 1970.
[4]Edward L. Hudgins, ed., *The Last Monopoly: Privatizing the Postal Service for the Information Age* (Washington: Cato Institute, 1996), p. 140.

chronicled in an extensive, impartial, and unbiased manner by the President's Commission on Postal Organization in the 1968 Kappel Commission report. That public policy treasure trove dissected the Post Office of the 1960s and laid out the potential policy options and alternatives for reform available to the federal government.

It is useful initially to focus on the regime crafted by Congress for postal wage and work rule determination, collective bargaining, and dispute resolution. What efficiencies or inefficiencies has the PRA process placed on the functioning of the Postal Service? Is there any politically acceptable "magic bullet" available to today's reformers in the Congress that could hold out hope for improving the labor-management efficiencies of this institution?

Terms of employment and work rules, and the way they are determined, have a tremendous influence on the morale and aspirations of the nearly 900,000 postal workers. As the Kappel Commission researchers found in 1968, the classic monopoly arrangement of the Post Office before enactment of the PRA provided for direct governmental control of the most significant managerial prerogatives and functions:

> Congress controls the essential element of employer/employee relationships: wages, working conditions, and fringe benefits;—of postal service, by defining the classes of mail and the rates which may be charged for each;—of postal deficit, by directing that certain classes of mail be charged at less than cost and that operations be conducted in such a way as to limit Post Office Department [POD] management's flexibility.[5]

The Kappel Commission also recognized that the POD's "principal failure is one of management." As it summarized,

> The organization of the Post Office as an ordinary Cabinet department guarantees that *the nominal managers of the postal service do not have the authority to run the postal service.* The important [labor and] management decisions of the Post Office are beyond their control and therefore cannot be made on the basis of business judgment.[6] [Emphasis in original.]

In enacting the PRA, Congress in effect deregulated postal labor-management relations and removed direct governmental determi-

---

[5]Annex to *Toward Postal Excellence—The Report of the President's Organization*, Vol. 1, Report of the General Contractor (Cambridge, Mass.: Arthur D. Little, Inc., 1968), p. 112.

[6]*Toward Postal Excellence*, p. 33.

nation of "wages, hours and other terms and conditions of employment" for nonmanagement employees of the Postal Service. That was accomplished through adoption of free collective bargaining, dispute resolution procedures, and the statutory comparability standard for the guidance of the bargaining parties and resolution neutrals. What is fascinating about the PRA is that in eschewing direct governmental determination of labor conditions by congressional action, Congress also rejected the Kappel Commission's recommendation that

> In the event of an impasse over a contract question or pay dispute which the parties *are unwilling to submit to binding arbitration or to resolve by some other agreed-upon means*, the issue would be referred to the President of the United States . . . [who] would be free to establish whatever ad hoc methods he chooses to resolve the matter.[7] [Emphasis added.]

Similarly, Congress did not give the Postmaster General unilateral authority to impose a final bargaining solution in such disputes. Further, the presidentially appointed Postal Board of Governors was not given any decisive unilateral authority either. Likewise, Congress did not vest any authority to set postal wage levels in the presidentially appointed members of the Postal Rate Commission, who from time to time are requested by the Board of Governors "to submit a recommended decision on changes in a rate or rates of postage or in a fee or fees for postal services." (39 U.S. Code § 3622(a).) *No* direct congressional action, *no* presidential action, and *no* presidentially appointed Board of Governors or Postal Rate Commission was given any authority in the PRA to resolve postal bargaining disputes to set wage and benefit levels for the then-650,000 nonmanagerial Postal Service employees whose salaries and benefits constituted around 80 percent of postal expenditures. That was deregulation of postal labor relations on a grand scale!

In 1970, whether Congress had repealed the postal monopoly and chartered the Post Office Department as a strictly private corporation, or structured it like any of the hybrid business forms available at the time, such as the Tennessee Valley Authority, it had to deal with the fundamental question of how to set "wages, hours and terms, and conditions of employment" for the enterprise. It seems apparent that in 1970 neither the federal executive nor legislative

[7]Ibid., p. 60.

branch wanted to remain "in the loop" in setting postal terms of employment. That was especially true in light of a March 1970 nationwide postal strike. President Richard M. Nixon sent 30,000 troops to New York City to help deliver mail and break the strike.

Similarly, if every vestige of governmental monopoly had been eliminated by Congress in 1970 and a private corporation chartered, it is more likely than not that the 650,000 unionized postal employees would have opted for collective bargaining in the new corporation through the election processes set forth under the National Labor Relations Act or through voluntary recognition by the new private employer. What the nation did get in § 10(a) of the PRA was mandatory recognition by the Postal Service of the labor organizations "hold[ing] national exclusive recognition granted by the Post Office Department, [and a directive that it] shall negotiate an agreement or agreements covering wages, hours and working conditions. . . ." In effect, the country got a deregulated postal labor-management system to set labor wage rates and working conditions based on private-sector models of collective bargaining—the system identical in major respects to the union/private-sector model that would have been established had the monopoly been ended and the institution privatized in 1970.

Indeed, Congress in 1970 accepted the clearest recommendation of the 1968 Kappel Commission on labor relations reform:

> Conditions of employment for nonmanagerial employees would be established by collective bargaining between postal labor and management. . . . The Corporation should protect present pay levels; it should negotiate the future pay of postal employees taking into account competing wage levels, the principle of comparability, where possible, or a similar standard of equity. . . . We are confident that management and unions working to achieve their common aim of better public service and improved working conditions will be able to resolve most issues.[8]

Although the Kappel Commission did not recommend final and binding interest arbitration as the sole means of resolving bargaining disputes, it did not rule out any role for arbitration upon the agreement of both parties. What Congress did mandate in § 10(a) of the PRA and in 39 USC § 1207 was not only collective bargaining but also a dispute resolution system culminating in a conclusive and binding

[8]Ibid., pp. 58–59.

interest arbitration and continuation of the government ban on strike activity. (39 USC § 410(b)(2).)

The PRA authorized full bilateral collective bargaining with a default mechanism of ad hoc interest arbitration chaired by a single citizen neutral to resolve bargaining disputes (see 39 USC § 1207(c).) The PRA further left the postal parties free to design their own brand of dispute resolution "procedures by mutual agreement." (39 USC § 1206(b).) Finally, the PRA continued the traditional ban on strikes in the federal government. Thus, Congress provided a nongovernmental mechanism to determine terms and conditions of employment while granting the parties maximum latitude to create their own process consistent with the suggestions of the Kappel Commission.

With the 1970 PRA, Congress removed from the hands of government direct determination of "wages, hours and terms of conditions of employment" for hundreds of thousands of citizen-employees of the Postal Service, clearly advancing the goal of "limited government." By banning compulsory unionism in the Postal Service (39 USC § 1209(c)), Congress clearly advanced the principle of "individual liberty." Finally, by providing interest arbitration to resolve contract disputes (39 USC § 1207(c)(1)) and retaining the prohibition of strikes (39 USC § 410(b)(1) and 5 USC § 7311) within the Postal Service, Congress clearly opted for a peaceful resolution of bargaining disputes.

But in spite of that substantial deregulation, Congress did establish some guidelines for contract terms consistent with the Kappel Commission's recommendation: that the new postal corporation "should negotiate the future pay of postal employees taking into account competitive wage levels, the principle of comparability, where possible or a similar standard of equity. . . ." Congress offered sharper language in § 1003(a) of the PRA: "It shall be the policy of the Postal Service to maintain compensation and benefits for all officers and employees on a standard of comparability to the compensation and benefits paid for comparable levels of work in the private sector of the economy." (39 USC § 1003(a).) In 39 USC § 101(c), Congress stated that "As an employer, the Postal Service shall achieve and maintain compensation for its officers and employees comparable to the rates and types of compensation paid in the private sector."

Unrealistic System Expectations

The Kappel Commission can be criticized for its idealized, indeed, nearly utopian view of the potential benefits that would be realized by introducing a full collective-bargaining process to the Postal Service.[9] The Commission oversold that concept to Congress. After all, its own data established clearly that in 1968 postal unions had literally no bargaining relationship with the POD and virtually no history of cooperative dealings on the basis of any mutual trust or respect with management. The Commission itself, commenting on a Kennedy administration executive order that introduced a very restricted form of collective bargaining for the federal government, concluded:

> Judging from the frequency and intensity of complaints by representatives of both postal unions and management, Executive Order 10988 has been less than a success in the postal service. In many interviews with the Commission, both labor and management have challenged the good faith of the other. . . . It is nevertheless clear that the relationship between labor and management in the Post Office is generally unproductive.[10]

Yet relying on the views of its prime labor consultant, Robert R. Nathan Associates, the Commission leaped to the conclusion that "Many of the problems in this area [lack of good faith on the part of postal labor and management] stem from the exclusion from bargaining of most items bargainable between management and labor in the private sector."[11] Nathan advised the Commission that if the postal parties only had "the ability to negotiate basic money issues . . . [management could buy] union cooperation in improved management or productivity."[12] Consequently, the Kappel Commission observed that "We are confident that management and unions working to achieve their common aim of better public service and

---

[9]I have taken the view that the Commission's overall effort was grade A and highly influential and valuable to Congress. The insights that permeate the work are in no small measure the product of its experienced membership and staff led by Murray Comarow, its distinguished executive director, who has given me and many Postal audiences the value of his honest, forthright, and penetrating commentary of the contemporary Postal scene.

[10]*Toward Postal Excellence*, p. 20.

[11]Ibid.

[12]Ibid.

improved working conditions will be able to resolve most issues" through free collective bargaining.

Scant empirical data supported that claim for collective bargaining in 1968. Further, that claim in effect directly contradicted the Supreme Court's 1960 classic description of the American labor relations model of the collective-bargaining process that it articulated in *NLRB v. Insurance Agents (Prudential Insurance Co.)*, 361 U.S. 477 (1960):

> Collective bargaining, under a system where the government does not attempt to control the results of negotiations, cannot be equated with an academic collective search for truth. . . . The parties—even granting the modification of views that may come from a realization of economic interdependence—still proceed from contrary and to an extent antagonistic viewpoints and concepts of self-interest. The system has not reached the ideal of the philosophic notion that perfect understanding among people would lead to perfect agreement among them on values. The presence of economic weapons in reserve, and their actual exercise on occasion by the parties is part and parcel of the system. . . . The truth of the matter is . . . the two factors—necessity for good-faith bargaining between parties, and the availability of economic pressure devices to each to make the other party incline to agree on one's terms—exist side by side.[13]

The American collective-bargaining model of the 1960s was adversarial and opportunistic, based on the self-interest of the parties involved. The Kappel Commission's notion that the postal parties, once armed with collective-bargaining rights, would submerge their special interests in favor of the common good of third-party consumers is counterintuitive and lacking in support.

Resolution Record

How, then, has the bargaining system functioned in practice? In every postal dispute resolution case between 1981 and 1996 in which I have participated, every neutral arbitrator has looked to the levels of wages and benefits prevailing for "comparable levels of work in the private sector of the economy" on which to base decisions. Neutrals have rejected every union attempt to identify the prevailing

---

[13]*NLRB v. Insurance Agents (Prudential Insurance Co.)*, 361 U.S. 477, at pp. 488–89, 1960.

wage level by reference to a labor subset, for example, of "white males employed in large unionized firms" in the economy. Neutrals have rejected union invitations to compare postal wage levels only with the highest wage levels that can be found in the economy. As one neutral wrote in the 1993 Valtin award, they looked instead to the private sector as a whole consistent with a clear reading of the PRA and its legislative history.

The course of action followed by neutrals has benefited every postal consumer in the nation. It also serves to underscore the wisdom of the framers of the PRA. To guard at least in theory against either postal labor or management misusing the monopoly to extract "market rents" (excessive wages or profits) from consumers, the comparability principle protects the public interest by requiring the Postal Service to operate as if it were subject to the discipline of the competitive product market.[14] The PRA provides a regulatory framework whereby the Postal Service has the policy goal of providing the public with a vital service in a cost-efficient manner. (39 USC § 101.) Although the Postal Service is a labor-intensive rather than capital-intensive enterprise, *controlling postal costs ultimately turns on paying competitive wages and benefits.* Professor Michael Wachter of the University of Pennsylvania has explained through his testimony to postal neutrals since 1981 that "The payment of a noncompetitive compensation premium dissipates the potential benefits of economies-of-density in the delivery function, and causes the universal price [for postal products] to be higher than it would in a competitive market."[15]

The key notion that has been stressed by Professor Wachter to neutrals hearing dispute resolution matters is that "the goal of the comparability mandate is to force the Postal Service to operate as if it were in competitive markets, thus protecting the interests of postal consumers and insuring universal service at cost-efficient prices. The goal is not to provide protection for noncompetitive postal prices and wages."[16]

---

[14]Michael Wachter, Barry Hirsch, and James Gillula, *The Comparability of the U.S. Postal Service Wages and Benefits to the Private Sector: Evidence from the Total Compensation Premium, New Hire Wage Increases, Quit Rates, and Application Rates,* July 10, 1995, Exhibit IV(E) p. 14 in testimony before the Stark Board.

[15]Ibid., p. 15.

[16]Ibid.

Inflexible Labor Policies

Commentators from time to time refer to costly postal work rules to suggest that the Postal Service is inefficient and bureaucratic and, in effect, is an abusive monopolist. To a certain extent, work rules, whether determined unilaterally by the employer or bilaterally by the employer and labor, will inevitably control and organize the way work is performed within a firm. For the Postal Service, it is instructive once against to look at history through the lens of the Kappel Commission report.

Robert R. Nathan, the Commission's primary labor consultant, extensively studied the Post Office in 1967 and 1968 and compared it with American Telephone & Telegraph, the Chicago and Northwestern Railroad, United Parcel Service (UPS), and REA Express. He summarized his findings about POD management in rather bleak terms: "Management is essentially bureaucratic . . . recruited almost exclusively from within the postal service (except for patronage appointments), thereby strengthening stability, continuity, and tradition, with less emphasis on management ability and skill."[17] Nathan went on to note that both seniority and political acceptability were the deciding factors in promotions, considerations that created an environment in which "employees, though committed to a high standard of service, are more concerned with job tenure than with better individual performance, and more concerned with ease and convenience than with advancement based on increased responsibilities."[18] Nathan concluded that "There is little incentive in the existing personnel framework for employees individually to do more or better work."[19]

Nathan recommended that "pay and promotion incentives be reoriented to stimulate improved productivity by rewarding superior performance as well as dependability and continuity of service." Yet the early postal collective-bargaining agreements saw neither labor nor management do anything to recognize "individual or group incentives" nor to compensate for "increased responsibility and arduous conditions of employment." Instead the parties installed the old

---

[17]Robert R. Nathan Associates, Inc., *Personnel Administration and Labor Relations: A Report to the President's Commission on Postal Organization,* Washington, 1968, p. 2.
[18]Ibid.
[19]Ibid.

government "step increase program," and added a cost of living clause and a general wage adjustment for all bargaining unit employees in the 1971 and 1973 agreements. This compensation practice has essentially continued to the present day. Nathan was ahead of his time in calling for "pay for performance" as a rational way of providing incentives to postal employees. But postal labor and management are a long way from creating such a system.[20] Nathan commented in 1968 that "*The weakness of incentives* of compensation, promotion and pay is one of the principal barriers to rising productivity and efficiency in the postal service."[21] [Emphasis in original.] The case remains the same today.

In 1991 Postal Service management did design and offer to all unions in collective bargaining a performance bonus system called "Striving for Excellence Together." To their credit the National Rural Letter Carriers Association and the National Postal Mail Handlers Union, AFL-CIO, voluntarily accepted the so-called SET Program and wrote it into their collective-bargaining agreements in 1991. However, the two largest postal unions, the APWU, AFL-CIO, and the NALC, AFL-CIO, categorically rejected the SET Program in collective bargaining. When the NALC and APWU interest arbitration was later convened before neutral Chairman Richard Mittenthal, the Postal Service again offered the SET Program as an add-on to the compensation program. When both NALC and APWU denounced the SET pay-for-performance concept, Chairman Mittenthal did not foist it on the unions over their objections. By their short-sighted, anachronistic approach to modern compensation concepts, the two major postal unions missed the opportunity for postal workers to share potentially in many millions of dollars generated subsequently by the SET program.

Limitations on working hours and workforce flexibility rules contained in collective-bargaining agreements also are key determinants of how postal work is organized and thus of its relative cost to the consumer. In 1967, slightly more than two-thirds of the then-715,000

[20]The National Rural Letter Carriers Association has long adopted evaluated routes that inter alia set pay rationally based on delivery stops, mail volume, and distance traveled. Since 1996, supervisory and management earnings also have been tied to firm performance and individual accomplishment. But for nearly 30 years, postal labor has not embraced incentive- or performance-driven pay systems.

[21]Robert R. Nathan Associates, Inc., p. 9.

total paid postal employees were "regular career employees," that is, essentially full-time workers. Part-time workers with flexible hours made up the other one-third of the workforce, or 235,000 workers.[22] Commenting on this situation, Nathan stated,

> It is also true that in general there is more flexibility than management *has been able or willing to use,* as evidenced by the wide variations in management and efficiency among Post offices.[23] [Emphasis added.]

It is instructive to compare the Postal Service's work rules with those of present-day firms like UPS and Federal Express (FedEx), the major providers of parcel and expedited mail, with the Postal Service a minimal competitor in those markets. Those private firms rely *principally on part-time workers for in-plant sortation and loading of vehicles,* which are lower-cost components in their overall labor cost structure. But after passage of the PRA, Postal Service not only did not retain one-third of its employees as part-time, with flexible hours, it actually lost ground.

Postal management agreed in its first labor contract in 1971 with the union's demands that "The Employer shall man all Post Offices and facilities with 200 or more man years of employment with 90 percent full-time employees." (Article VII Section 3 1971 Agreement.) Reducing operational flexibility even more, management further agreed that those full-time postal employees were to work "eight (8) hours per day within ten (10) consecutive hours." (Article VIII Section 1, 1971 Agreement.) In the 1973 labor agreement flexibility was further restricted when postal management agreed "that in all offices with more than 100 full-time employees in the bargaining units the normal work week for full-time regular employees will be forty hours per week, eight hours per day within nine consecutive hours." (Article VIII Section 1, 1973 Agreement.) Those voluntarily agreed-to operational restrictions remain in effect today with an exception noted as follows.

The 1971 agreement also established a guarantee of at least four hours of pay whenever employees are called in outside their regular work schedules (Article VIII Section 8). The 1973 agreement established that a full-time regular worker called in on his or her non-

[22]Ibid., p. 26.
[23]Ibid., p. 22.

scheduled day "will be guaranteed eight hours work or pay in lieu thereof." (Article VIII, Section 8, 1973 Agreement.)

Thus in 1971 and 1973 Postal Service management surrendered substantial part-time operational flexibility to the unions and since then has never been able to secure any relief from those restrictions in collective-bargaining negotiations. Private competitors like UPS and FedEx, which are normally thought of as efficient employers, manage their inside operations by massing and matching *part-time work groups* with variable volumes of packages. On the other hand, the Postal Service masses full-time sortation personnel to handle its variable mail volumes, with only limited part-time employees, who historically average 38 hours per week, to supplement the full-time work force. Under this work rule setup, high overtime usage is the only practical way of handling volume surges.

The problem of mandatory overtime reached a boiling point in 1984 when Postmaster General William Bolger agreed to penalty overtime payments of double time for hours over 60 in a work week, along with complicated overtime payment procedures that have plagued postal operations during the intervening 15 years.

Flexibility limitations voluntarily accepted by the Postal Service in early collective bargaining have added incalculable operational costs to the Postal Service over the past three decades. Until bar-code technology meaningfully changes the capital-labor ratio for mail distribution and ultimately allows for reductions in labor demand, the Postal Service will have virtually no way to correct the 1971 and 1973 voluntary bargaining missteps.

In 1991, in an interest arbitration dispute with its clerks and city carriers unions, the Postal Service offered innovative and comprehensive arguments in support of its bargaining demands for more flexibility in work-rule policies. Neutral Chairman Richard Mittenthal, on the basis of the evidence, was persuaded to change the historical 90–10 full-time/part-time ratio that had prevailed since 1971 to 80–20 for the clerks and 88–12 for the carriers. Mittenthal also allowed for another type of noncareer contingent employee, referred to as a "transitional employee," to be used to assist the Postal Service in adjusting to the introduction of bar-code technology. Those workforce flexibility breakthroughs could not, in my judgment, have occurred through collective bargaining with the unions, but were the product of the interest arbitration portion of the postal labor relations model.

Organized labor is well-known for historically trying to slow the introduction of new labor-saving practices in industries such as railroads and the building trades. But to postal labor's credit, such artificial work-rule restrictions did not appear in early Postal Service labor agreements. Article IV of the 1971 Agreement, entitled "Technological and Mechanization Changes," gave the Postal Service the right to introduce new processes after advance notice to the postal unions. In subsequent years, although spirited rights arbitrations have been common over the labor rates or craft assignment of the new mechanization, the Postal Service has retained the right to introduce technological advances as fast as the new work processes for those technologies could be developed.

But in 1971 the postal unions successfully negotiated protection against involuntary layoffs, a provision that at least theoretically offsets the potential benefits that might accrue from introducing new labor-saving technology. Such broad protection against layoffs has continued in subsequent agreements and distinguishes the Postal Service from nearly all employers in the private sector. While postal employment levels have consistently been more than 700,000 since the 1970s and in fact have grown to more than 800,000 in the past five years, there remains the possibility in the next century that communications market breakthroughs will force major reductions in the postal labor force.

The Postal Service currently has only limited rights to cut employment levels. But under Article VI of the 1978 labor agreement, postal management won in interest arbitration the right to lay off employees with less than six years of continuous employment. The Postal Service has *never utilized this right* in the intervening 20 years. The price it paid to secure even limited layoff rights was high as the arbitrator granted uncapped cost of living adjustment (COLA) payments to union employees. That poorly conceived trade has subsequently cost postal consumers billions of dollars.

What Is to Blame?

A review of postal work rules shows that the interest arbitration process is clearly not at fault for many of the Postal Service's labor rigidities. The major postal work rules were installed through voluntary collective bargaining in the 1971 and 1973 national agreements. Interest arbitration in the fullest sense of the term did not occur in the Postal Service until 1984. By that time, most of the work rule damage had long been done. In fact, some of the postal work rules voluntarily incorporated into the labor agreements had origins going back well before the passage of the PRA, which were simply carried over into the post-PRA labor agreements. A few examples illustrate the point.

The 25 percent premium for work performed on Sunday, including any Sunday shift time that flows back to Saturday or ahead to Monday (Article VIII Section 6), came in the 1971 Agreement; it had been the law for much of the federal government for many years before the PRA. Likewise, the 10 percent night shift differential rate (Article VIII Section 7) for work hours between 6 p.m. and 6 a.m. had been the law in the federal government before PRA.

Those differentials could not be changed in collective bargaining. However, they have been addressed partially in interest arbitration cases. For example, by 1995 the night differential rate for a veteran clerk or carrier amounted to $1.71 per hour. In an interest arbitration case in October 1995 involving the APWU, AFL-CIO, the Postal Service made its case to the satisfaction of neutral arbitrator Jack Clarke that the night shift differential rate was demonstrably too high by private-sector standards. Chairman Clarke ordered a reduction of that differential to a flat rate $1.58, effective November 22, 1997. Unfortunately, the neutral in that case did not see fit to confine the 25 percent Sunday premium amount to only that 24-hour period of Sunday. That premium rate still applies to Sunday shift overlaps on either Saturday or Monday.

The Arbitration System

The PRA enabled postal labor and management to design their own grievance systems but required an opportunity for a fair hearing on adverse actions (disciplinary actions) (39 USC § 1001(b)) and authorized binding third-party arbitrations as a means of concluding the process (30 USC § 1206(b).) This arrangement in theory was a huge improvement over the labyrinth appellate structures existing under the Post Office Department because it enabled a neutral, outside arbitrator to decide appeals, whether they concerned the propriety of discipline imposed or management compliance with collective-bargaining terms.

What neither the Kappel Commission, its contractor Robert R. Nathan Associates, or Congress foresaw was that grievance and appeal filing would become a cottage industry within the Postal Service. Individuals and union representatives file huge numbers of grievances. Postal workers are allowed by work rules to pursue their complaints "on the clock," that is, they receive their salaries for their postal work even as they expend considerable official time pursuing grievance matters under the terms of the labor agreements. Postal unions aggressively appeal every conceivable disciplinary matter or alleged contract violation committed by postal management. And perhaps postal management has been too ready to use its "grievance denied" stamp and pass the grievance up to a higher stop in the process. The result is that the total grievance backlog awaiting arbitration by 1998 approached nearly 100,000 cases.

The General Accounting Office (GAO) roughly pegged the cost of running the postal grievance-arbitration system in 1992 at about $200 million.[24] Enormous amounts of productive work time are lost as union representatives, grievants, and managers process the flood of grievances and participate in meetings to resolve disputes. Clearly a better, more efficient system must be agreed to bilaterally by the bargaining parties to correct the present system.

There have been attempts to improve the efficiency of the process and to cut costs. As early as 1973 an experimental, informal expedited arbitration program was put into effect to resolve disputes more quickly. (Article XV, Section 4, of the 1973 Agreement.) That program, which was adopted on a permanent basis in subsequent contracts, has resulted in thousands of lower-cost, informal expedited arbitration hearings. It is unreasonable to expect that postal dispute resolution processes in disciplinary matters can be meaningfully reduced as courts have held that postal employees have a proprietary interest in continued employment that is entitled to due process protection and the grievance arbitration system satisfies their due process rights.[25]

---

[24]U.S. General Accounting Office, *U.S. Postal Service Labor-Management Problems Persist on the Workroom Floor*, vol. II, (Washington: Government Printing Office, 1994), p. 38.

[25]*Winston et al. v. U.S. Postal Service*, 585 F.2d 198 (7th Cir. 1975); *Malone v. U.S. Postal Service*, 526 F.2d 1099 (6th Cir. 1975).

A number of suggested reforms might make for a more efficient and fair grievance-arbitration process. They would include the following:

1. Make local postal managers and supervisors directly accountable on their performance evaluations if they support disciplinary actions that ultimately are reversed as lacking "just cause" by a neutral arbiter, or who are found willfully to violate contract work rules. Such a move would constitute a giant step toward assuring that contractual promises entered into with postal labor will be abided by.

2. As part of the merit pay program, reward managers and supervisors who establish records of winning arbitrations, settling backlogged cases, and complying with contract work rules.

3. Encourage union and management personnel jointly to study and agree that precedents set by arbitration decisions will be the "law of the issue" and control disposition of future cases. A group of prominent former presidents of the National Academy of Arbitration could be impaneled to make such determinations when agreement proves elusive. Such precedent-based rules would reduce the number of cases and the time and money now wasted on duplicative ad hoc arbitration.

4. Make the loser pay all arbitration fees and costs, including reasonable advocacy expenses for the winning side as determined by the neutral arbiter.

5. Institutionalize joint interest-based problem-solving techniques and training for all local post office personnel, including management, local union leaders, and rank and file workers, in hopes that in the future all sides will be able to work out local problems short of filing formal contract grievances.

6. Require third-party mediation of all grievances filed before any written appeals.

7. Require a $50 filing fee for any written grievance appeals, which fee is recoverable as part of a remedy if the case is settled in favor of the grievant or if that individual is found to have prevailed in arbitration.

8. Institute a system that allows workers with multiple infractions of rules to be dismissed, perhaps through a "three strikes and you're out" rule.

9. Have contract language that prevents arbitrators from modifying imposed penalties if just cause exists as to the conduct at issue.

10. Award employees. Postal employees who comply with all work rules and are discipline-free for one year, probably the majority, could be given their birthdays off or a $100 savings bond—to nail down the point that cooperative work behavior is appreciated.

In sum, there is a need for postal collective bargainers to think outside the box, to find more creative alternatives to the traditional postal grievance-arbitration system. Cosmetic pilot programs or a feel-good tweaking of the process in the past has not made the system more efficient.

Other Labor Regulations

The old Post Office Department historically maintained a prodigious number of handbooks and manuals that obviously affected the terms and conditions of employment. In 1973, the unions agreed that "the employer shall have the right to make changes [in handbooks and manuals] that are not inconsistent with this Agreement and that are fair, reasonable and equitable." (Article XIX—1973 Agreement.) To make such changes, postal managers must give advanced notice to the unions and meet with union representatives to discuss the implications of the change. If unions believe the change violates the Agreement or the principles of Article XIX, they can go through a grievance process. The provision for changes has been used frequently by postal authorities over the intervening years and remains an intelligent and efficient way of allowing handbook and manual changes to terms and conditions of employment that meet the fair, reasonable, and equitable test during mid-contract periods.

In the 1973 Agreement the Postal Service also gained the unilateral right to subcontract. In 1973 subcontracting was not quite the hot-button issue it is today for organized labor. In the 1990s, management in many industries aggressively pursued strategies designed to control overall costs such as downsizing, double-breasting (for example, maintaining separate nonunion business entities operating in the same line of business as a unionized sister company), and restructuring the size and scope of business. Subcontracting has also been a major employer cost-control tactic. For example, when Bell Atlantic was spun off from AT&T, it faced numerous disputes with the Communications Workers Union over its extensive use of contract installers for local residential services. Other major AFL-CIO affiliates have had tough collective bargaining over subcontracting and preserving union bargaining unit jobs.

Article XXXII of the Postal Service's 1973 Agreement gives the employer the right to subcontract after giving "due consideration to public interest, cost, efficiency, availability of equipment, and qualification of employees."[26] It further requires management "to give advance notification" to the involved union on subcontracting "which will have a significant impact on bargaining unit work . . . being considered." Finally, the article requires the employer to meet with the union before a "final decision" is made. The Postal Service has been rather judicious in its use of its subcontracting right over the years, as evidenced by the fact that the union work force has continued to grow with no layoffs. But the clause has been invoked more recently when the Postal Service established new operations, for example, remote encoding centers technology, call centers, and most recently the dedicated Priority Mail network initiative.

Subcontracting once again was a concern in 1998 Postal Service labor negotiations for the APWU, AFL-CIO. Ultimately, the subcontracting issue with APWU in 1998 was resolved by the execution of a largely symbolic memorandum of understanding in which the Postal Service acknowledged that it had no new planned subcontracting initiatives to undertake in the 1998–2000 period. Although subcontracting may be a political annoyance to the APWU, the union has not seen any "significant [downside] impact on [its] bargaining unit" owing to the clause. In fact, it can be demonstrated the opposite has occurred.

By innovative use of "contingent employees," whose more market-based compensation levels made doing remote encoding work

---

[26]Article XXXII of the 1973 Agreement states as follows:

Section 1. The Employer will give due consideration to public interest, cost, efficiency, availability of equipment, and qualification of employees when evaluating the need to subcontract.

Section 2. The Employer will give advance notification to Unions at the national level when subcontracting which will have a significant impact on bargaining unit work is being considered and will meet to consider the Unions' views on minimizing such impact. No final decision on whether or not such work will be contracted out will be made until the matter is discussed with the Unions.

Section 3. A joint committee is established at the national level to study the problems in this area leading towards a meaningful evolutionary approach to the issue of subcontracting.

in-house somewhat more economically attractive than continuing the subcontracting arrangement, the APWU prevailed on postal management in 1993 to bring the subcontracted remote encoding work back in-house. By that understanding, contingent employees would constitute 70 percent of a work crew, and regular postal employees would constitute the other 30 percent. Rather than experiencing downsizing by subcontracting, the APWU saw 25,000 new contingent employees added to the APWU-represented work force. That innovative result was a win-win affair for both parties. But it is improbable that the Postal Service ever would have seen the work ultimately performed at labor rates closer to competitive private-sector market levels for key entry operations if it had not used its subcontracting rights under Article XXXII and taken the flack to exercise the right in a responsible manner.

The 1971 Agreement also provided the employer with the right to implement changes in any current or new "work measurement systems or work or time standards" after giving advanced notice to the involved unions along with the right to challenge the changes in arbitration *after implementation* (Article XXXIV—1971 Agreement). Although the right has been rarely used by postal management in nearly three decades, it remains an instrument for potential productivity enhancement and service improvement. Unions no doubt would object to use of the controversial article, claiming it violated the principle of a "fair day's work for a fair day's pay" in the Article. But it remains a peaceful and principled way to change the status quo on work standards and bring new efficiencies to the system.

The Wages of Postal Workers

How has the USPS labor regime affected the level of postal wages? Compared with the rise in average salaries for other American industries for the period 1956 to 1967, the Kappel Commission in 1968 concluded that postal salaries "have not only kept pace with, but have risen somewhat more than, those in the rest of the economy."[27] The Commission's labor consultant Robert Nathan remarked, "In general, the [1968] postal wage rates fall within the range of high and

[27]*Toward Postal Excellence*, p. 25.

low prevailing rules for unskilled and semi-skilled labor—the labor pool from which the Post Office mainly recruits."[28] Nathan added that

> Fringe benefits [in the Post Office Department] are comparable to those of most other large employers, with a 10% differential for night work on which most clerks and mail handlers start. These rates are generally competitive with other users of semi-skilled and unskilled manpower in the larger northern and western labor markets, judged by the ability of Post Offices to fill their complements . . . and by an evaluation of wage rates of other segments of the economy.[29]

March 1970 saw a postal workers' strike that started in New York City and soon spread to other metropolitan areas. Unlike the response of President Reagan when confronted with an illegal strike by air traffic controllers, President Nixon did not discharge postal strikers; in fact, he had his Postmaster General enter into a 1970 strike settlement agreement with the postal unions that granted a 6 percent wage increase retroactive to December 27, 1969. The administration and labor unions agreed to support jointly a legislative reorganization of the Post Office Department, allowing for collective bargaining and providing an additional 8 percent wage increase on the effective date of the new legislation. Accordingly, postal union strike militancy led to a 14 percent wage hike added to the "generally competitive" postal wage levels prevailing in 1968, according to Kappel Commission researchers.

In light of the history, it is not surprising that between 1970 and 1984, under the PRA's collective-bargaining regime, postal unions adopted policies of "no contract-no work" and implicitly if not explicitly threatened another national postal strike during national contract negotiations to enforce healthy wage demands. Economic terms agreed to in the 1971, 1973, 1975, and 1978 Agreements thus were motivated in part by the fear of a strike. As a result, economic settlements during that period were excessive in comparison with the rate of growth of private-sector wage levels. By my calculation, postal rates of wage growth for the 1970–80 period exceeded those in the private sector by nearly 19 percent. Not surprisingly, the Postal

---

[28]Robert R. Nathan Associates, Inc., p. 34.
[29]Ibid.

Service accumulated deficits from operations that reached $4.267 billion by the close of FY 1981.[30]

According to the NALC, AFL-CIO, a senior city letter carrier received nominal wage increases of 14.7 percent for the two-year 1971 Agreement, 21.8 percent for the two-year 1973 Agreement, 22.4 percent for the three year 1975 Agreement, and 31.1 percent for the three-year 1978 Agreement.[31] In addition, the 1971 Agreement provided for the introduction of cost-of-living allowances, and continued periodic step increases for all but the top-step employees in each pay grade. Further, the employer's share of health benefit premiums went from an average of 40 percent of the six largest health benefit plans' subscription charges used by the federal government to compute its contribution to cover its employees' health benefit premiums[32] to 75 percent by 1975.[33] Ostensibly the Postal Service was following the private-sector practice of employers paying a greater share of health care premiums. But that occurred at a time when total premium costs were relatively low. However, when health benefit costs skyrocketed starting in the late 1980s, virtually all employers moved to restrain those bills. The Postal Service was no exception to that trend, as we shall see in due course.

Reaction to High Costs

In 1980 the Postal Service commissioned Professor Wachter to undertake a comprehensive study of the Postal Service and its relative position in the labor market. His independent findings startled postal management because he advised that it had not done a thorough job of reading or interpreting the PRA's comparability principle. Using statistical analysis of the Current Population Survey data, Wachter concluded that postal workers earned a wage premium comparable to that of private-sector workers.

Postal management first used the Wachter analysis and data in its 1981 collective bargaining with the APWU, AFL-CIO, and NALC,

[30]USPS Exhibit 5a to testimony of Chief Financial Officer Michael Riley to the Stark Board in July 1995.

[31]NALC Exhibit 37 before the Stark Board in 1995.

[32]The various health benefit plans' subscription charges used by the federal government under 5 U.S.C. 8901 to compute the government contribution to cover health benefit premiums for government employees.

[33]Article XXI, Section I, of the 1975 Agreement.

AFL-CIO, who were bargaining jointly. A voluntarily negotiated and ratified agreement was reached that year in which those postal workers accepted a combination of lump sum cash bonuses and general wage increases.[34] The result was that, on average, wage levels for those workers' wages would grow approximately 4.7 percent points more slowly than those in the private sector for the 1981–84 period.

In 1981 the National Postal Mail Handlers Union opted to use the full dispute resolution procedure of the PRA in an attempt to break the pattern set by the 550,000 postal clerks and carriers. The Wachter comparability data were presented in interest arbitration. That year neutral Donald Goodman's decision merely "moved the furniture around," letting stand the pattern set early that year in the wage settlement with the other unions. The unions could not use interest arbitration to undermine voluntary collective-bargaining results.

By 1984 the members of the Postal Board of Governors were fully aware that Wachter's analysis revealed a postal wage premium estimate of 23 percent and that newly hired postal workers received on average a huge 63 percent wage increase over their last full-time private-sector employment. Accordingly, the Board of Governors instructed postal management to propose in collective bargaining a contract that actually reduced postal earnings levels over the 1984–87 contract period. The clerks and city carriers union countered by demanding a huge, double-digit wage increase. The economic dispute went before neutral arbitrator Clark Kerr, a distinguished labor economist, who held in the interest arbitration case after extensive litigation that "discrepancies in comparability" existed and that

---

[34]That was the last national Postal negotiation in which a serious threat of strike was advanced by the major unions. On the night of July 20, 1981, after the parties reached a salary increase deal on $650 per year, a serious dispute erupted over whether that was a bonus each year or a general base wage increase. When the dispute lingered on into the morning hours of July 21 and nearly precipitated a strike, a compromise was reached whereby for each year a $300 base increase and a $350 bonus was paid. In 1981, interest arbitration was simply not an acceptable alternative to the two largest postal unions. The reader is reminded that *no government* dictated the terms of the 1981 Postal bargaining crisis. The parties bilaterally found their way out of the morass they found themselves in on July 20, 1981, and a neutral citizen-arbitrator provided the binding resolution of the mail handlers case. The 1981 experience illustrates the deregulated PRA mechanism for the wage and benefit determinations for Postal employees in a manner that continued uninterrupted mail service.

new postal wage rate increases should be governed by the principle of "moderate restraint," which he defined

> as a slowing of wage increases, as against the private sector, by 1% a year or for 3% in total over the life of this contract. In the opinion of the Chairman, this does not dispose of the problem. Moderate restraint may also be necessary in future years to approximate the guidelines of comparability as established by Congress.[35]

Some closing of the wage gap occurred in the 1984–87 period because of Kerr's authorization of new lower starting rates for new hires. But the Kerr award signaled other important policy points. First, economic change through interest arbitration, an inherently conservative process, would be incremental and not revolutionary. Second, when confronted with substantial economic evidence and argument, interest arbitration could be an instrument for meaningful change where the collective-bargaining parties did not and perhaps could not find a bilateral politically acceptable compromise. Kerr's award, consistent with the public interest, pointed the parties in a new economic direction to comply with the comparability mandate. And third, the Kerr award legitimized the PRA's dispute resolution procedures for all postal unions, and the threat of a costly and disruptive national postal strike passed thereafter from the scene. The decisions by arbitrator Arnold Zack in the 1985 mail handlers dispute and by Marlin Volz in the 1985 rural letter carriers dispute followed literally the rationale and holdings of the Kerr award on comparability and "moderate restraint."

In 1991 Wachter found that the postal wage premium was 21.8 percent, compared with 23 percent in 1984. When he added in the fringe benefit premium, the total compensation premium hit 31 percent. The average new-hire wage premium was reduced somewhat by the Kerr award, to 54 percent, down from 63 percent. In light of those findings, postal management emphasized in collective bargaining and interest arbitration the impact of wages on postal pricing levels and the willingness of postal consumers to accept higher prices.

The 1991 Mittenthal award acknowledged the existence of the wage premium in explicit terms and thus awarded only moderate general wage increases and lower starting rates for new hires,

[35]U.S. Postal Service, 83 LA 1105, 1111 (1984).

granted the right of postal management to use noncareer low-cost transitional employees, granted more favorable full- to part-time ratios to the Postal Service, and provided an opportunity for management to litigate in further interest arbitration hearings over appropriate contribution rates to health benefit premiums. The postal unions in the 1990 round of national labor negotiations steadfastly refused to accept the proposition of any health care benefits cost-shifting to employees. The health benefit premium-sharing dispute was resolved by the 1993 Valtin award, which *reduced* the USPS average contribution rates to health benefit premium from 90 percent to 85 percent over the 1994–97 period. Once again, the postal interest arbitration process awarded significant economic change dictated by the public interest without any interruption of postal services to the nation.

In the 1995–96 series of interest arbitration battles, the postal unions continued to argue for substantial wage hikes in spite of clear evidence of a "wage premium." But the Stark, Clarke, and Vaughn awards, consistent with the public interest, produced "moderate restraint" over all economic packages that saw *postal wages grow about 2 percentage points more slowly per year than overall wage growth in the private sector* over the 1994–98 period. Such moderate increases awarded by the Stark, Clarke, and Vaughn awards contributed directly to rate stability, to reducing the accumulated postal deficit, and to moving the Postal Service closer to statutory wage comparability. In addition, the 1996 Clarke award saw the first reduction in night shift differential rates in 25 years. That award froze wages for 25,000 transitional employees for the life of the agreement and reduced new-hire transitional employee wage rates, though it did grant, to that noncareer category, access to health benefit coverage, with employees paying the entire premium on a pretax basis. Those moderate awards, along with a favorable business cycle for the period, helped the Postal Service realize operating surpluses in the 1994–98 period.

Many of the foregoing views and characterizations of postal bargaining results and interest arbitration awards admittedly were formed by my personal observations and involvement in the process, which concluded with my retirement in 1998. However, the process marches along and most of us now know that the Postal Service reached voluntary agreement on a two-year labor agreement with the APWU, AFL-CIO, which was ratified in late 1998. More recently, we know that an interest arbitration award issued in September 1999 by Chairman George R. Fleischli resolved the Postal Service's bargaining dispute with the NALC, AFL-CIO. Finally, we know that collective bargaining is currently under way with the National Rural Letter Carriers Association for approximately 100,000 bargaining unit members. For me, fully analyzing the 1998–99 postal round of collective bargaining will be deferred until a later time. Suffice it to say that the latest Employment Cost Index numbers issued by the U.S. government on October 28, 1999, show that private-sector wages and salaries grew at 3.2 percent from September 1998 to September 1999. From that growth perspective as well as the perspective regarding the principle of moderate restraint discussed at length and crafted to achieve compliance with Congress's definition of wage and benefit comparability with the private sector, I view the recent bargaining developments as deeply disturbing. Postal consumers should, too.

Conclusion

What can we generally conclude about the postal collective bargaining or interest arbitration model adopted by Congress in the PRA of 1970? To begin, adversarial collective bargaining has resulted in postal wage levels far higher than the compensation and benefits paid for comparable levels of work in the private sector of the economy. (39 U.S.C. § 1003(a).) Further, the voluntary bargaining process has kept work rules generally inflexible and not accommodated the change necessary for a competitive entity. On the other hand, the mechanism by which interest disputes ultimately are resolved has served the public interest well by settling bargaining controversies when voluntary agreement between labor and management is not possible, without the interruption of essential mail service. The interest arbitration default mechanism has established a positive track record of serving the public interest.

The citizen neutrals who have served in the postal dispute resolution process have, through their awards, made needed incremental changes in the public interest that have improved the postal system as a whole. They have confronted crucial economic issues such as wage comparability, health care benefits, bonuses, and pay premiums, as well as noneconomic issues including work-force structure and use of contingent employees. The citizen neutrals have performed with integrity and professionalism and genuinely tried to get it right.

The adversarial voluntary postal collective-bargaining system clearly is the weak link in the labor regime statutory process, with most disputes since 1984 settled by arbitration. Yet there are examples of cooperative, productive collective bargaining forged between employers and unions in the private sector. The Saturn–General Motors experience is often cited as one of the best examples of labor-management cooperation.

But postal blue ribbon commissions, summit conferences, and intervention by the Federal Mediation and Conciliation Service over the years have failed miserably to move labor and management to overcome narrow self-interest, entitlement attitudes, and a status quo mentality that seems to permeate the postal bargaining relationship. In reality, only Congress is in a good position to assert the public interest, to require change in the current postal collective-bargaining/dispute-resolution regime for the better. In my opinion, the best reform would be minimalist in nature and designed to fine-tune the current model.

Congress should begin by barring the Postal Service from seeking new rate increases until the Secretary of Labor and Director of Federal Mediation and Conciliation Service certify that postal management and unions have adopted a meaningful and comprehensive program, with measurable criteria, for achieving a number of goals that have been recommended by the GAO.[36] Such a program should include requirements that the bargaining parties undertake the following:

1. Give employees greater responsibility and make them more accountable for results by clearly defining the composition and structure of work teams and the measurements of team success.
2. Provide incentives that reward employees in work units for corporate and improved unit performance.
3. Give employees training to work better as members of work teams and to focus on serving the customer better.

[36]U.S. General Accounting Office, *U.S. Postal Service Labor Management Problems Persist on the Workroom Floor* (Washington: Government Printing Office, 1994).

4. Select and train supervisors who can serve as facilitators/counselors who motivate employees positively, recognize and reward employees for good work, promote teamwork, and deal effectively with poor performers.
5. Counsel, train, and, if necessary, remove supervisors and employees who do not meet goals.

Postal unions and management owe a duty to the country to justify the special economic status that they enjoy; to rise above adversary relations, self-interest, and political considerations; to take postal labor management relations to a new plateau of cooperation; and to realize more fully the policy benefits initially envisioned by the Kappel Commission in 1968 when it recommended collective bargaining as the cornerstone of its reform of postal labor-management relations.

7. Consequences of Competition

Robert H. Cohen

A monopoly for the carriage of letters was originally imposed by Charles I in 1635 to prevent seditious communications. British monarchs soon learned that a letter-mail monopoly had economic value because it could be used to extract rents. That led to the granting of the postal franchise in exchange for a fee or as a reward to friends and allies.

Originally, postal services simply transported mail between cities. Senders and recipients dropped off or received their mail at a central point. It was not until the 19th century that posts began to collect and deliver mail.[1] Today, it is the universal delivery network with its obvious economies of scale that is used to justify the postal monopoly. The most frequent argument given for the monopoly is that it is required to ensure universal service. It is also argued that the monopoly is necessary to prevent "cream skimming," delivering only to the most profitable routes, which would subtract from the economic benefit (scale economies) of the universal delivery system. In other words, the monopoly makes mail service more affordable.

My colleagues and I have written three papers addressing those arguments, and in this short paper I present a summary of them. The studies are published in the series of books on postal economics edited by Michael A. Crew and Paul R. Kleindorfer. They are also available on the Postal Rate Commission's Web site, www.prc.gov.

Robert H. Cohen is the director of the Office of Rates Analysis and Planning at the Postal Rate Commission. All figures in the tables are compiled by the author from PRC data.

[1]Collection is largely a by-product of the delivery system.

Table 1

Selected Statistics for City and Rural Delivery (FY 1989)

	City Routes	Rural Routes (residential, business, and mixed)
Possible deliveries[a] (millions)	78.10	20.50
Minutes per day per possible delivery (in and out of office)	1.04	1.07
Seconds per piece	12.50	14.90
Pieces per day per possible delivery	5.01	4.30

[a] Possible delivery is a residence or business that can receive mail.

Rural Cross-Subsidies

Our first paper[2] addressed the argument that it is necessary to cross-subsidize rural delivery with profits from urban delivery in order to maintain universal service. The argument presupposes that rural service is unprofitable. The claim is so often repeated that it has become the conventional wisdom. As we all know, the conventional wisdom is often wrong.

Our analysis capitalized on the fact that the U.S. Postal Service (USPS) has separate city delivery and rural delivery crafts and maintains separate data systems for them. We used data from 1989 to compare the cost of city and rural delivery and to calculate the profitability of rural delivery. We began by generating comparative city and rural delivery statistics, some of which are shown in Table 1.

Rural carrier time per possible delivery is 3 percent higher than for city delivery; the two are virtually equal if the time devoted to retail services provided by rural carriers only is eliminated.[3] The reasons include the following:

- Rural routes are the functional equivalent of the most efficient kind of city route (curbline routes). These routes account for

[2] See Robert Cohen, William Ferguson, and Spyros Xenakis, "Rural Delivery and the Universal Service Obligation: A Quantitative Investigation," in *Regulation and the Nature of Postal Delivery Services*, eds. Michael A. Crew and Paul R. Kleindorfer (Boston: Kluwer Academic Publishers, 1993).

[3] Rural carriers provide retail services; city carriers do not.

Table 2
Cost of Direct Labor and Vehicles for
City and Rural Delivery

	City	Rural
Per box per day	44.6	41.5
Per piece	8.9	9.7

only 21 percent of city routes; the remaining involve carriers on foot, and are much less efficient.

- Rural recipients do not receive any door delivery and must have a box on the carrier's line of travel. The line of travel requirement causes many boxes to be bunched at crossroads, which makes them less costly to service. (The line of travel requirement is also a manifestation of a lower quality of service than that received by city delivery recipients.)

Rural carriers are paid somewhat less than city carriers but their vehicle costs are higher. Labor plus vehicle costs are compared in Table 2, where we ignore the substantial number of contract rural carriers who cost the Postal Service about half as much as ordinary rural carriers.

We analyzed the effect of population density on rural delivery by distributing rural route data into quintiles based on number of boxes per mile (of route). Those data are summarized in Table 3. As expected, time per piece increases as population density decreases.

Table 3
Selected Rural Delivery Statistics Population Density Quintile

Boxes	Miles	Pieces per Box (day)	Time per Box (minutes)	Time per Piece (seconds)
1.	2.88	4.04	1.56	33.15
2.	5.90	3.79	1.14	18.10
3.	9.20	4.19	1.06	15.16
4.	14.20	4.67	0.98	12.53
5.	26.27	4.59	0.87	11.41
All	8.00	4.30	1.07	14.97

Table 4
Profit (Loss) from Rural Delivery by
Quintile

Quintile	Profit (%)	Total ($ millions)
1.	(15.8%)	($121)
2.	0.9	10
3.	10.6	137
4.	20.4	281
5.	23.3	361
All	10.8	669

Thus, the least dense quintile (1) stands out as being the most costly in carrier time per box and per piece of mail delivered.

Some areas served by rural carriers are increasingly becoming urbanized. Because the Postal Service seldom converts an area from rural delivery to city delivery, some rural routes are more typical of urban routes. The preponderance of those routes is in quintile 5, the most dense. Boxes per mile in quintile 5 are more than three times as large as the average for all quintiles.

We next modeled route profitability by quintile. In this model, we took into account the revenue of the mail delivered, its nondelivery attributable costs (including collection, processing, transportation, and retail service), and its total delivery cost.[4] The results are summarized in Table 4.

It can be seen that rural delivery is profitable in every quintile save the first, which constitutes only 2.5 percent of all addresses served by the Postal Service. Even eliminating the most densely populated fifth quintile, rural delivery is profitable. When considering the $121 million loss for delivery to quintile 1, it should be borne in mind that recipients within the quintile send a substantial amount of profitable mail.

To put the $121 million in perspective, Postal Service expenditures in 1989 (a year in which it essentially broke even) were $39 billion.[5]

---

[4]Attributable costs may be thought of as direct costs. Total cost includes direct and overhead cost.

[5]The Postal Service is today a $60 billion enterprise.

Thus, the loss caused by delivery to the most remote areas of the nation is three-tenths of 1 percent of total expenditures. Because rural delivery generally is profitable, it does not seem that a monopoly is necessary to ensure rural delivery. As will be discussed later, it is not likely that even a profit-seeking postal service that did not enjoy a monopoly would abandon delivery to the first quintile.[6]

Economies of Scale

Our next paper, "A Measure of Scale Economies for Postal Systems,"[7] analyzed the question, Does the postal monopoly make mail more or less affordable? In a nonsubsidized postal service, the customer benefits when returns to scale are maximized by having a single firm (a monopoly) provide delivery. On the other hand, monopolies harm consumers when they protect technically inefficient behavior and allow economic rents to be extracted. This paper sets up a framework to examine the question, Do the economies of scale in the delivery function exceed the technical inefficiencies and economic rents of the postal monopoly?

Recent empirical research confirms the widely held belief that economies of scale exist in the delivery of mail. Other functional components of the Postal Service are presumed here not to exhibit significant scale economies, although that has not been demonstrated.

Carrier street time has been extensively studied by the Postal Service. Conceptually it can be broken into components shown in Table 5. Route time is the time required to walk or drive a route, but making no deviations to deliver mail.

Access time is the time it takes a carrier to deviate from the route to make a delivery. Load time is the time it takes a carrier to put the mail in the receptacle. Route time is fixed and load time is 100 percent variable with volume. Access is partly fixed and partly variable. Analysis of extensive delivery data shows that a 10 percent increase in current volume would increase access cost by 0.6 percent.

---

[6]Perhaps the first thing a competitive post office would do would be to replace rural carriers with contract carriers in quintile 1.

[7]See Robert Cohen and Edward Chu, "A Measure of Scale Economies for Postal Systems," in *Managing Change in the Postal and Delivery Industries*, eds. Michael A. Crew and Paul R. Kleindorfer (Boston: Kluwer Academic Publishers, 1997).

Table 5

Carrier Street Time (1993)

Function	Cost	Percentage of Total
Route time	2,950	29.3
Access time	5,205	51.7
Elemental load time	1,912	19.0

We measured the scale economies in the Postal Service by comparing the cost of providing delivery by a single firm with that of two equally efficient firms. We began with the total cost of delivery by the USPS. Next we determined the cost of delivery if performed by both the incumbent and a second firm assumed to be equally efficient. We assumed that the two firms share the market equally, each delivering a random half of the mail. We assumed each firm services the entire country each delivery day. Each firm would have the same route-time costs. The number of accesses by the two firms would be greater than the total experienced by the incumbent alone because some delivery points will receive mail from both firms on the same day. Each firm would have half the load time of the incumbent because each delivers half the mail.

Summarizing our analytical results, route time would double, load time would not change, and access cost would increase. Using a Postal Service empirically based model, access cost would grow by 61 percent. Under the duopoly scenario described, total street time cost would increase from $10 billion (the cost for the monopoly deliverers) to $16 billion. Thus, $6 billion[8] represents the benefits from scale economies in delivery.[9]

But labor costs also must be taken into account when comparing a monopoly and duopoly. In 1993, the average postal worker under collective bargaining received $35,001 in pay and allowances plus $7,713 in fringe benefits. That compares with the median annual earnings (without fringe benefits) in 1993 of $24,076 for all full-time workers in the United States. Michael B. Wachter of the University of

---

[8]These figures use FY 1993 data.

[9]If the USPS were more efficient, the current street cost of $10 billion would be less and the resulting calculation of duopoly street costs would be less. Similarly, if the USPS were less efficient, the benefits of the scale economies would be greater.

Pennsylvania and his colleagues concluded that in 1993 there was a wage- and fringe-benefit premium for the postal bargaining labor force of 29.5 percent with respect to comparable workers in the private sector.[10] That amounted to $9 billion in 1993. Thus, the monopoly rents, $9 billion, exceed the benefits of scale in the delivery system, $6 billion, by $3 billion.[11]

Technical efficiency in the USPS has not been analyzed. To the degree that the Postal Service is technically inefficient, those costs should be added to the $9 billion in rents in order to compare the costs and benefits of the delivery monopoly.

Cream Skimming

Our last paper[12] analyzed the potential for cream skimming in the United States. It is common for postal administrations to argue that without legal protection of their monopoly, cream skimmers would capture their high profit routes and leave them with their less profitable (and money losing) routes. They claim that universal service at affordable prices would then become infeasible.

That argument actually is being tested in Sweden, which eliminated its postal monopoly and has a significant competitor in several parts of the country. Sweden Post is required to provide universal service.[13] New Zealand and Argentina have more recently given up their postal monopoly. A new German law will eliminate the

---

[10]Michael B. Wachter, Barry T. Hirsch, and James W. Gillula, *The Comparability of U.S. Postal Service Wages and Benefits to the Private Sector: Evidence from the Total Compensation Premium, New Hire Wage Increases, Quit Rates, and Application Rates*, Report prepared for the U.S. Postal Service (Washington: USPS, July 10 and August 14, 1995). Dr. Wachter has done a number of studies on the Postal Service's labor costs under contract to the USPS. Critics of previous Wachter studies claim that they ignore the fact that the Postal Service pays minorities the same as it pays white males. The critics argue that it is the Postal Service's minority employees (not white male employees) who earn more than their private-sector equivalents, and that situation only means that the Postal Service does not discriminate.

[11]Wachter's wage premium for the delivery network alone, however, amounts to only $2.3 billion, which is much less than the value of the scale benefits in delivery.

[12]See Robert Cohen, William Ferguson, John Waller, and Spyros Xenakis, "An Analysis of the Potential for Cream Skimming in the U.S. Residential Delivery Market," in *Emerging Competition in Postal and Delivery Systems*, eds. Michael Crew and Paul Kleindorfer (Boston: Kluwer Academic Publishers, 1999).

[13]It is interesting to note that, in the face of competition, Sweden Post abandoned geographically uniform prices for bulk mail.

Table 6
Selected Daily Average Statistics for Residential City Routes

Quartile	Profit	Piece	Cost Delivery	Volume
1	$248	7.74	39.94	3,485
2	50	12.0	52.0	2,206
3	(25)	15.4	56.8	1,692
4	(110)	23.5	64.7	1,131
All	41	12.5	51.7	2,128

monopoly in that country at the end of 2002. Thus, we will soon learn if what appears to be a natural monopoly actually needs legal protection to provide universal service at affordable prices.[14]

In this paper we assumed that all legal barriers to entry into the postal market are eliminated.[15] We asked these questions: How much more efficient would a potential competitor have to be to overcome the scale economies of the USPS? How much volume might they be able to capture, and in which markets? What effect would the loss of volume to cream skimmers have on the resulting prices the USPS would have to charge to maintain universal service?

The analysis uses city delivery statistics from FY 1989 but uses cost data from FY 1996. The cost per residential delivery route is $266 per delivery day.[16] We calculate the daily profit for each of the 13,212 routes in our sample in a manner similar to the way we calculated the profit of rural routes earlier. This time we array the data by quartiles. Selected statistics are shown in Table 6.

Clearly the profitability of a route is related to its volume and that in turn is closely related to the income of the recipients of the route.[17] Surprisingly, 46.5 percent of the routes are not profitable. Thus, it is

[14]Each of those postal administrations reduced its count dramatically before the elimination of the monopoly.

[15]Barriers include both the letter-mail monopoly and the mailbox law, which prohibits anyone other than the Postal Service from placing anything in a mail receptacle. The United States is the only industrial nation with such a law.

[16]The amount includes all fringes, supervision, vehicle, and space-related costs for the standard workday of eight hours for a city carrier.

[17]See the appendix to the published paper.

argued that a monopoly is necessary to ensure service to those households.

A competitive postal service that refused to serve households on unprofitable routes would impose large transaction costs on its customers to separate mail and to secure suppliers to deliver its remaining mail. Such firms would be at a considerable disadvantage to those providing universal service. Larger transaction networks (be they mail, packages, overnight, or telephone) are more valuable to customers and providers than are smaller networks. It is for sound business reasons that Federal Express and United Parcel Service provide universal delivery service. A major business asset of the USPS and all other national posts is that they provide service to every address in the countries they serve. Thus, there is a business incentive for any postal provider (who is not simply a cream skimmer) to offer universal service within the territories it serves.

Routes that are unprofitable when served six days per week would become profitable when served less frequently. In a competitive environment, the Postal Service easily could retain universal service, but perhaps not a universal service standard.[18] Delivery less frequently six days per week would certainly be preferable to abandoning delivery altogether. Of course, if the Postal Service was simply to abandon delivery to unprofitable routes, it would not have to refuse, return, or destroy mail destined to those routes. Delivery firms with lower costs than the Postal Service's would emerge to serve them and the Postal Service could hand off its unprofitable mail to them.[19] Under any foreseeable circumstances, universal delivery would not cease.[20]

Because a cream skimmer would have to serve bulk mailers with sufficient volumes for areas they serve, they would need to serve mailers with mail presorted to carrier route to keep transaction costs reasonable. There are 40 billion pieces of that mail (slightly less than 20 percent of total volume).

---

[18]It is interesting to note that United Parcel Service recently began delivery less frequently than daily to certain residential areas.

[19]Costs would be lower by dint of lower wages and/or less frequent delivery.

[20]The concept of a universal service obligation may really mean more frequent delivery than economically warranted for households living on unprofitable routes. That obligation, of course, is in addition to providing retail services to rural communities.

It is doubtful that cream skimmers would wish to target routes other than the top quartile of routes ranked by carrier route volume. Those 40,000 routes are scattered over half the 30,000 five-digit ZIP Code areas in the United States. From an operational and marketing standpoint, cream skimmers would have to serve markets with at best a large proportion of routes in that quartile. We ignored that practical difficulty and so build a best case for cream skimmers.

The top 25 percent of routes when ranked by carrier route volume deliver 57 percent of all carrier route mail received by households. Thus, about 22 billion pieces of mail (11 percent) are at risk to cream skimmers.

Cream skimmers could cut their costs by reducing frequency of delivery. Although that saves fixed delivery costs, it runs the risk of not providing adequate service for mail that must be delivered within a one-, two-, or three-day window.

A cream skimmer's cost per piece would be a function of its cost of labor and productivity. The latter depends on the technology employed. Since 1989, the USPS has made major investments in automated carrier sequencing equipment for letter mail. That equipment has brought down the cost of walk sequencing letter mail, which was done manually by carriers in 1989.[21]

Carrier route advertising mail is the most vulnerable target for cream skimmers. The USPS incremental (or avoidable) cost for such mail is about 7 cents per piece. In a competitive market the USPS could respond to cream skimmers by lowering its prices, with 7 cents being the floor. Most probably it would offer selected discounts to large-volume carrier route mailers who would otherwise use cream skimmers. Thus, cream skimmers would most likely have to have costs less than 7 cents per piece to compete with the USPS on a cost basis alone.

Our analysis calculated how much more efficient in wages and productivity a cream skimmer would have to be at a given frequency of delivery to have per-piece costs lower than those of the USPS. If a cream skimmer were to capture only 25 percent of the available market, its costs would have to be 40 percent of the Service's at a two-day frequency to be below 7 cents per piece. With 50 percent of the avail-

---

[21]For example, from 1989 to 1996 the time carriers spent in the office declined from 41 percent to 34 percent. The trend is continuing.

able volume at a two-day frequency, a cream skimmer's costs would have to be no more than 60 percent of the Postal Service's to remain below the Postal Service's average incremental costs.[22] Inasmuch as we have built the best-case scenario for cream skimmers, it appears that they would have difficulty succeeding.

If cream skimmers captured 10 percent of the available carrier route mail, the increase in the first-class rate by the Postal Service to make up the lost overhead contribution would be 0.1 cents. If they captured 100 percent, the increase would have to be 1.2 cents. Thus, cream skimming is unlikely to affect the affordability of universal delivery. Moreover, the negative impact on postal finances would likely be offset to a great extent by the effect of competition on the Postal Service's efficiency, service performance, and product innovation.

[22]See the full paper for a complete exposition of the analytical results.

8. Fatal Flaws in the Postal Service's Structure

R. Richard Geddes

To discuss potentially "fatal flaws" in the U.S. Postal Service's (USPS) organizational structure, it is necessary to define our terms. In an economic sense, "flaws" can be understood as aspects of the current structure that raise the organization's overall social costs. Such flaws become fatal when the costs of the current structure increase to such an intolerable level that the arrangements are altered and the Postal Service's form is changed.

A reasonable benchmark for comparison is the cost of providing the same services through a set of voluntary arrangements. Thus a good way to approach the fatal flaws question is to describe the nature of the USPS using the economics of contracts and property rights that has been applied to private firms, with a special emphasis on restrictions on contractual arrangements surrounding ownership and competition with the USPS. Next it would be useful to discuss the reasons why those arrangements might be expected to lead to higher social costs. And finally it would be worthwhile to consider the reasons why political change may be slow in coming.

The Nature of the USPS

A firm, whether public or private, can be understood as a legal entity composed of a set of contracts between constituents.[1] These contracts include suppliers of inputs such as capital, labor, and materials, as well as customers. The contracts specify the rights and

R. Richard Geddes is an associate professor in the Department of Economics of Fordham University.

[1]See, for example, Michael C. Jensen, "Organizational Theory and Methodology," *Accounting Review* 50 (1983): 326.

responsibilities of resource owners regarding the division of labor, the sources of capital, and the ownership of residual earnings (the "residual claims") of the firm. For this reason the firm is sometimes referred to as a "nexus of contracts." The subtleties of the arrangements for various organizational forms are only now beginning to be appreciated.

The nature of any institution is determined by the details of the contractual arrangements. For example, a private "open" corporation is defined by the free transferability of its ownership shares. By contract, the owners of the corporation need have no role in the organization other than supplying capital and voting on officers. That form of residual claim allows for specialization in ownership of shares (investing) as well as in management. A partnership is defined by the fact that its residual claims are restricted to two or more individuals who also manage the firm. A sole proprietorship is defined by the fact that its ownership is restricted to one person, who is also the manager. Since management and ownership are separate in the corporation, a challenge is to encourage managers to operate the firm in the interest of the owners. That need creates a special type of economic problem called the "agency problem," as discussed in more detail later.

To understand the nature of the USPS then, we need to examine details of the contractual arrangements defining this organization. The arrangements are highly complex and multifaceted in an organization the size of the USPS. However, there are two critical elements that make the USPS distinct. First, it is government owned, and second, it is a legally mandated and regulated monopoly with its own powers to regulate potential competitors.

Monopoly Statutes

Through the Private Express Statutes of 1845, the USPS was given a legal monopoly over letter mail.[2] The monopoly extends to most of first-class and a portion of third-class mail,[3] and has been discussed

---

[2]George L. Priest, "The History of the Postal Monopoly in the United States," *Journal of Law & Economics* 18 (1975): 33–80.

[3]The USPS recently instituted a new mail classification system. For a description of the new mail classes, see the *1996 Annual Report of the United States Postal Service*, pp. 39–40.

frequently in detail by commentators.[4] Without repeating that discussion, a few points related to institutional economics are in order. The economics of contracts emphasizes the reciprocal nature of transactions. Although the monopoly statutes typically are viewed as a restriction on other companies from competing with the USPS, they also effectively prohibit customers from contracting with alternative suppliers. That is, the monopoly statutes can be understood as a restriction on the freedom of contract of every potential customer of alternative delivery firms for those services. The welfare of all the consumers is therefore affected, because with greater freedom to contract they would enjoy more consumer surplus (through lower prices, better quality services, a greater range of services, etc.). It is not simply a matter of lost profits for competitors. Because potential customers are poorly organized politically, the unrealized consumer surplus is frequently lost in the policy debate.

It is also important to note the "voluntary" nature of contracting restrictions in a typical corporation versus those defining the USPS. Although all contracts involve restrictions, the stockholders, bondholders, managers, and others who joined together to form a corporation accept those restrictions voluntarily. But no living Americans explicitly agreed to restrict their transactions with competitors of the USPS. Additionally, an individual who violates the monopoly statutes will feel the full weight of the federal government's enforcement powers rather than the typical remedies in contract law.

Government Ownership

A second critical element defining the USPS is the nature of its ownership. Generally, the ownership of any asset is said to consist of three elements: the right to use the asset; the right to appropriate the returns on the asset; and the right to change its form, substance, and location.[5] Within the context of a firm, the first element translates

---

[4]See, for example, Douglas K. Adie, *Monopoly Mail: Privatizing the U.S. Postal Service* (New Brunswick, N.J.: Transaction Publishers, 1989); Peter J. Ferrara, *Free the Mail: Ending the Postal Monopoly* (Washington: Cato Institute, 1990); Edward L. Hudgins, *The Last Monopoly: Privatizing the Postal Service for the Information Age* (Washington: Cato Institute, 1996).

[5]Erik Furubotn and Rudolf Richter, "The New Institutional Economics: An Assessment," in *The New Institutional Economics* 1, eds. Erik Furubotn and Rudolf Richter (College Station, Tex.: Texas A&M Press, 1991).

into an exclusive property right, or "exclusivity." The second is the right to the residual claim or net cash flows of the firm, that is, the profits. The third implies that the owner has the right to transfer ownership of the share to another party, or "transferability," as well as specific "control rights" over how the firm is run.

In contrast, ownership in a government-owned entity like the Postal Service is held by the public or "in common." The rights here are demonstrably different from private property rights when analyzed in the context of the three elements identified earlier:

- The public property right is not exclusive. That is, there is common ownership based only on citizenship.
- The firm's owners are not given direct ownership rights to the residual cash flows of the firm. That is, they are not "residual claimants" of the firm.
- The ownership right is not transferable.

The owners of a government firm thus have ownership rights only in the narrow sense that they can transfer them by changing citizenship, acquire residual cash flows through tax reductions or rebates (and face residual losses through deficits or tax increases), and influence resource allocation within the firm (e.g., investment and financing) through an indirect voting-to-bureaucracy mechanism. As fewer rights are associated with ownership in government corporations, those rights are attenuated relative to private ownership. Restrictions on the tradability of ownership shares can be understood as a restriction on buyers of those shares, that is, on investors, or suppliers of capital.

Social Costs of Monopoly

There are a number of reasons why the restrictions on contracts described may lead to higher social costs and thus represent flaws in the Postal Service's institutional structure. The first is the social costs of monopoly.

Much effort has been expended by economists in studying monopoly, and its social costs are well articulated. As they are not unique to the USPS, a few are discussed below.

Allocative Efficiency

The standard economic model of monopoly implies that the firm will raise price above the competitive level and reduce quantity produced to below the competitive level. The result is too little of the good being produced in equilibrium, and creation of a social welfare loss. That is, the firm will produce less output at a higher price, so resources are misallocated in the sense that too few are devoted to the activity. That is perhaps the most obvious theoretical cost of monopoly.

It can be argued that rate-of-return regulation ameliorates such effects. While regulation might constrain the price of mail to below that of an unconstrained monopolist, it is unlikely that it is as effective as competition in encouraging firms to achieve productive efficiency or to force them to effectively use new technologies, governance structures, and so forth as described below. Additionally, it is unlikely that regulation will achieve prices as low as those forthcoming under competition.

Productive Efficiency

The incentive to produce output in the least costly manner is attenuated in any firm that faces reduced competition. Under competition, firms that do not use the best available technology or the optimal choice of inputs will not be able to price products as cheaply as others and will be driven out of business. Without market discipline, a firm is likely to face substantially higher unit costs than in a competitive market.

Governance Structures, Service Quality, and Innovation

The economics profession is beginning to appreciate the wide variety of ways in which monopoly rate-of-return regulation affects the behavior of a firm. Focus was traditionally on price and cost, but it is now clear that a large array of beneficial activities is attenuated by regulation.[6] Referring to industries in which deregulation occurred, Clifford Winston of the Brookings Institution states:

> The intensified competition resulting from deregulation causes firms to make innovations in marketing, operations, technology, and governance that enable them to become more efficient, improve their service quality, introduce new products and services, and become more re-

---

[6]Clifford Winston, "Economics Deregulation: Days of Reckoning for Microeconomists," *Journal of Economic Literature* 31, no. 3 (September 1993):1263–98, and Clifford Winston, "U.S. Industry Adjustment to Economic Deregulation," *Journal of Economic Perspectives* 12, no. 3 (Summer 1998): 89–110.

sponsive to consumers' preferences. One might suspect that regulation could foster innovations because firms were more profitable in this environment and thus had the resources to devote to innovative activity. I point out, however, that regulation generally did not significantly increase industry profitability.[7]

Competition set loose by deregulation appears to have numerous benefits—suggesting that the social costs of monopoly rate-of-return regulation are, relative to competitive markets, substantially higher than previously thought.

Social Costs of Government Ownership

Although it may be equally important, less attention is paid to the social costs of restrictions on transferability of ownership than to the problems of the Postal Service's monopoly status. Nevertheless, the costs of government ownership are likely to be quite high. A main component falls under the heading of agency costs. They are the costs to a corporation of controlling its managers and the costs of the managers deviating from "optimal behavior," that is, behavior that maximizes the value of the firm.

Under voluntary contracting, a number of mechanisms have evolved to help control agency costs in modern corporations. The transferability aspect of private ownership is critical for corporations' existence. When combined with rights to residual cash flows, transferability provides not only the ability but also the incentive to control managers effectively. Transferability and residual claimancy form the basis for markets in ownership rights, from which several important control mechanisms stem. Although many have been identified, only a sampling will be discussed here: stock market prices, debt ratings, and takeovers.

Stock Prices

Transferability of ownership shares creates a market in those rights, which continuously price or value a firm. Those prices furnish valuable signals about the effectiveness of current management in maximizing firm value, as they rapidly reflect the expected impact of managerial decisions on current and future profits. Owners do not need to be experts in analysis of managerial decisions to discern the

[7]Winston, 1998, pp. 95–96.

quality of managers; they need only observe the stock price. Changes in stock price lead to gains or losses for shareholders, who have an incentive to hold managers accountable for such changes. Stated simply, the stock price provides an instantaneous, easily understood measure of the performance of managers, and therefore exerts considerable pressure on them to limit agency costs. Additionally, the existence of tradable stock facilitates managerial pay packages that encourage them to avoid wasting firm resources. Managers can receive pay in the form of the stock itself; restricted stock (which cannot be sold for a specified period of time); or options, the value of which is closely related to the stock price. The other side of the coin is that managers can be removed when the stock price (and thus the firm's value) falls abnormally low.

Because government-owned firms do not, by definition, have ownership shares which are tradable, their shares are not priced. The value of the firm is therefore calculated rarely (and then very inaccurately) rather than continuously. Agency costs are increased because the effect of managerial decisions on cash flows, and hence firm value, is not discernable through stock price signals. Also, it is impossible to pay managers in a manner linked to the stock price, or to remove them when firm value collapses. Thus, managerial decisions are more likely to go unscrutinized, and agency costs will increase relative to private ownership.

Debt Ratings

Private corporations that issue tradable stock also issue debt. Capital structures composed of either all equity or all debt are rarely observed. The issuance of publicly traded debt helps lower agency costs through the specialized assessment of default risk, and it is often associated with tradable ownership shares.[8] For example, banks that issue credit specialize in the evaluation of credit risk. The granting or denial of a credit line provides a signal to owners about the riskiness of a firm's investment decisions. Banks frequently review their credit decisions, thus updating the signal. Indeed, large corporations often purchase debt ratings from agencies such as Moody's, Dunn & Bradstreet, or Standard & Poor's. Those firms have a powerful incentive to maintain the integrity of their ratings. Since own-

[8]See, for example, Eugene Fama, "Contract Costs and Financing Decisions," *Journal of Business* 63 (supp. 1990): S71.

ers can easily observe ratings on debt to infer the riskiness of managerial investment decisions, such specialized evaluation of default risk on debt lowers agency costs. Debt ratings by banks and others constrain careless investment decisions by managers, forcing them to undertake only those projects within an acceptable risk category.

Government-owned corporations do not issue debt secured by the firm's net cash flows. Instead, the tax revenues of the relevant jurisdiction guarantee the debt. The capital market thus does not provide discipline through debt assessment for any financing activity conducted by government managers unless those decisions materially affect the ability of the jurisdiction to extract tax revenue. Ratings assigned to government-issued debt are more likely to reflect the willingness of the jurisdiction to tax citizens to repay bondholders than the riskiness of managerial investment decisions per se. Debt ratings of government firms therefore provide poor information to firm owners about the prudence of managerial decisions, thus raising the cost of monitoring managers in government firms.

Takeovers

Management teams compete for control of firm assets through the purchase of rights on the market. This is the takeover market, and it is facilitated by the transferability of ownership. Competing management teams can circumvent entrenched boards and managers to gain control of a firm through control of the voting rights attached to the firm's common stock. Takeovers are a costly but effective way of allowing competition among managers for control, therefore ensuring that assets are employed in their highest-valued use.[9] Competition for control implies that poor management teams will be replaced when the cost of their inefficiency exceeds the transaction costs of a takeover. The market for corporate control encourages managers to use the firm's assets effectively, and therefore lowers agency costs.

Takeovers of government-owned firms are not possible because tradable ownership shares do not exist. Owners are not able to buy shares on a market with the intention of replacing entrenched managers. Thus, lack of tradability implies that it is costly, if not impossible, for competing management teams hoping to gain control of the

---

[9]Henry Manne, "Mergers and the Market for Corporate Control," *Journal of Political Economy* 73 (1965): 110.

firm's decisionmaking process to do so. The disciplining effect of tender offers, mergers, and proxy fights is eliminated. Without such disciplining effect, the agency costs of managerial behavior are likely to be considerably higher than in privately owned corporations.

Fatal Flaws

The flaws in the institutional arrangements defining the USPS suggest that the social costs of that government monopoly are high compared with competitive, private-sector institutions. The term fatal can also be given meaning within that context. It implies the need for a change in the Postal Service's structure so that government coercion is no longer used to restrict contracting with competitors or investors. A change in either of the restrictions, that is, deregulation or privatization, would profoundly alter the nature of the USPS. Standard contract law would then govern those relations.

Such changes clearly require action on a political level. If political agents are rational, they will respond to the costs (to them) and benefits (to them) of alternative institutional arrangements. That is, flaws will become fatal when the political benefits of the USPS exceed its political costs. As the costs noted are highly dissipated throughout society (rather than concentrated in one easily identified group), politicians are unlikely to be sensitive to increases in those costs. Alternatively, the political benefits of monopoly and government ownership accrue to small, highly organized, politically effective groups. Politicians are likely to be highly sensitive to the dissipation of those benefits. It will therefore require extraordinarily high social costs to initiate meaningful institutional change. Indeed, politicians have been willing to tolerate the substantial costs of such arrangements to date.

Numerous predictions of the Postal Service's demise have been made on the basis of the costs as discussed, and similar arguments. They have proven false. While the Postal Service's institutional structure may not be economically redeeming, it is surprisingly durable politically. Unless the distribution of political costs and benefits changes, it is unlikely to expire any time soon. To paraphrase Mark Twain, "reports of the Postal Service's death are greatly exaggerated."

9. The Future of Messaging

Michael J. Critelli

Trying to summarize the future of messaging is a daunting task. However, there are noteworthy observations that may help us make sense of what is happening.

To articulate some themes running through all of my remarks, I would note the following:

1. Despite tremendous technological advances in communications media, communications efficiency and effectiveness for one-to-one communications have not advanced all that much. The limiting factors, as they always have been, are the ability of senders to understand what will move recipients to action and the mind share or attention span limitations for all of us as message recipients.
2. Newer technologies that enable more rapid communications do not overcome this mind share limitation and have other attributes that prevent them from totally displacing older, slower communications tools. The older tools keep improving to retain their place in advanced societies.
3. Message costs are large, growing, and out of control in most organizations, and will need to be subject to serious reengineering efforts.
4. Neither the government nor postal authorities should give up on paper-based communications or favor some communications tools over others. All have their places, and the marketplace should decide.

My first theme is that creation of new communications tools and advances in older tools are not significantly improving communications effectiveness and efficiency.

Michael J. Critelli is the chairman and CEO of Pitney Bowes Inc.

The reason for this situation is that although we have increased our ability to generate more messages, we have not significantly increased our capacity to receive and respond to them. Ultimately, the main principle set forth in Aristotle's *Rhetoric* is still valid: The ability of senders to understand recipients is the key to effective communication. That reality is not enhanced by more messages; if anything, more messages mean less focus on each individual message.

Let us step back and understand why there are more messages. First, technology makes it easier and less expensive to originate a message.

Second, the development of wireless communications has created opportunities to send and receive messages at places and during times that used to be message free. Cellular telephones and pagers enable us to call or be reached virtually anywhere at any time.

Third, because of deregulation and competition, we have choices where none previously existed. Think back to 20 years ago to an age of monopoly services and regulated pricing for other services even where there was competition. Today, we have a bewildering array of options for all but electric utility service, and that will be deregulated within the next few years. Multiple competitive vendors repeatedly communicate with us to solicit our business, and we reach out for the many available choices.

Fourth, we have moved from an economy in which we pay fully in advance for most goods and services to one in which we pay while we are using those same goods and services. That arrangement means frequent periodic financial communications between us and the vendor or a third-party credit provider.

Fifth, market power has shifted from vendors to customers. Because of customer power, vendors communicate frequently to improve customer convenience and satisfaction or to build customer loyalty. Think about how different the world was before frequent flier programs and customer satisfaction surveys.

Sixth, although home shopping started more than 100 years ago with mail-order catalogs, it has grown explosively in the last 20 years with the advent of outbound telemarketing, the Home Shopping Network, and now the Internet.

Finally, contrary to the popular belief of many that younger, better-educated, high-tech consumers will communicate exclusively through electronic media in the future, the Institute for the Future, a

consulting and market research firm based in Menlo Park, California, has found that a new consumer is emerging. This new consumer
is indeed younger, better educated, wealthier, more computer liter-
ate, and online more than three times a week. This new consumer
sends and receives more messages by far than everyone else and,
most surprisingly, receives 57 percent more mail than those who do
not fit that definition. The new consumer demands choice up front,
and loyalty and care after a purchase decision.

In short, for all those reasons, we are sending and receiving more
messages than ever before. In a study funded by Pitney Bowes, the
Institute for the Future found that in 1998 all of us who work sent
and received more than 190 messages a day, up from 178 a year before, and up significantly over the last several years.

Despite such a volume increase in messages and broad availability of a variety of communications tools, we are not necessarily ac-
complishing more with all those messages. With a few exceptions
such as using our driving time to answer voice mail, we are not necessarily realizing all of the productivity gains promised by the new
messaging tools.

In terms of message content from physical mail, though direct
marketers are targeting us better than ever, their efforts are deemed
successful if 98 percent of us reject their messages. Organizations of
all kinds have a harder time making their increasingly voluminous
communications achieve their desired ends, whether with employees, customers, or other stakeholders. To some degree, the problem
is message overload. However, to a profound extent, recipient
cynicism and distrust make message communication far more
challenging.

Moreover, because of increased message volume, the efficiency
and effectiveness of individual messages are declining, despite the
development of so many tools that have the potential to reach recipients faster, more effectively, and in so many places. If we look at
how particular media are used today, versus how they were used a
generation ago, there is a significant increase in communications volume to complete a single transactional activity. For example, in the
past, a telephone call usually led to a two-way conversation in which
a particular set of messages was communicated. Today, it is more
likely that the same set of messages will be conveyed by a sequence
of one-way communications into a voice mailbox or answering ma-

chine. It could easily take several one-way messages to complete the same activity that used to occur in one call. We also check voice mail more frequently during a day, and send more faxes and e-mails.

When new media are used, particularly if the sender cannot validate receipt at the time the message is sent, multiple confirming messages may be originated. It is not uncommon for an e-mail to be followed by a telephone call requesting confirmation of e-mail receipt, with a follow-up transmission of a physical mail version of the e-mail message.

The reason for the gap between message-sending capability and efficiency is that the increased volume of messages is being funneled to recipients with an inherently limited mind share and attention span.

Message overload turns our nine-to-five workdays into less productive time, in which we have to juggle our profit-bearing work with the demands of managing a river of messages. Our serious knowledge work is done in the evenings and on weekends. Because of overload, face-to-face communications, probably the gold standard for message senders, vies for schedule time with the time that a recipient needs to sort through e-mail, voice mail, fax, and physical mail messages, and it increasingly loses.

Other media that have the ability to help us break through to others and help others reach us have not realized the promise inherent in their increased transmission capability and cost-effectiveness. Telephone communication is a lower-cost, higher-quality medium that has been enhanced by the penetration of cellular technology. However, because of the fact that recipients are not able to manage their schedules to receive live telephone calls, telephone communication has turned increasingly into a series of one-way time-delayed communications into a voice mailbox or answering machine. Part of the reason is that would-be recipients are away from their workstations. However, many recipients who could take a live call forward their calls to voice mail simply to minimize interruptions. The popularity of call waiting and caller ID features in telephone systems is further evidence of the strong need recipients feel for message control.

Fax and e-mail transmissions have long since ceased to be able to achieve the communication urgency and immediacy inherent in their speed of transmission. They become part of the message clutter, as they have become more universal, more convenient, and less costly.

Physical mail has retained its credibility and impact to a much greater extent than many experts would have predicted, according to a study conducted by the PaperCom Alliance. It is valued by recipients because of its universal accessibility, its versatility in the media that can be used to deliver the message, the portability of its output for a recipient, and the perception that the recipient has more control over the timing of the response. It is also trusted because the recipient has more visual information about the sender, not the least of which is the sender's identifiable physical address and the sender's choice of physical material and content. Moreover, recipients often believe that if a sender has to incur significant cost to prepare a mail piece, that gives the sender more credibility and substantiality. Indeed, one of the attractive elements of a postage meter has been the professional appearance it gives an envelope.

Nevertheless, since technology has brought down the cost of creating a piece of mail and reaching many more recipients, we have a greater proportion of mail thrown out before it is opened than ever before. Recipients make quick judgments on the value of a mail message based on the physical appearance of the outside of the envelope. This can be seen as a defensive mechanism to save time, which is the one commodity that never expands, rather than a judgment on the inherent value of the message.

Expedited mail is very popular because senders can get mail to a recipient at a predictable time, recipients have better control over the timing of the receipt, and with many carriers, both have the ability to do end-to-end tracking and tracing. One of Pitney Bowes's most successful products introduced in the last four years is a software-based system called Arrival.

Arrival is a system used in mailrooms and shipping rooms to manage messages and packages from the moment of receipt by a large organization to the moment they arrive at the recipient's desk or room. Once again, we see the power of recipient message control. I suspect that one of the reasons recipients pay attention to expedited mail when they try to screen out messages from other media is that, given the cost of expedited messages (usually several dollars a message), they implicitly trust that the sender is trying to communicate an important message.

My second theme is that no new or existing medium has any inherent technological ability to capture scarce recipient mind share. To the degree that any medium does succeed, that success will be of many factors, only some of which are technology based.

There is a perception that we are moving inevitably from older to newer technologies and, particularly, from paper to electronic communications. We particularly hear that paper-based communications will pass because of the new way younger people use electronic messaging tools. That is an oversimplification of a complex reality.

As noted, every communications tool has strengths and limitations. Audio telephone communication is limited because of its inability to communicate via visual cues or tangible physical objects. Fax transmission produces tangible, visual output at the rate of a few seconds a page, but it is a one-way communications medium. Although the receipt by an addressee's facsimile machine can be confirmed, receipt by the addressee is not inherently able to be confirmed by an ordinary fax machine. E-mail does not produce a tangible output, and, over most systems, addressee receipt cannot be confirmed.

The other common characteristic of telephone communications, fax transmission, and e-mail is that all require both senders and recipients to have a device capable of sending or receiving the message over some kind of network. Such capability is second nature to those of us in built-up, advanced countries. It is not something to take for granted in emerging markets.

Physical mail can have paper, audio, or video communications components, but it is inherently slower and, in the absence of expedited services with specified recipient confirmation, its timing and confirmation of receipt are not guaranteed. Certain technologies improve the attractiveness of certain kinds of physical mail delivery, but none make it any faster than the fastest transportation time between the location at which the physical mail message is created in tangible form and the recipient's point of receipt. Physical mail also has a universality of access for senders and recipients. Other than postage costs, it has little inherent sender cost and no recipient cost, which fact makes it advantagous for many citizens, particularly those in less technologically advanced communities.

The Internet is most frequently invoked as having created a revolution in messaging. However, its impact is more complicated than is often understood. In many respects, Internet applications have involved the substitution of virtual activities for face-to-face activities: a virtual library that supplements or displaces a physical library; electronic commerce for face-to-face retail; virtual communities and chat lines in place of face-to-face communities; and remote news and entertainment activity in place of live or group activity in front of a television set or other entertainment medium. It disconnects senders and recipients of messages from physical addresses and substitutes e-mail addresses and chat line names for physical addresses, except when electronic commerce is involved.

However, the effectiveness of e-mail over the Internet is limited today by Internet economics: it is a "free" medium relative to per-message usage charges. As is the case with most resources perceived to be free, demand continues to outrun capacity. The Internet may eventually be the exception to the rule because of heavy investments in capacity expansion, but that has not happened yet. The information superhighway, like motor vehicle superhighways, experiences congestion at peak hours and breakdown when accidents occur, and frequently is under repair. The Internet is a powerful communications medium, but it is unlikely totally to displace other forms of communication.

Ironically, the Internet has a number of attributes that make it a new tool for originators of marketing messages to learn more about possible message recipients. Whether the marketing message is delivered by e-mail, a Web page, or physical mail, Internet tools permit senders to capture a great deal more information about us, without our knowledge and consent, than is available through other media.

Each medium will play as large or as small a role in the future of messaging as the sum of factors affecting their attractiveness may dictate. The volume of wired telephone communications will increase to the degree that the pricing reflects the very low incremental cost of an individual message. At the same time, telephone service providers need to find ways of capturing profitable revenue beyond charging for plain-vanilla voice messages.

Wireless communication will increase in use to the degree that it becomes nearly universal, more reliable, and more compatible over more markets. The balkanization of the U.S. cellular market and the incompatibility of U.S. cellular systems with those in use in most of the rest of the world need to be addressed.

E-mail is certainly becoming the communications medium of choice in the academic community and within many large organizations. Its ability to be the primary communications medium between businesses will depend on its ease of use for individuals and the degree of difficulty and cost that organizations experience in trying to support e-mail networks.

Physical mail and other paper-based communications will continue to become more attractive as technology improves their capabilities. The advances in desktop publishing, address database management, mail finishing, and decision support systems for postal and carrier service selection will make them more cost-effective.

Besides the technological and economic factors noted, one of the findings of the Institute for the Future studies on messaging over the last several years is that organizational culture and senior management preference determine the predominant form of communications originating in most organizations. Some organizations elect to be e-mail cultures, some use voice mail, and some communicate on paper.

However, government policies and practices and the vitality of postal authorities can have the greatest impact of all on which media perform the best in the future. For example, physical mail will ultimately succeed only to the degree that postal authorities can continue to improve mail delivery systems to ensure that mail is delivered reliably, securely, and within a time frame that meets mailer expectations, particularly as new media become universal.

Postal authorities also have to offer a variety of products that meet varying customer needs. In this country, first-class mail is a high-quality universal service, but, to an increasing extent, customers demand services tailored to their special needs in both delivery commitment and price. Technologies such as digital metering enable time-specific delivery and the ability to do end-to-end tracking and tracing.

Postal authorities also need to minimize the external costs they impose on mailers and recipients through regulations or processes that may reduce postal costs but increase external costs. They need to give incentives for downstream access through hybrid mail systems that let electronic communications systems carry the message closer to the destination point and use physical mail creation systems that improve mail preparation quality and deliverability. They also need to be more focused on outsourcing and work-sharing discounts to stimulate greater mail volume. In the PaperCom study, business executives acknowledged the high value of physical mail, but also expressed concerns that it would not continue to grow, even over the next three years. Clearly, the U.S. Postal Service cannot take its formidable customer loyalty for granted.

All messaging systems will be affected by the degree to which they can gain more information about recipients, including their needs for goods and services and their message receipt preferences. Privacy laws will increase the complexity of any effort to gain information about potential recipients, and it is unclear at this point how much momentum will drive increased difficulty of getting private information.

My third theme is that messaging costs in large organizations will continue to grow, and, as a result, will eventually be subject to major reengineering efforts.

Message communications costs are large, growing, and out of control in most large organizations. In Fortune 500 companies—according to a study sponsored by Pitney Bowes and conducted by the Institute for the Future—they cost, on average, more than $120 million per company per year for direct, in-house communications expenses. And those costs do not include indirect support costs or outsourced expenses such as advertising agency communications costs.

Most organizations do not understand the full costs of different kinds of communications. The costs are spread over many cost and profit centers, usually in small amounts. The activities that trigger those costs occur at one place, but the responsibility for paying the costs is usually in another part of the organization. Other than physical mail, few media require full advance payment; most are billed in arrears to provide as few usage barriers as possible. Moreover, with respect to fax, telecommunications, and e-mail costs, there are significant network support costs that are virtually impossible to quantify and relate back to individual messages.

Ultimately, that situation must change. To be more competitive, organizations of all kinds must reduce costs and increase the effectiveness of vital business processes, and they must find a way to get the most value from messaging processes at the lowest possible cost. The tools to map those processes and define their costs and their value to organizations are at the earliest stages of development, but eventually all organizations will redefine their messaging processes to comport with business competitiveness realities.

My conclusion today is that there is no inevitable or natural outcome.

Ultimately, the proportion of future messages carried by one medium versus another will depend on the extent to which those in businesses or governments that support a particular medium successfully invest in business designs that make it more likely that senders reach recipients when and how recipients want to be reached.

A great deal of effort is going into providing access to the Internet and to e-mail communications. To some degree, there appears to be a preference for newer communications tools over older ones in government policy and investment decisions. Ultimately, governments cannot pick winners in communications technology any more than they could pick winners in domestic industries they attempt from time to time to protect.

In closing, I would refer back to Aristotle's wisdom: The audience for messages will vote by their actions on which messaging tools will grow. Just as power shifted from government to people and from vendors to customers, all of us as message recipients will ultimately play a much more important role in the race for message tool superiority.

Ultimately, we must let the marketplace and the people decide.

PART III

UNWINDING MONOPOLIES

10. The Post Office and the Digital Switch: Observations on an Outmoded Industry

Thomas J. Duesterberg

France is a wonderful place to observe the stubborn persistence of the past into the present. When I was a student in Paris in the early 1970s, it was amusing to observe one of the vestiges of labor union intransigence in the public sector. It took the form of manual ticket punchers who controlled entry to the subway, just as they had done since the inception of the system. Decades of bruising ideological and political combat were required before that quaint but monumentally inefficient tribute to the working woman (most of the jobs were held by women—hence the term *"poinconneuses"*) gave way to an automated ticket reading system. The process took so long that the intermediate generation of technology based on tokens, and long used in London and New York, was largely bypassed.

The French postal monopoly will undoubtedly outlast the American, but one certainly has to resort to history and cultural anthropology rather than economics to explain the persistence of an outmoded and inefficient communications technology. Previous work, some presented in the 1995 Cato conference on the U.S. Postal Service, has convincingly made the case that there is no rational economic argument for maintaining a protected monopoly.[1] Moreover, Peter Ferrara summarized a strong case that maintaining the monopoly is a drag on U.S. economic performance, increasing consumer costs by

Thomas J. Duesterberg is the president of the Manufacturers Alliance/MAPI, and previously was a senior fellow and the director of the Washington, D.C., office of the Hudson Institute.
[1]A good recent synopsis of the economic and political case for ending the postal monopoly is J. Gregory Sidak and Daniel E. Spulber, *Protecting Competition from the Postal Monopoly* (Washington: AEI Press, 1996).

up to $12 billion per year.[2] Maintaining a subsidized monopoly with almost 900,000 workers not only raises costs, but also stifles innovation in one of the most dynamic sectors of the modern economy, digital telecommunications.

We might help build the case for ending the postal monopoly by looking more closely at the recent history of the telecommunications industry, one of the last of the so-called network industries to make the transition from protected monopoly to competition. Competition has unleashed the dynamic forces of innovation in telecommunications. The modern telecommunications sector has all but accomplished the project of displacing the Postal Service as a platform for communications in the 21st century. Nonetheless, the process of introducing competition in that sector has been a messy one, beset by major policy errors having real economic costs. We can learn valuable lessons from what Alfred Kahn, the former chairman of the Civil Aeronautics Board and a regulatory expert, has called the "miasma" of telecommunications deregulation as we contemplate the end of the postal monopoly.[3] So I will first survey some of the ways the telecommunications sector has rendered the Postal Service obsolete while creating a highly dynamic industry that contrasts strongly with the moribund postal service. Second, I will explore a few of the lessons to be drawn from the flawed process of telecommunications deregulation as we try to map out the politics and economics of ending the postal monopoly.

The Growth of Digital Telecommunications

Despite the determined efforts of some regulators, politicians, and industry players, strong competition has taken root in telecommunications, often in areas not anticipated by regulators. Since the breakup of AT&T in 1984, the process of technical advance and convergence with the information technology industry has been nurtured by the constructive and destructive forces of competition.[4] As

---

[2]See Peter Ferrara, "Postal Service Problems: The Need to Free the Mails," in *The Last Monopoly: Privatizing the Postal Service for the Information Age*, ed. Edward L. Hudgins (Washington: Cato Institute, 1996), pp. 23–32.

[3]Alfred E. Kahn, *Letting Go: Deregulating the Process of Deregulation* (East Lansing, Mich.: MSU Public Utilities Papers, 1998), pp. 145–46.

a result, the telecommunications industry has begun to resemble the dynamic computer industry more than the static Postal Service. The "positive feedback cycle" of dynamic growth that Bill Gates identified in the computer sector is now being played out in telecommunications.[5]

The unparalleled success of the personal computer industry was of course driven by the constant and rapid expansion of memory capacity and computing power starting in the late 1970s. Today we pay $1,000 for a personal computer 13 times more powerful than the mainframes that sold for $4.7 million in 1971.[6] As computers became faster and more powerful, there was a vast need for new programming and new content to take advantage of computing power. So the hardware revolution gave impetus to both software and various forms of content industries. Later, software and content developers started to drive the hardware makers by constant upgrades in their products requiring ever-bigger and ever-faster machines.

The telecommunications analogue to such a symbiotic process is the interaction of digital content with bandwidth, or the capacity to transmit large amounts of data across distances. New Internet applications such as e-commerce, distance learning and medicine, and interactive video applications of course depend on the deployment of even more transmission capacity or bandwidth.

Fortunately, the convergence spawned by digital telecommunications is now beginning to produce the same sort of symbiotic relationship with content providers to spur progress. Competition in bandwidth is now widespread. Observers, especially those in Washington seeing with the blinders of regulators, have tended to focus only on the old copper-wire, physical network as a source of bandwidth. That perspective is of course colored by the history of the Internet, which started on a copper-wire backbone and distribution network.

Yet what is going on in the real world is that new, high-bandwidth platforms are being deployed widely, at declining cost. In late 1998, new telecommunications firms obtained more than $5.1 billion in

---

[4]For a good primer on those forces, see Peter Pitsch, *The Innovation Age* (Washington: The Hudson Institute and Progress and Freedom Foundation, 1996).

[5]Bill Gates, *The Road Ahead* (New York: Viking, 1995), p. 46.

[6]See "Time Well Spent: The Declining Real Cost of Living in America," *1997 Annual Report of the Federal Reserve Bank of Dallas* (Dallas, Tex., 1998), pp. 16–18.

debt financing, according to Dow Jones investment information.[7] And newer forms of digital telecommunications are starting to dwarf the public switched-telephone network as platforms for Internet applications.

Consider cable television. Microsoft, Intel, AT&T, and others have sunk billions of dollars into transforming cable to interactive networks capable of transmitting data at up to 100 times the speed of normal phone lines, and at much lower cost. Cable modems now give high-speed, two-way voice and data connections to more than 500,000 customers, and Donaldson, Lufkin, Jenrette analysts predict that figure will grow to 13 million in four years.[8] Additionally, satellite-delivered video signals have enough bandwidth to deliver hundreds of program channels. Digital Direct Broadcast Satellite services are one of the fastest-growing consumer electronic products in history. Nearly 14 million people now take their video signals directly from satellites—and the bandwidth is ample to deliver data as well.[9] Terrestrial broadcasters too have hinted strongly that they will use some of the new spectrum given to them by Congress to deliver data to customers—opening up yet another broadband pipe to the home.

The wireless telephony industry is also putting huge amounts of capacity online through both terrestrial and satellite systems. In 1999 wireless capacity in the United States will be able to handle all voice and data requirements now sent by the traditional wireline telecommunications system, according to the WEFA Group.[10] The spectrum auctions of the past few years have produced a truly competitive wireless marketplace, which is lowering prices and leading to a proliferation of new services to pay for infrastructure investment. Projections by the Yankee Group indicate that wireless telephony prices will decline in the United States over the next few years from about 44 cents per minute to around 18 cents per minute in 2003. Prices will on average decline by 15 percent to 20 percent annually over the next

---

[7]See Seth Schiesel, "Phone Upstarts Scramble for Capital," *New York Times*, November 8, 1998, p. BU–4.

[8]See Thomas J. Duesterberg and Peter K. Pitsch, *The Role of Competition and Regulation in Today's Cable TV Market* (Indianapolis, Ind.: Hudson Institute, 1998), pp. 26–28.

[9]For up-to-date reports on subscribers, see www.SKYREPORT.com.

[10]WEFA Group, "Economic Impact of Deregulating U.S. Communications Industries" (Bala-Cynwyd, Pa.: WEFA Group, 1995), pp. 28–29.

five years.[11] In highly competitive markets, some with six or more providers, prices for nationwide calling plans have dipped to 10 cents per minute for large users. As AT&T hopes, at those rates users could well start substituting wireless for everyday telephone service that has been copper-wire based for more than 100 years.

Fiber-optic cable is also being laid at a dizzying rate, more than 1,000 miles per day, according to George Gilder. New-wave division multiplexing technology is advancing the delivery speed of fiber to the terabit (trillion bits per second) range, enough to deliver every extant issue of the *Wall Street Journal* in less than one second.[12] Satellite systems, some designed for fast data, others for voice and interactive applications, also are being financed and coming online. Gilder estimates that telecommunications bandwidth is now doubling every six months; the law of the telecosm, as he labels it, is three times faster than Moore's law for computing power. Another study, by Insight Research, puts the doubling time for bandwidth at 18 months, and estimates the cost of transmission falls by half every two years.[13]

The abundance of bandwidth that is appearing, in both largely deregulated sectors like wireless and satellite and more regulated segments like cable and fiber-optic backbones, is facilitating an explosion of new services and more competition in old ones. The wireless sector is the clearest example of the phenomenon. With six or more providers in many metropolitan areas, and with bandwidth expanding to three times ISDN speeds in the near future, wireless is competing in both telephony and data markets. Strategy Analytics, a Boston research firm, estimates that wireless subscribers in the United States will increase to 126 million by 2003, and minutes of use will grow by 35 percent per year.[14] According to Technology Futures, an Austin forecasting firm, terrestrial wireless systems beginning service in 1999 will offer up to 384 kilobits per second (kbs) speeds, facilitating the faster Internet connections that companies

[11]Data provided by Crispin Vickers, The Yankee Group (1998).

[12]George Gilder, "Telecosm Outlook 1998: Piping Hot," *Forbes ASAP* (February 23, 1998), pp. 111–20.

[13]Ibid., p. 112. See also "Study: Expect 25 Terabits per Second by 2002," *Fiber Optic News* 18, no. 41 (October 19, 1998).

[14]Charles Mason, "PCS Carriers Leverage Price Advantage," *ASAP* (Advanstar Communications, September 15, 1998), p. 19.

like Motorola and Qualcomm are promoting (with the help of Microsoft) for their new generation of mobile phones. Qualcomm is already testing systems offering megabit per second (Mbs) speeds over its networks. Satellite data systems such as Teledesic and Celestri will reach data transmission speeds of up to 16 Mbs when they become operational in a few years.[15] Mobile, high bandwidth Internet connections are just the latest in a series of platforms that are spurring more opportunities for voice and data communications. New applications like mobile Internet and interactive video are just the leading edge of a feedback system in which new applications emerge to exploit the plethora of bandwidth.

Postal Implication

What all this means for the "second wave" technology of the Postal Service ought to be fairly clear: It is fast becoming obsolete in addition to being inefficient. A few data points help put this draconian statement in perspective. Since about 1970, the nominal price of a first-class stamp has quadrupled, growing by about 10 percent in real terms, while the inflation-adjusted price of a long-distance phone call has declined by 88 percent and the price of a unit of computing power has declined by a factor of 10 million. The price of a cellular phone has fallen by 98 percent since 1984.[16]

Despite more than $5 billion invested in automation equipment in recent years, the number of full-time postal employees has grown by about 5 percent since 1994. At the same time, the volume of mail delivered has been stagnant, growing at about 1 percent per year in recent years for first-class mail. Each full-time employee of the Postal Service moves, on average, about 223,000 pieces of mail per year. By contrast, each America Online (AOL) employee moves more than 13.8 million e-mail and instant messages per year and facilitates about 43 million "hits" on Web pages per year. For AOL usage is expanding by more than 20 percent annually, per customer, and its subscribers have more than doubled in the last two years.[17] If one ex-

[15]See Lawrence Vanston, "Wireless High-Speed Data to Climb into the Ring Soon," press release by *Technology Future, Inc.* (1998), www.tfi.com.

[16]Data from Dallas Federal Reserve Board, "Time Well Spent," and U.S. Postal Service, www.usps.com/history.

trapolates simply from AOL data, Americans now send more than 48 billion e-mails and 423 billion instant messages per year, well in excess of four times the number of pieces of mail sent via the Postal Service. Americans also access about 1.5 trillion Web pages per year. One Internet backbone provider, Frontier Corporation, recently calculated that its traffic had grown by 300 percent in just six months, another indicator of how new bandwidth capacity is stimulating expanded use of the medium.[18]

E-mail and Internet access are just two of the forms of direct substitution for the types of communications, both personal and business, previously handled by the postal monopoly. Yet the proliferation of bandwidth is generating—in a classic supply-side experiment—newer ways to communicate and do business. We have already noted the growth of mobile Internet products, including digital phones and palm pilots, that widen access to the Internet. Electronic commerce also is growing much more rapidly than anticipated. It is up more than 200 percent, to a projected $13 billion this year. Forrester Research estimates that e-commerce could jump to 6 percent of GDP by 2005.[19] Customers can not only order products over the Internet, but receive delivery of such products as computer software, music, and video products, a change that is slowly eroding the parcel post business of the Postal Service as well. A recent *New York Times* story discussed electronic billing systems that are being tested and deployed. Although the *Times'* estimate that 60 percent of all first-class mail consists of bills and payments is surely exaggerated, it is another staple of the postal monopoly business that will be displaced in the near future.[20]

On a more speculative note, Marc Andreesen recently offered the prognosis that Internet operators would soon start giving away personal computers as a means to lure Internet users.[21] Andreesen's company, Netscape, of course pioneered the giveaway of computer

---

[17]Data available at www.AOL.com.

[18]"Frontier Global Center Sees Dramatic Traffic Increase—Reaches 6 Billion Page Views per Month," *Business Wire* (October 7, 1998).

[19]See "The Net Is Open for Business—Big Time," *BusinessWeek*, August 13, 1998, p. 108.

[20]Denise Caruso, "Digital Commerce," *New York Times*, November 16, 1998, p. C–5.

[21]Anthony Effinger, "Free PCs? Expert Says They're on the Way," *Arizona Republic*, September 19, 1998, p. E–9.

programming as a technique to win users to Internet browsing, paying for it with advertising and other services. That concept may not be illusory, if another recent survey showing that more than 18 million households in the United States now use the Internet for shopping, and if the promotional material for a new business to deliver movies to theaters using satellite systems, are both accurate.[22]

Given the explosion of new users and new products, and expanded use of digital communications as bandwidth is deployed, it is easy to comprehend why use of the postal system is stagnating. What is even more revealing is that the telecommunications system, dynamic as it has been, is still shackled by a regulatory apparatus and regulators intent on preserving their control over the industry. Telecommunications would be even more dynamic and innovative absent the myriad cross-subsidies and regulatory burdens now weighing upon it. As we look ahead to ending the postal monopoly, several lessons should be learned from the experience of telecom deregulation.

Lessons from the Telecom Deregulation Experiment

Despite the dynamism and growth of the telecommunications industry since the breakup of AT&T and the landmark Telecommunications Act of 1996, the shackles of regulation still impede even more rapid innovation and efficiency in the system.[23] Local telephone companies are not allowed to offer long-distance service, massive subsidies for various classes of users are still in place, prices are managed in ways that diminish efficiency and discourage innovation, and regulatory authorities seek to extend their reach over new technologies instead of phasing out controls as the Telecommunications Act allows. As a consequence, various industry players quite understandably try to protect their existing advantages or seek rents in new ways at the expense of efficiency. In so doing they retard rather

---

[22]"18.4 Million U.S. Households Participating in E-Commerce," *Xinhua News Agency*, September 10, 1998; and Cine Comm Digital Cinema press release, "Cine Comm to Introduce Digital Delivery of Theatrical Films to Exhibitors," November 17, 1998.

[23]I have tried to catalogue the problems in Thomas J. Duesterberg and Kenneth Gordon: *Competition and Deregulation in Telecommunications: The Case for a New Paradigm* (Indianapolis, Ind.: Hudson Institute, 1997).

than advance the goal of a market-driven system, which was the explicit purpose of the Telecommunications Act.

Some of the errors and miscalculations plaguing the process of telecommunications deregulation are relevant to thinking about how to end the postal monopoly. Perhaps the most obvious and egregious error of the telecom deregulators—the legislators who wrote the relevant statutes as well as those who implemented them—was trying to *micromanage* a transition from a regulated or an administered industry to a state of competition. In his important book on the future of utility deregulation, Alfred Kahn recounts how he and his colleagues learned that lesson in their efforts to deregulate transportation:

> I have . . . recounted how we came to the realization in the case of the airlines, beginning with the intention of moving gradually and deliberately; discovering that doing so created more problems than it solved; and how the process, once initiated, took on a life of its own, until there appeared to be no halfway house between comprehensive regulation on the one side and something close to total deregulation on the other.[24]

Micromanaging a technologically complex industry such as telecommunications has proven even more difficult than it was for transportation. For example, in its zeal to level the playing field, the Federal Communications Commission has taken it upon itself to try to *create* competition through a system of preferences and subsidies instead of letting market forces operate. Its labors have been focused on creating wireline competition for local telephone services. The FCC has imposed below-cost resale prices on incumbent operators while maintaining a system of cross-subsidies which keeps prices in rural areas low and urban areas high.[25] The quite predictable result has been a dearth of so-called facilities-based competition, as it has simply been more attractive to enter markets through the favorable resale terms mandated by the FCC than to build a separate system. One unintended consequence is that the incumbent local telephone companies have lagged behind in offering advanced services like broadband technologies, partly resulting from fear that competitors would simply purchase them for resale and undercut their business opportunities. That in turn has provided a type of arbitrage opportunity for the cable and wireless operators to fill a need for residen-

[24]Kahn, p. 16.
[25]Ibid., Ch. 3.

tial high-speed services; it gives them a lead in the promising new sector.

Related to the inherent difficulty of micromanaging is the iron law of modern bureaucratic life: Once given authority to administer an industry, those to whom it is entrusted will fight tenaciously to keep and expand it. That proposition is so self-evident as to require little elaboration. The best single example from the telecommunications process is the universal service requirement.[26] Seizing on rather vague language in the Telecommunications Act, "for the preservation and advancement of universal service," the FCC, goaded on by interested parties in Congress, industry, and self-appointed consumer groups, has engineered a massive expansion of a subsidy program with very modest origins. In implementing a new program to expand the subsidy to cover high-speed computer connections to every classroom in the country, every rural health facility, and many remote households, the FCC has imposed an administrative tax of more than $2 billion per year (and headed higher) without the constitutionally mandated consent of Congress. And the FCC's chairman, William Kennard, has even bigger plans for the universal service program. Using the vaguely apocalyptic language so useful for bureaucratic imperialists, Kennard recently concluded in a major speech:

> Our country is struggling with a vast digital divide. It's a division between those who have access to modern technology, and those who don't; a division between the well-to-do and the poor, the well educated and those who did not finish high school; those who face no physical or cognitive impediments and people with disabilities; and a racial division, because African-Americans and Hispanics stand on the wrong side of the divide in all income groups. I believe we all want to conquer the Digital Divide.[27]

The self-evident solution for Kennard is expanding the universal service program to address this vast litany of contemporary social problems, a prospect that could prove expensive indeed. Paying for

---

[26]Much has been written about the subject. A good place to start is Lawrence Gasman, "Universal Service: The New Telecommunications Entitlements and Taxes," Cato Policy Analysis no. 310, June 25, 1998; see also Duesterberg and Gordon, *Competition and Deregulation*, Ch. 3.

[27]Federal Communications Commission, "Remarks of William Kennard . . . to the National Association of Regulatory Utility Commissioners," Orlando, Fl., November 11, 1998.

such a program, of course, is already a major political dilemma, but it is also, according to Alfred Kahn and others, one of the major impediments to ending the vast system of cross-subsidies that saps efficiency and impedes innovation.[28]

Universal service is of particular relevance to the discussion, because "The Postal Service views [it] as the justification not only for retaining its existing monopoly over letter mail, but also for expanding its operations in and into competing markets."[29] As J. Gregory Sidak and Daniel E. Spulber point out in their excellent book on the postal monopoly, the Postal Service is now exploiting a parallel concept of universal service to justify cross-subsidies that harm competitors in related markets like express mail and parcel delivery.[30] If the telecommunications example is used as a model, we can expect to see further expansion of subsidized services and undermining of competition in the increasingly competitive markets for delivery of information and physical packages. Indeed, the Postal Service is already experimenting with e-mail, electronic payments systems, and electronic access to its services.[31]

The baneful example of universal service exposes another hard lesson from telecommunications deregulation, although the underlying problem is lamentably widespread in contemporary America. The legislative language of the 1996 Telecommunications Act was so vague and suggestive that it created two related problems. First, it delegated broad discretion to the regulators to interpret its meaning. Second, it was so imprecise that it almost invited litigation to settle differing interpretations. Examples of the first problem are the universal service provisions and the all-important rules for competition in long-distance service. The latter problem is symbolized by the ongoing battle now at the Supreme Court for final decision over the rules governing interconnection of new firms with incumbent local telephone operators. While Congress obviously cannot foresee every contingency likely to arise in the course of introducing competition, it surely could have been explicit about the direction given to those charged with implementing the bill. By shrinking from that respon-

---

[28]Kahn, Ch. 5.
[29]Sidak and Spulber, p. 71.
[30]Ibid., pp. 100–101.
[31]See U.S. Postal Service, "Postal Service Merges onto Information Superhighway: Introduces Internet-Based Services," Press Release No. 90 (September 2, 1998).

sibility, Congress only encouraged the natural predisposition of the regulators to micromanage business and to aggrandize their own authority—ironically, in the name of deregulation!

One of the reasons alleged for such reticence by Congress is the political difficulty of introducing competition, a problem that could easily be negated by relying on empirical experience. The underlying fear of Congress when deregulating has always been, of course, being blamed if higher prices result from the process. Some operators and consumers—that is, those most subsidized—will certainly experience new burdens as subsidies and inefficiencies are wrung out of the system by competition.[32] Others will see lower prices. Study after study has shown the economic necessity of "rebalancing rates," a euphemism for ending subsidies and moving prices toward real costs.[33]

What is too often obscured by the hand-wringing angst of politicians and regulators is that there is not as big a public relations problem as feared. In the first place, prices have been raised in the past by both the federal and state authorities without, in the words of Alfred Kahn (who was also a state commissioner in New York), any "reported fatalities among the commissioners."[34] The federally imposed subscriber line charge was without serious political repercussion, as were efforts by the states of Illinois, California, Massachusetts, Michigan, and Wisconsin to raise residential rates while taking the pressure off business rates for local telephony.[35] One should also note that, where competition has appeared, such as in wireless telephony, prices have declined steadily. That experience in the telephone industry has been replicated in other network industries. Substantial consumer welfare gains have been documented from the network industry deregulation process. The historical evidence ought to give courage to feckless politicians worried about a momentary surge of protest and outrage from professional consumer advocates whenever residential telephone prices are untethered from the omniscient hand

---

[32]See Kahn, Ch. 6.

[33]The Brookings Institution recently issued a paper by centrist economists endorsing the notion. See Robert Litan and Roger Noll, "Unleashing Telecommunications: The Case for True Competition," *Brookings Institution Policy Brief No. 39* (Washington: Brookings Institution, November 1998).

[34]Kahn, p. 131.

[35]See Duesterberg and Gordon, pp. 40–43, 82, and 90.

of central planners.[36] The price of a first-class stamp—if that poses a relevant question in the digital age—is more likely to fall than to rise after the demise of the postal monopoly.

The final lesson to be drawn from the experience of telecommunications deregulation is that maintaining subsidies and inefficient pricing—no matter how well intentioned—distorts investment and discourages innovation. That proposition is nearly tautological and probably requires little elaboration. Two examples will suffice. Return once again to Alfred Kahn's analysis of the government requirement that established telephone companies to price resale of telecommunications services to new entrants artificially low. Such prices, he argues,

> in a very real sense discourage competition itself, in the name of encouraging it: if potential competitors can obtain from incumbents, at regulatorily prescribed prices, not just facilities and services that are naturally monopolistic but any and all others present and future that could feasibly be supplied independently, the incentive for incumbents to innovate and for competitors to provide their own will be attenuated.[37]

Thus the local telephone companies have been severely handicapped in offering the cutting edge of telecommunications, high bandwidth services, and the American public has been deprived of their competition for these services for years. Further, subsidies for rural telephone operators have discouraged innovation in providing telephony to those areas. Wireless operators, for instance, have been excluded from competing in that arena, at least as carriers of last resort, by the subsidized wireline prices. Peter Ferrara, drawing on the empirical experience of real businesses as varied as pizza delivery and overnight express, estimates that prices could be cut in half if competition were allowed for rural routes.[38] As the Postal Service seeks to enter new electronic messaging businesses we should certainly be wary of what its subsidized service can do to undermine one of the most dynamic sectors of the American economy.

---

[36]For a discussion of the benefits of deregulation across industries, see Robert Crandall and Jerry Willig, *Economic Deregulation and Customer Lessons for the Electric Industry* (Fairfax, Va.: Center for Market Process, George Mason University, 1997).

[37]Kahn, p. 48.

[38]Ferrara, p. 28.

Conclusion

I have argued that the rapid deployment of bandwidth and the concomitant stimulus to new digital services adds even more weight to the argument in favor of ending the postal monopoly. I think the frustrating experience of trying to micromanage the transition to competition, while maintaining a complex system of subsidies in the telecommunications industry, also argues for a quick dissolution rather than a gradual phaseout of the postal monopoly. Any attempt to micromanage a transition will be beset by the same sorts of problems and misjudgments affecting telecommunications, including attempts to subsidize entry into new businesses. The case for simply ending the postal monopoly is even stronger because, despite what it would like to be, the Postal Service is what futurists Alvin and Heidi Toffler call a "second wave" or classic industrial-age industry, not a dynamic digital age industry.[39] Preserving an inefficient, centralized, bureaucratic organization as large as the Postal Service simply diverts resources away from more efficient solutions to the communications requirements of the modern economy, imposes an unnecessary welfare burden on the American people, and subsidizes competition to one of the most dynamic parts of the U.S. economy.

[39] Alvin and Heidi Toffler, *Creating a New Civilization: The Politics of the Third Wave* (Washington: Progress and Freedom Foundation, 1994)

11. Privatizing the U.S. Postal Service

Michael A. Crew and Paul R. Kleindorfer

In testimony before the House of Representatives Subcommittee on Postal Service concerning H.R. 22, we argued that the proposal for a form of price-cap regulation was unlikely to yield significant benefits as long as the U.S. Postal Service (USPS) remained a public enterprise. More than a year has passed and H.R. 22 has been revised. However, the Postal Service appears no closer to privatization. The purpose of this paper is to restate and expand the arguments for privatization and to examine some scenarios for the operation of a privatized Postal Service. In section one we discuss briefly the current state of postal service, including developments in other countries and the reason change is required. In section two we examine reasons privatization should be an integral part of postal reform. In section three we sketch our views about the direction that regulation might take for a privatized postal service, the U.S. Postal Service, Inc. (USPSI). For some our proposals will not go far enough, as they retain the regulated monopoly in modified form. Section four concludes the discussion.

The Current State of Postal Service

The Postal Reorganization Act of 1970 provided the basis for the current organization of the USPS and the Postal Rate Commission. The organization has had numerous successes during the last quarter of a century. The regulatory process has emphasized procedural fairness, allowing competitors and mailers a strong voice in the set-

Michael Crew is a professor of economics and the director of the Center for Research in Regulated Industries at Rutgers University. Paul Kleindorfer is the Universal Furniture professor at the Wharton Risk Management and Decision Processes Center.

ting of rates and the shaping of new services. Despite the apparent cumbersome, legalistic structure of the regulatory process, it has not stifled innovation. USPS is a world leader in volume of mail, work-sharing discounts, bulk mail, automation, and downstream access. In addition, the rates for basic first-class mail are among the lowest in the advanced economies.

Despite significant successes, postal service in the United States cannot continue in its present form because of major exogenous changes that are not compatible with the current system. The changes include chiefly the emergence of microelectronics, optical fiber, and computer-based alternatives such as the Internet, which have revolutionized traditional communications and advertising.[1] The changes can be a significant source of opportunity for growth in postal and delivery services, but taking advantage of the opportunities will require a move to a more commercial, businesslike approach to postal service and the incorporation of regulatory innovations such as incentive regulation. H.R. 22 recognizes those needs and the dangers of not heeding them.

The United States is not alone in moving toward postal reform. Postal administrations worldwide have been moving toward more commercial operations, including adopting organizational and tech-nological innovations developed in the private sector over the past several decades of increasing global competition.[2] The rationale for more commercial operations is simple: Increased competition from other communication modes, and alternative delivery services, have meant that the traditional civil service bureaucracy coupled with the traditional regulatory process respond too slowly to emerging mar-ket realities. What is required is a market-oriented approach to align

---

[1] For a discussion of recent technological and marketing trends in postal and deliv-ery services worldwide, see Michael A. Crew and Paul R. Kleindorfer, *Managing Change in the Postal and Delivery Industries* (Boston: Kluwer Academic Publishers, 1997).

[2] For a discussion of international trends and issues in postal reform, see Michael A. Crew and Paul R. Kleindorfer, *Commercialization of Postal and Delivery Services* (Boston: Kluwer Academic Publishers, 1995); and Crew and Kleindorfer, 1997, supra. Very re-cently, the Communications Workers Union in the United Kingdom has put forward its proposals for mail ("Freedom to Deliver—Posting the Way to Greater Success," CWU, London, February 1997), which propose turning the United Kingdom Post Of-fice into an independent corporation within the public sector, and the creation of an independent regulatory agency administering a scheme of price-cap regulation.

the incentives and operations of economic agents involved in postal and delivery services with the needs of their customers. In short, exogenous changes in both markets and technologies of postal and delivery services imply an unavoidable requirement for a significantly greater business orientation in the postal sector.

The changes required to achieve an increased commercial orientation are not just internal to the USPS, but also involve reforms in the regulatory process. It is important to note at the outset that national postal administrations will continue to enjoy residual market power for some time. That means that regulation will continue to have an important role in balancing increased commercial incentives for static and dynamic efficiency while restraining the exploitation of market power. Postal service is not unique in that regard, and we have seen a similar evolution in other network industries that have undergone the transformation from traditional cost-of-service regulated monopolies to more competitive structures. Indeed, the experience from such industries as telecommunications and energy is of considerable value for the postal sector, as such experience has provided the direction for understanding the necessary regulatory innovations to achieve the transition to greater competition. The general character of the innovations has been to provide greater autonomy to the incumbent service provider for pricing and product innovation, while encouraging competitive entry into all parts of the value chain except for those displaying the natural monopoly attributes of overwhelming scale or scope economies. In postal service, as in electric power and telecommunications, it is only in the area of local delivery that a strong case can be made for the existence of natural monopoly.

The experience in other countries and other industries suggests the key themes that should guide the introduction of reforms in the postal sector. First, the aforementioned transformations to greater commercialization and streamlined regulatory governance are central. Second, in order for the USPS to align its internal incentives with market requirements, its employees must be given both the rights and the responsibilities of "residual claimants" in USPS. That implies a stronger link of the economic results of the Postal Service to the salaries and wages of employees. In particular, the combination of current labor-relations practices and cost-plus regulation has led to a situation in which USPS employees have enjoyed a significant premium over similarly situated employees in the private sector.[3] Under increasingly competitive conditions that state of affairs would not be able to continue for long were the Postal Service not a public enterprise with a statutory monopoly and with its finances underwritten by the U.S. government. However, with public enterprise the static inefficiencies implied by the wage differential can continue. Similarly, the beneficial effects of competition and technological change will be attenuated under public enterprise. To attain the potential benefits of technological change, competition, and price-cap regulation, privatization is required. H.R. 22 in its present form fails to take the most important step toward reforming the USPS. Compared with privatization, most of the changes proposed are cosmetic. Let us now examine some of the consequences of making privatization the centerpiece of postal reform.

Privatization—The Centerpiece of Postal Reform

The forces of technological change, increased competition, and a different attitude toward monopoly regulation mean that the time is ripe for serious reform of the postal sector. In the United States reform is under way with H.R. 22. However, H.R. 22, while subscribing to the notion of regulatory reform and incorporating some recent developments in "regulatory technology," in particular price-cap regulation, misses the opportunity for serious regulatory reform in that it fails to grasp the nettle of privatization. Privatization of the USPS and postal service in other countries is the key element to successful, efficient, and innovative postal networks.

There are no strong technological, strategic, or economic reasons why postal service should be publicly operated. While it may be difficult to make a case for privatizing the armed services, there are no such strategic considerations with postal service. Postal service is a network industry. Other network industries—for example, electricity, gas, and telecommunications—are privately owned and oper-

---

[3]Jeffrey M. Perloff and Michael L. Wachter, "A Comparative Analysis of Wage Premiums and Industrial Relations in the British Post Office and the United States Postal Service." *Competition and Innovation in Postal Services*, eds. Michael A. Crew and Paul R. Kleindorfer (Boston: Kluwer Academic Press, 1991), estimated the magnitude of the postal employee wage premium at 28 percent.

ated.[4] Postal service is arguably less important to the economy than any of the other network industries. It would be much more painful if the lights went out for half a day than if postal service ceased for an extended period. There would be inconvenience if the mail did not get delivered but the ready availability of (imperfect) substitutes would mean that severe disruption could be avoided.

Operating USPS as a public enterprise is a political matter that is in the hands of the federal government. It remains a public enterprise despite the many advantages in having a privatized Postal Service. For example, a private-sector postal service would be subject to different competitive rules than would a public enterprise, and it would have the potential of being more efficient than a public enterprise. To some extent, H.R. 22 recognizes the potential of putting private enterprise to work in the USPS by changing the competition rules and by subjecting USPS to price-cap regulation. Both measures are artifacts of privately owned, regulated companies. However, H.R. 22 fails to privatize the USPS, the vital step that is necessary for legislative changes to bring about their intended benefits. We will not get involved in the details of H.R. 22 but will be concerned with the consequences arising from the failure to privatize.

Price-cap regulation (PCR) is the most significant change in regulation embodied in H.R. 22. It differs from traditional cost-of-service regulation in that it does not restrict the profit that the firm can make to the cost-of-service, including an allowed rate-of-return on its capital. PCR sets the maximum price level[5] that the regulated firm may charge and then allows the firm to keep the profits that it makes. It also allows the firm to raise its prices over time by a specified amount, namely, the annual increase in the index less X, where X is a percentage deduction from the annual increase in the index. Thus PCR appeals to the firm's incentive to maximize profits and, in so doing, to minimize costs and otherwise operate efficiently. The efficiency of PCR comes in the form of lower costs as a result of the operation of the profit motive. To be effective, PCR requires the profit motive, which requires residual claimants if it is to operate. Absent

---

[4]Water utilities are mostly publicly owned but there is a trend toward privately managed operations through contracts with privately owned utilities.

[5]That level is normally based on a price index, for example, the Laspeyre index, which allows the firm to set its prices within the limits of the index.

residual claimants, PCR lacks the incentives for efficiency that support its implementation.

Residual claimants readily exist in that case of private companies whose objective is profit. The stockholders are the recipients of the residual in that case, namely profits. Management, by means of appropriate executive compensation schemes—for example, stock options—can be made to face incentives such that they share the stockholders' objective to maximize profits. The capital market also operates to provide further incentives to management to maximize profits. The market punishes poor management by driving down the price of the stock and by the threat of takeover.

With public enterprise there is effectively an absence of residual claimants. The government's interest is entirely too diffuse. Moreover, with public enterprise the discipline of the capital market is absent. H.R. 22, in proposing PCR, fails to take into account the absence of residual claimants in the public sector. In addition, it completely ignores lessons learned elsewhere. It is no coincidence that incentive regulation, and specifically price-cap regulation, has been applied almost exclusively to privately owned companies rather than public enterprises. Notably in the United Kingdom, price-cap regulation was the regulatory scheme adopted for the newly privatized enterprises—not only among network industries such as gas, electricity, telephone, and water, but also for other industries such as the British Airports Authority. The U.K. Post Office was not privatized and not subject to price-cap regulation.

Similarly, in the United States, price caps have applied primarily to telecommunications companies. The fact that those companies are privately owned largely explains the potential of price caps in achieving more efficient operation than cost-of-service regulation does. Under price caps, shareholders and top management, as residual claimants, have the opportunity to enjoy the extra profits that result from increasing the efficiency of operations. However, if the Postal Service were subject to price-cap regulation with no change in ownership or residual claimants, there is no guarantee that efficiency will be improved, as there would otherwise be no, or at best weak, residual claimants to benefit from increased profits. Indeed, additional profits arguably might be counterproductive, in that they might send a signal to postal employees that the Postal Service could pay more. Unlike a private company, the Postal Service, absent any other strong residual claimants,[6] would have little incentive to stand firm, as management would have little to gain from doing so.

In addition, a public enterprise is not subject to the pressure of competition in the same way that a private company is, in that it is insulated from bankruptcy. The insulation from the discipline of bankruptcy also means that a public enterprise, unless strongly reined in by the government, can get into competitive ventures on favorable terms and therefore compete unfairly and inefficiently with privately owned companies.[7]

Absent privatization, there is no strong residual claimant to ensure a proper allocation of scarce resources. Some efforts can be made to establish residual claimants by allowing for strong management incentives and profit targets as, for example, has been the case in Australia and New Zealand, where the post offices have been public enterprises, though the latter is now privatized. However, the government's powers to punish failure are weak compared with those of the market. Thus, in Germany and the Netherlands, the incentives for efficiency may be stronger, as in both cases either a schedule for privatization is in place or some portion of the stock is already privately owned. The implications for the USPS are clear. Absent privatization or a schedule to privatize, the benefits to be expected from incentive regulation are likely to be reduced significantly.

---

[6]It is difficult to argue in a credible manner that taxpayers are meaningful residual claimants.

[7]The revised H.R. 22 recognizes some of the problems in that it has a number of provisions requiring clear accounting separation of competitive and noncompetitive products. However, the approach proposed in H.R. 22 may be exceedingly difficult to administer. Given the common resources used to provide many of the most obvious competitive products, attempts at separation will undoubtedly lead to many complexities and additional regulations in sorting out what resources are used for various products and what cost responsibilities are to be assigned to the products. The potential for strategic behavior to discourage entry exists in public enterprise, as a recently documented example of cross-subsidies of competitive products by monopoly products in the case of the Federal Reserve Board illustrates (See Ken S. Cavalluzzo, Christopher D. Ittner, and David F. Larcker, "Competition, Efficiency and Cost Allocation in Government Agencies: Evidence on the Federal Reserve System," *Journal of Accounting Research* 36, no. 1 [Spring 1998]: 1–32). Thus, we would not be sanguine about the ability of regulators to achieve either efficiency or clear separation in the provision of competitive and noncompetitive products if the USPS continues as a public enterprise.

Similarly, in the absence of privatization and residual claimants there is little incentive on the part of postal management to address the issue of the current labor relations framework within which the USPS operates. Unless there is a change in labor practices, the improvements in efficiency are likely to be small or nonexistent. The current system involves binding arbitration. Thus, approximately 80 percent of the Postal Service's costs are effectively subject to the decision of an arbitrator. The arbitrator is not obliged to abide by the price cap. The arbitrator may award significantly in excess of the rate of increase allowed by the price cap. If that happens, the Postal Service would have no alternative but to seek rate relief on the grounds of impending financial exigency! With that system of labor relations, which arises from the public enterprise status of the USPS, there is little likelihood that the benefits of cost economy promised by price caps will be achieved in the Postal Service.

Regulation of U.S. Postal Service, Inc.

In this section we will sketch a possible scenario for the future of a privatized postal service, the aforementioned United States Postal Service, Inc., USPSI.[8] Like H.R. 22, we see USPSI as a continuing regulated monopoly. Like H.R. 22, we would propose changing the monopoly from the current arrangement, which forces private carriers to charge at least $3.00 or twice the USPS postage, whichever is greater, for express deliveries. However, our approach would be to limit the monopoly beyond the proposals in H.R. 22. We would confine the monopoly to a monopoly in local delivery.

We see our proposal as part of an evolving process. Entry has been taking place in postal service and fixed network industries over the last 10 years or so. Indeed, the USPS faced entry into its business at an early stage in the form of work-sharing, namely discounts for presorting. Unlike privately owned companies, it did little to oppose entry in that form. Similarly, its parcels business was devoured by United Parcel Service and Federal Express, which came to dominate courier service. Now postal administrations in Europe and the

---

[8]We are confining our attention to regulation of USPSI and will not discuss major open issues, that is, finance and labor relations. See Richard D. Froelke, in this volume, for some ideas on possible reform as a prelude to "privatization" of postal labor relations.

United States are beginning to face more serious threats to their traditional and basic letters business. The issue of regulatory governance when entry is allowed is now becoming as important as it is in the other network industries.

Entry by competitors in network industries has not been complete, as not all parts of the value chain are natural monopolies. Some parts of the industry can be successfully subjected to competition but there is a residual monopoly, bottleneck, or essential facility. As we argued in Crew and Kleindorfer (1998), making network industries more competitive may require the acceptance of some residual monopoly. We argued that, in such circumstances, the feasible approach was to recognize the inevitability of some regulation of the residual natural monopoly. The approach we proposed was to pare the residual monopoly to the minimum and regulate, using a form of price-cap or incentive regulation. That is the approach we would propose for the regulation of USPSI.

Currently, the postal monopoly or reserved area is usually defined in terms of a weight or monetary limit. For example, the British Post Office has a monopoly on letters priced below one pound sterling. H.R. 22 proposes lowering the American limit but is not expected to make more radical changes in the approach. In addition, the Postal Service has a mailbox monopoly. We take a more radical approach to the regulation of USPSI. We would argue that many of the upstream services such as collection, transportation, and mail processing could be subjected to increased competition, with local delivery remaining as a regulated monopoly. The postal monopoly would be confined to the local delivery network only. Local delivery would be the core or residual monopoly. USPSI would take on the role of a supplier of services wholesale and not have any retail customers. Postal administrations would provide only the local delivery networks and the sortation needed for local delivery.

Although we are not going into the details at this stage, we should emphasize that our proposal would not affect the rights of couriers and parcel operators to deliver as they currently do. They would be under no obligation to use USPSI's network for their existing services. USPSI would have a monopoly on local delivery of letter mail and small packets up to some dollar limit. That dollar limit would likely be less than the current limit of $3.00 or twice the USPS rate—whichever is higher. For example, it might be in the range of $2.00.

The problem with the proposal is that potentially it would leave most residential postal customers high and dry for some services. Unlike the other network industries, it is unlikely that in postal service the competitive market has the potential to rebundle the services required for residential and other small customers to obtain fully integrated or end-to-end service. In postal service there may be major problems of bundling together with the various parts of the postal value chain needed to provide end-to-end single-piece service for residential or other small customers. The reason is that a postage stamp, unlike a utility bill, is a low-value item leaving little scope for competitors to bundle the services necessary to provide single-piece service. That is likely to be an even more important problem in rural areas, which receive service only because of cross-subsidization. Those areas are vulnerable not only when it comes to delivery but also when it comes to collection. Similarly, very small residential customers, the Aunt Minnies, might be almost completely cut off from sending letters absent the "lifeline" offered by postal administrations. We are saying, in effect, that we cannot see much if any interest in end-to-end single-piece service for residential customers. However, because of potential scale economies arising from their collection networks, most postal administrations could handle that kind of business and receive a contribution over variable costs. We would therefore argue that the postal monopoly should consist of local delivery but that USPSI would also be required to provide end-to-end single-piece service.

The requirement to provide end-to-end service results not in an increase in postal monopoly power but rather an increase in a postal administration's universal service obligation (USO). Although it would be obliged to offer end-to-end single-piece service, there is nothing to stop consolidators from collecting mail from small customers into large batches of mail for presorting or bar coding. For large users that is done now. Some small customers might have that option if the market offered sufficient profit to make it attractive to entrepreneurs. Indeed, customers who would be targeted for the option would likely be postal administration's profitable customers; that is, the potential for "cream skimming" would exist. However, the gains from competition here are likely to be greater than the losses from cream skimming. Given that the postal administration has a monopoly in local delivery, through which it would fund its

USO, we are not concerned that such losses, if any, would affect the financial viability of the postal administration or threaten its ability to meet its USO. Another reason for taking such a route is that funding the USO in the postal context, through uniform pricing and the local delivery monopoly, would likely be preferable to setting up a universal service fund, as is the case in telecommunications.[9]

As in the case of H.R. 22, USPSI would be subject to a form of price-cap regulation or incentive regulation. Again without going into details, it is clear that the choices are between pure price-cap regulation and hybrid price-cap regulation.[10] Pure price-cap regulation allows the regulated firm to keep any profits it earns within the price-cap constraint. Hybrid price-cap regulation allows the firm to retain only a percentage of the profits it makes above a certain return on its assets. Such hybrid forms of regulation provide considerable flexibility. We do not examine specific proposals here. Our basic point is that none of the forms is likely to outperform the current cost-of-service system in the absence of privatization.

Irrespective of the form of price-cap regulation adopted, setting the starting point is a critical part of the process. The most likely approach is to have an initial rate case that essentially takes a traditional cost-of-service approach based on expected expenses and a rate of return on the invested capital or rate base. It would establish the initial prices that would then become subject to a price-cap index. The individual products would have to be placed in "baskets" for purposes of the price cap.[11] One approach would be to have two regulated baskets, for example, an "access" basket and a "single-piece" basket. Each basket would be subject to the price-cap index. The index would be based on, say, the CONSUMER PRICE INDEX minus

[9]We have examined the USO in Michael A. Crew and Paul R. Kleindorfer, "Efficient Entry, Monopoly, and the Universal Service Obligation in Postal Service," *Journal of Regulatory Economics* 14, no. 2 (September 1998):103–25.

[10]Those terms are discussed in Michael A. Crew and Paul R. Kleindorfer, "Incentive Regulation in the United Kingdom and the United States," *Journal of Regulatory Economics* 9, no. 3 (May 1996): 211–25; and Donald J. Kridel, David E.M. Sappington, and Dennis L. Weisman, "The Effects of Incentive Regulation in the Telecommunications Industry," *Journal of Regulatory Economics* 9, no. 3 (May 1996): 269–306.

[11]The index would apply to each basket separately. For example, if USPSI chose to raise one basket by less than the allowed amount, that would not be allowed as a credit to the other basket. One of the purposes of baskets is to restrict cross-subsidization of competitive products by monopoly products.

X. Setting the X factor would be important. It would have to recognize that, unlike telecommunications, technological change and demand growth are not rapid. That would imply a significantly lower X factor than those common in telecommunications. After a period of, say, five years, the price-cap period, prices, and X factor would be reviewed, following standard practices in the implementation of price-cap regulation.

Conclusion

We see considerable potential for increased efficiency arising out of our proposal. One expected consequence of the proposal would be to promote innovation not just on the part of USPSI but on the part of competitors who would introduce new products to reflect the new situation. Because of the central importance of delivery in our proposal, we would expect USPSI to be especially innovative in its approach to improving its local delivery networks. One likely consequence would be an increase in potential organizational innovations, as well as more rapid development and adoption of new technologies. For example, one area of organizational innovation is the potential for much more contracting out. USPSI might auction off franchises for local delivery networks to independent contractors. USPSI would, in effect, take on the role similar to that of McDonald's, of a franchiser of local delivery networks. Some of the networks would be operated by franchisees while others would be owned and operated by USPSI. The role of USPSI, as a franchiser, would include quality control. It would have to set standards for the franchisees and monitor the franchisees to see that the standards were being achieved. It would also be able to benchmark the performance of franchisees against one another and against networks it still continued to operate.

Normally the franchisee would operate out of a post office or other postal facility. However, the choice of different franchise arrangements is considerable. In some cases USPSI might provide the trucks as well as the physical facilities. In other cases the franchisee might provide all trucks and facilities; there are various possibilities in between. Franchising would have the effect of reducing employment by UPSPI compared with employment at the current USPS. However, total employment is unlikely to decline dramatically, as the franchisees would require labor. It is expected, however, that competitive pressures would result in cost savings and other efficiencies on the part of franchisees.

We could go on at length as to the potential benefits from privatization of USPS and the creation of USPSI. However, we should conclude with a dose of reality. We recognize that privatization of the USPS, as in the USPSI, is no more than a dream at this stage. That does not reduce our belief that it should happen. Whether it will happen is a political matter. That would get us into the realm of public choice theory, which is beyond the scope of this paper. However, that approach may provide the opportunity for fruitful research into the political feasibility of privatization.

We conclude that the case for privatization is strong. Although we recognize that a powerful case does not imply political feasibility we also know that political decisions arise from ideas. Privatization of the Postal Service is an idea whose time is overdue.

12. The Global Postal Reform Movement

James I. Campbell Jr.

While significant progress in terms of reform has been made in other public service sectors, the postal service is one of the last bastions of the old order.

World Bank study, 1996[1]

At the end of the 20th century, a wave of technological advances has brought into question the long-term viability of the core functions of national post offices. Electronic conduits for written documents are improving rapidly. Physical delivery services are becoming more specialized and better tailored to the needs of specific customers. With modern telecommunications and air transportation, the feasible scale for delivery networks has expanded beyond national boundaries. A monopolistic, government-owned provider of plain vanilla postal services is ill-adapted to thrive in the new environment.

In all developed countries, postal systems are feeling the effects of the climatic changes. Modernization of the postal sector has evolved into a broad international movement. Step by step, political leaders, civil servants, postal officials, leading mailers, and scholars are forging a new approach to national postal policy. Although mixed in different proportions in different countries, the common elements of postal reform are reduction or elimination of the postal monopoly, restructuring of the national post office as a normal company, substantial privatization of the ownership of the post office, and diver-

James I. Campbell Jr. is a special counsel for postal affairs at the International Express Carriers Conference. This paper reflects the author's personal views and should not be construed to represent the views of his clients.

[1]Kumar Ranganathan, *Redirecting Mail: Postal Sector Reform* (Washington: The World Bank, 1996). An excellent survey of postal reform strategies and the need for reform, especially in developing countries.

sification of the business of the post office. Although there exist several surveys of postal policies in developed countries,[2] this paper offers an overview of the movement as a whole to clarify the ways postal reforms in different countries have formed a coherent pattern.

The year 1988 may be conveniently selected as the starting date for the movement because of a confluence of key decisions taken in widely separated parts of the globe. In New Zealand, a government committee recommended the unprecedented step of repeal of the postal monopoly. In Australia, the government decided to transform the national post office into a corporation subject to taxes and duties like any private company. In the European Union, the European Commission began major competition and policy investigations that ultimately catalyzed adoption of a new Postal Services Directive and, more important, far-reaching reforms in several member states. Meeting in Canada, the world's top postal officials resolved to establish the International Post Corporation as a new mechanism for coordination of international mail services. Events set in motion by those decisions have influenced each other and, a decade later, continue to reshape postal policy at both the national and international levels.

New Zealand

The first country to address the full implications of new technologies for postal policy was New Zealand. In 1986, New Zealand transformed the New Zealand Post Office into a corporation, New Zealand Post, owned by the government. At the same time, the government began a comprehensive review of the case for continuing or abolishing the postal monopoly. Pending completion of its review, in 1987 New Zealand established a price limit for the postal monopoly of NZ$1.75 and a weight limit of 500 grams (1.1 pounds). In other words, a private operator was allowed to transport a letter out of the mail if its service met either of two conditions. A private operator could carry a letter whenever it charged more than NZ$1.75 per letter, about 4.5 times the stamp price. Alternatively, a private operator

---

[2]See the Price Waterhouse study, *A Strategic Review of Progressive Postal Administrations* (February 1995 and February 1996 update); Australia, National Competition Council, *Review of the Australian Postal Corporation Act 1989,* Vol. 2, Appendix 4 (February 19, 1998), a survey of postal reform in other countries.

could carry a letter weighing more than 500 grams regardless of the price charged. The government review of the postal monopoly resulted, in 1988, in a recommendation to repeal the postal monopoly after a two-year transition period during which the price limit of the monopoly would be reduced in stages. The government committee noted "there are no precedents for deregulating the letter post" but concluded "this is not a strong argument against deregulation."[3]

New Zealand Post opposed deregulation of the postal monopoly. It considered that it was already "exposed to competition from a wide range of substitutes and competing services, such as telephone, telex, fax, electronic mail, and nonregulated services." New Zealand Post also suggested that deregulation was unnecessary as a stimulus to improved postal service. It pointed to recent service improvements and the low level of postage rates in New Zealand compared with those in other developed countries. New Zealand Post further warned of jeopardy to universal postal service, "cream skimming" of urban mail by competitors, withdrawal of postal services from rural communities, a threat to the uniform national postage rate, and probable closure of more than 25 percent of post offices.[4] In the following decade, the same arguments, in virtually identical form, have been repeated again and again by post offices opposed to postal reform.

The New Zealand government was undeterred. It recognized the need to close uneconomical post offices, but rejected New Zealand Post's other claims. In anticipation of deregulation, in February 1988, New Zealand Post was allowed to close more than one-third of its post offices, retaining local shops to take over counter operations. New Zealand Post also substantially increased its annual charge for home delivery in rural areas. In 1990, the government amended the postal law by reducing the weight limit on the postal monopoly from 500 grams to 200 grams (7 ounces) and lowering the price limit to NZ$0.80 over a two-year period (i.e., by December 1, 1991). At the end of the transition period, the price ceiling for the postal monopoly

---

[3]*Report of Officials Committee to the Cabinet State Agencies Committee*, summary paper, paragraph 19 (1988). Repeal of the postal monopoly over three years was the middle ground among three options presented, and the one implicitly endorsed by the committee. The committee considered and rejected out of hand continuation of the postal monopoly without change.

[4]Ibid., full report, paragraphs 40–41.

was less than twice the stamp price. Outbound international mail was also deregulated, and New Zealand Post was required to provide more detailed annual reports on its finances and quality of service.[5]

After the 1990 act, momentum toward full deregulation of the New Zealand postal monopoly stalled temporarily. A public outcry over the rural delivery charge prompted a Parliamentary inquiry, which concluded that rural banking services (which had been provided by the Post Office) were more of a problem than rural postal services. Nonetheless, elections changed the party in power, and the new government decided to postpone abolition of the postal monopoly. Full deregulation came in 1998, when a comprehensive postal reform act, supported by New Zealand Post, abolished the postal monopoly and imposed basic obligations on private operators.[6]

The effect of the reforms on New Zealand Post has been positive. After 1990, New Zealand Post improved efficiency and introduced new services. In 1995, after five consecutive years of 5 percent growth in letter volume, New Zealand Post abolished the rural delivery fee and lowered its first-class stamp price from NZ$0.45 to NZ$0.40. New Zealand Post continues to provide universal service under an agreement with the government that limits the maximum stamp price to NZ$0.45 but does not require uniform national rates. New Zealand Post has expanded into a number of related businesses including the delivery of unaddressed advertising, e-mail preparation, express and freight services, and consulting. New Zealand Post has earned a profit every year since 1986. Its declared goal is to be recognized as "the best company in New Zealand." There are, however, no plans to sell the shares of New Zealand Post to the public.[7]

[5]Postal Services Amendment Act of 1990.
[6]Postal Services Act of 1998.
[7]New Zealand Post, *Annual Report 1998*, p. 5. See also Elmar Toime, "Competitive Strategy for New Zealand Post," in *Competition and Innovation in Postal Services*, eds. Michael Crew and Paul Kleindorfer (Boston: Kluwer Academic Publishers, 1991); Elmar Toime, "Service Performance in the Postal Business," in *Regulation and the Nature of Postal and Delivery Services*, eds. Michael Crew and Paul Kleindorfer (Boston: Kluwer Academic Publishers, 1993). Mr. Toime is the CEO of New Zealand Post. More recently, growth in letter volume has slowed (to 2.4 percent in 1998) and on-time delivery has slipped slightly (from 96 percent in 1996 to 94 percent in 1998).

Australia

In Australia, postal reform followed a course roughly similar to that in New Zealand, but lagging by two or three years. In 1988, while New Zealand officials were contemplating repeal of the postal monopoly, the Australian government was just getting around to restructuring the post office. In the Australia Post Corporation Act 1989, the national post office became Australia Post, a government-owned corporation subject to taxes and customs duties like a private company.

In 1991, the government asked an Industry Commission, a select group of experts, to undertake a serious inquiry into abolishing the postal monopoly. In an unusually scholarly report issued in 1992, the Industry Commission recommended abolition of the postal monopoly after one year. Rather than requiring Australia Post to provide universal service at a uniform postage rate, the Industry Commission proposed to allow variation in stamp prices provided no stamp exceeded a maximum rate equal to the previous uniform rate.[8] The government, however, was unwilling to go as far as the commission proposed. In the Postal Act of 1994, the price limit on the postal monopoly was reduced from 10 to 4 times the stamp price, and the weight limit reduced from 500 grams to 250 grams (8 ounces). The 1994 act also increased Australia Post's accountability for the quality of its services.[9]

In June 1997, the government launched another major review of postal policy. The National Competition Council (NCC), a five-member commission, was asked to propose practical steps for further improving competition, efficiency, and consumer welfare in the postal services sector while keeping in mind the public service commitments of the government. In February 1998, the NCC issued its final report, again a detailed and thoughtful study. The NCC recommended repeal of the postal monopoly for business mail and other measures to make Australia Post more like a business.[10] Once again, the government considered its review commission's proposal too politically daring. However, in July 1998, the government an-

---

[8]Industry Commission, *Mail, Courier and Parcel Services* (Canberra, 1992).

[9]Australian Postal Corporation Act 1989, as amended.

[10]Australia, National Competition Council, *Review of the Australian Postal Corporation Act 1989*, Vol. 1 (summary report), February 19, 1998, and Vol. 2 (detailed report).

nounced support for legislation that would reduce the price limit on the postal monopoly to A$0.45, the current stamp price, and the weight limit to 50 grams (1.8 ounces) as of July 2000.[11] After winning reelection in October 1998, the government is expected at some point to introduce legislation to implement the proposals.

Like New Zealand Post, Australia Post has thrived during the period of increasing competition. Postage rates have remained stable for more than six years, and Australia Post has earned substantial profits every year since 1987. On-time delivery has increased from 89 percent in 1989 to 94 percent in 1998. Australia Post has diversified into electronic and logistical businesses. In 1998, Australia Post estimated that almost half its revenue and more than two-thirds of its profits were earned in competitive markets.[12]

European Union

In 1988, the European Commission, the secretariat of the European Union (EU), began two related investigations into postal policy. The first was a legal inquiry prompted by private operators who complained that European postal administrations were conspiring to restrict remail competition (The U.S. Postal Service was also involved).[13] The focus of the *Remail* case was a series of meetings beginning in April 1987, in which post offices agreed on a multipronged strategy: adoption of a new schedule of interpostal charges for the delivery of cross-border mail (the "CEPT Agreement"), interception and discouragement of remail by resort to Article 23 of the 1989 Universal Postal Convention, and exhortation to post offices to refrain from working with those post offices and private operators providing remail services.[14] In response to the complaint, postal ad-

[11]Australia Post,"Review Outcome: The Government's Decision and How We'll Meet the Challenge" (July 1998).

[12]Australia Post, *Annual Report 1997–98*, p. 10. See also M. Castro, "Deregulation of Australia's Postal Services," in *Commercialization of Postal and Delivery Services*, eds. Michael Crew and Paul Kleindorfer (Boston: Kluwer Academic Publishers, 1995).

[13]*Remail* refers to mail that is produced in one country and transported by nonpostal means to a second country where it is entered into the domestic or international mail stream. Via remail, post offices, working with private operators, compete with one another for the distribution of international remail.

[14]The history and details of the anti-remail intrigues are provided in a Statement of Objections (i.e., a preliminary decision) issued by the European Commission in 1993. See Statement of Objections, Case IV/32.791 - *Remail* case (5 April 1993).

ministrations persuaded the European Commission to initiate a second inquiry, a broad review of European postal policy. By engaging the policy machinery of the Commission, postal officials hoped to delay competition by slowing down authorities working on the *Remail* case, and, during that delay, to establish a consensus that maintained universal postal service and overshadowed principles of competition law.

The policy offensive was supplemented by a commercial gambit. In late 1988, 15 leading European post offices, together with the post offices of the United States, Canada, Australia, and Japan, resolved to establish a new company to operate an international cargo airline for postal express shipments and to provide marketing and management services for international mail. The company, called International Post Corporation, opened its doors in Brussels in January 1989.

The hopes of postal officials were only partially realized. The European Commission agreed to delay a decision in the *Remail* case, but it also accepted most of the pro-competitive policy arguments put forward by economists, private operators, and large mailers. The Commission's conclusions and policy proposals were embodied in the *Postal Green Paper*, published in June 1992. The *Green Paper* and the Australian *Industry Commission Report*, issued a few months later, constitute the two major governmental policy studies of the early postal reform movement.

In the *Green Paper*, the European Commission recommended new limits to European postal monopolies: (1) Europe-wide price and weight limits; (2) liberalization of international mail, including intra-EU cross-border mail; (3) adoption of a legal presumption in favor of liberalization of printed advertising mail; and (4) liberalization of the collection and transportation of mail. In sum, the measures would have left post offices with a monopoly over the major part of their revenues while liberalizing the cross-border services that were most important to integration of the European Union (about 4 percent of all mail) and requiring member states to follow the "best practices" of their pro-competitive brethren. The *Green Paper* also urged greater regulatory oversight of postal services and transparency of accounts.[15] In the wake of the *Green Paper*, in April 1993, the Commis-

---

[15]See European Commission, *Green Paper on the Development of the Single Market for Postal Services* (Brussels: European Commission, 1992), chapters 8 and 9.

sion issued a preliminary decision in the *Remail* case that upheld the complaint of the private operators on all counts.

Despite the careful political balance struck in the *Green Paper*, postal reform proved far harder than the European Commission imagined. Political opposition from postal administrations and postal unions resulted in further delay and a substantial scaling back of the *Green Paper* proposals. In December 1997, five and a half years after publication of the *Green Paper*, the European Council finally adopted a Postal Services Directive that did little more than impose a price limit on European postal monopolies of five times the stamp price and a weight limit of 350 grams. Other deregulatory measures were postponed for another five years. In the same manner, in the *Remail* case, the European Commission in 1995 reversed its earlier findings in favor of private operators and declined to condemn the post offices. The Commission's rationale was that, even though post offices had violated European competition law, they had promised to mend their ways.

Although postal liberalization opponents were largely successful in getting the European Commission to scuttle the *Green Paper* and the *Remail* case, they could not force the genie of postal reform back into the bottle.[16] A long procession of public seminars and scholarly studies had produced a sea change in attitudes among the postal cognoscenti. Two series of scholarly seminars were especially important in the evolution of European postal thought. The first was organized by two American economists, Michael Crew and Paul Kleindorfer, beginning in 1990, the 150th anniversary of the postal innovations launched by the great English reformer Rowland Hill. A second series was convened annually from 1993 to 1997 by Wissenschaftliches Institut für Kommunikationsdienste, a German research group.[17] Such seminars provided the medium in which Euro-

---

[16]The Commission's decisions were annulled in part by the European Court of First Instance. See *International Express Carriers Conference v. Commission*, Joined cases T-110/95, T-133/95, and T204/95 (September 16, 1998). Appeals are now pending before the European Court of Justice, the supreme court of the EU.

[17]Papers from the five Michael Crew and Paul Kleindorfer seminars are available in four books: *Competition and Innovation in Postal Services* (1991), *Regulation and the Nature of Postal and Delivery Services* (1993), *Commercialization of Postal and Delivery Services* (1995), *Managing Change in the Postal and Delivery Service Industries* (1997), and *Regulation under Increasing Competition (1999)*, all published by Kluwer Academic Publishers, Boston, Mass.

pean officials learned from each other and from the more progressive reforms being carried out in New Zealand and Australia.

Postal managers and governmental officials at both European and national levels became convinced of the inevitability of competition as the future norm for the postal sector. By the mid-1990s, the growing threat from electronic substitutes hardened that conviction. The new conventional wisdom gave birth to several developments with far-reaching implications. Four deserve particular mention: the TNT joint venture, repeal of the postal monopoly in Sweden, privatization and expansion of the Dutch Post Office, and Postreform III in Germany.

TNT Joint Venture

In 1991, the post offices of France, Germany, the Netherlands, and Sweden—joined by Canada Post—shocked the international postal community by purchasing 50 percent of the worldwide express business of TNT, an Australian transportation conglomerate. It was as if Fay Wray had decided to marry King Kong. By creating a joint venture with a private express operator, those post offices gave up on the International Post Corporation. They concluded that IPC would never achieve the level of coordinated end-to-end management necessary to compete with international express services. In applying the competition rules of European law, the European Commission approved the TNT joint venture but imposed certain pro-competitive conditions, notably the requirement that the joint venture could not benefit from legal privileges available to public postal operators.[18] Although there remained skepticism over its commercial prospects, the joint venture confirmed the view of many governmental officials that the postal sector was being transformed into a competitive and international sector.

Sweden

In late 1992, Sweden became the first major European country to opt for abolition of its postal monopoly.[19] The government decided

[18]European Commission, Case No IV/M.102 - TNT/Canada Post, DBP Postdienst, La Poste, PTT Post and Sweden Post, Decision of December 2, 1991.

[19]In 1991, Finland became the first European country to abolish its postal monopoly, but that step attracted little attention because of Finland's small size and the absence of new competition.

to repeal the monopoly as of January 1, 1993, rather than suppress an upstart new entrant, CityMail. CityMail had pioneered a low-cost, twice-weekly delivery service for computer-generated mail in Stockholm, Sweden's largest city. Sweden Post supported termination of its monopoly because it concluded that without deregulation it could not obtain the commercial flexibility necessary to adapt to a changing market.

Demonopolization was followed by the Postal Services Act of 1994, which created a new legal framework for delivery services. Sweden Post was transformed into a normal stock company with all shares owned by the government. In the same year, Sweden Post applied value-added tax to all its products, like a private company. The government negotiated a three-year contract with Sweden Post for the provision of various public services.[20]

As competition intensified, Sweden Post sought to maintain its customers with an aggressive campaign of exclusivity clauses, tie-in arrangements, discriminatory discounts, and other pricing strategies. Those measures were condemned as anti-competitive by the Swedish Competition Authority. Nonetheless, the response of SPK was inadequate to protect competition. CityMail sought bankruptcy protection and was taken over by Sweden Post.[21] Although CityMail subsequently regained independence from Sweden Post with new financial backing, the Swedish experience suggests two lessons for other countries. First, contrary to postal protestations, the postal monopoly may be unnecessary to preserve universal service even in a country with very remote hinterlands. Second, demonopolization must be accompanied by a review and clarification of the role that competition rules will play in regulating the newly competitive market.[22]

[20]See Torsten Zillen, "Sweden Post: Public Operator on a Deregulated Market" (Euroforum conference, "The Liberalization of the European Postal Services," Amsterdam, 8–9 December 1994); Sweden, National Post and Telecom Agency, "Regulatory Framework for the Postal Market in Sweden" (October 1998) (a compilation of legal texts).

[21]See E. Nerep, "Current competition law issues in regard to the de-(re-) regulation of the Swedish postal services market—especially the problems of defining the relevant market and establishing price discrimination and predatory pricing" (October 1996); Swedish Competition Authority, "Postal Services: From Monopoly to Competition," Report Series R 1992:9 (October 1992).

[22]See M. Plum, "Antitrust or regulation for safeguarding competition in liberalised postal markets?" (June 1997).

The Netherlands

The Netherlands is the first, and so far the only, developed country to privatize a *majority* interest in its post office. In 1989, the Dutch post and telecommunications administration was transformed into Royal PTT Nederlan (KPN), a private law company operating postal and telecommunications services. In 1994, the Netherlands sold 30 percent of KPN to the public. In 1995, the Dutch government sold another 22 percent of stock to the public, bringing the government's share down to 48 percent.

Privatization allowed PTT Post, the postal subsidiary of KPN, to pursue an aggressive and innovative commercial strategy.[23] As noted earlier, PTT Post participated in the 1991 TNT joint venture. In June 1996, PTT Post bought out its postal partners in the joint venture (except for Sweden Post's small share).[24] In August 1996, PTT Post purchased TNT itself, thus acquiring complete control of the joint venture operations.[25] In June 1998, KPN "demerged" into two independent companies, KPN and TNT Post Group.[26] TPG is thus an amalgam of the national post office of the Netherlands and a global express company. Although privatized, TPG remains legally obligated to provide universal postal services in the Netherlands and continues to benefit from a legal monopoly over the carriage of letters weighing 500 grams or less and priced below certain limits. TPG has declared its support for termination of the Dutch postal monopoly provided potential competitors such as Deustche Post are likewise constrained to compete without monopoly support.

Germany

In December 1997, Germany completed the last phase of a three-stage postal reform program that took almost a decade to enact. In 1989, Postreform I reorganized the Ministry for Posts and Telecom-

---

[23]See P. Overdijk, "Postal Services: Competition in The Netherlands: Current Situation" (May 1996).

[24]European Commission, Case No IV/M.787-PTT Post/TNT-GD Net, Decision of July 22, 1996.

[25]European Commission, Case No IV/M.843-PTT Post/TNT/GD Express Worldwide, Decision of November 8, 1996.

[26]TNT Post Group, *1997 Annual Report*. An especially detailed report in light of the demerger.

munications by placing postal services, postal banking, and telecommunications in separate departments. Management of Postdienst, provider of postal services, was committed to a new board of directors with members from the private sector. The board introduced private-sector management and accounting practices and reorganized operations into four business groups: letters, cargo, post offices, and new business segments.[27] In 1994, Postreform II transformed Postdienst into Deutsche Post A.G., a normal corporation whose shares are owned by the government. Postreform II also amended the German Constitution to guarantee provision of "appropriate and adequate" universal postal services. Although progress toward additional reform slowed temporarily because of opposition from Deutsche Post and postal unions, in December 1997 the German parliament agreed on Postreform III. Postreform III abolishes the Ministry for Posts and Telecommunications and repeals the postal monopoly as of the end of 2002.[28]

Postreform III is arguably the most sophisticated postal reform in the world. The law recognizes universal postal service as an obligation of government, not a requirement imposed on Deutsche Post. Universal service is no longer to be funded by cross-subsidy from overpriced monopoly services. Instead, funds to cover the cost of universal service will be generated by a licensing scheme.

Every delivery service that provides carriage of addressed written communications weighing less than 1,000 grams (2.2 pounds) must obtain a license. No license is needed for services outside the "licensed area," including carriage of publications and unaddressed mail, document exchanges, and express services. Any service priced more than five times the stamp price is considered an express service. If the market fails to provide universal service within the li-

---

[27]See generally the German chapters in Price Waterhouse and Omega Partners, *A Strategic Review of Progressive Postal Administrations* (February 1995) and Price Waterhouse, *A Strategic Review of Progressive Postal Administrations: February 1996 Update* (February 1996).

[28]Postal Act (December 22, 1997). By June 1997, even economists for Deutsche Post were ready to concede: "In objective terms the present regulatory framework in the postal sector no longer bears close examination from the economic and legal point of view." P. Knauth and F. Dommermuth, "Reorganisation of the postal sector in Germany" (June 1997).

censed area, licensees may be required by a Regulatory Authority to provide basic postal service and are entitled to compensation for losses incurred. Compensation is to be paid from a fund composed of contributions from all licensees earning more than 1 million deutsche marks annually. Rates for postal services covered by license are subject to approval by the Regulatory Authority. Rates for carriage of other documents and parcels up to 20 kilograms (44 pounds) are subject to investigation for anti-competitive price discrimination. A licensee with dominant market position must provide unbundled services and post office box services for other licensees at cost-based rates.[29]

As in other countries where postal reforms have been enacted, Deutsche Post has taken advantage of its commercial freedom to expand into new businesses. In 1997, Deutsche Post purchased 18 percent of the independent Postbank and concluded a close cooperation agreement, thus partially undoing the separation of financial and postal services imposed by Postreform I. Deutsche Post also purchased parcel businesses in Austria, Poland, Belgium, and (in late 1998) the United Kingdom, establishing what Deutsche Post calls "a solid platform for its pan-European parcel mail business." In 1998, Deutsche Post purchased 25 percent of DHL, an American-born company that pioneered international express service. Also in 1998, Deutsche Post acquired Global Mail, a major U.S. exporter of international remail. Deutsche Post's goal, expressed in 1997, is nothing less than "to secure a strong position in the global logistics market."[30]

Future of the Postal Reform Movement

Where postal reform has started, it appears likely to continue. In the EU, the European Commission is expected to announce support for new Europe-wide limits on national postal monopoly laws after 2003. In the United Kingdom, after the Post Office has urged privati-

---

[29]Postreform III grants Deutsche Post an exclusive license, that is, monopoly, until the end of 2002 for the carriage of letters weighing up to 200 grams and advertising mail weighing up to 50 grams.

[30]Deutsche Post, *Annual Report 1997*, p. 49.

zation for several years,[31] the government is on the verge of introducing major postal reform legislation, possibly including privatization of a substantial percentage of the ownership. In 2000, the German government is planning to sell 49 percent of the Deutsche Post to the public. As noted earlier, additional reform legislation is expected in Australia. The postal reform movement is gaining converts as well among some developing countries.[32]

Some major countries, however, remain largely untouched by the postal reform movement. Of them, the most important, and perhaps most surprising, is the United States. Since 1995, the Postal Service Subcommittee of the House Committee on Reform has been studying postal reform and is considering modest reforms, for example, establishing a price limit on the postal monopoly of six times the stamp price and a weight limit of 12.5 ounces (350 g). The U.S. Postal Service, a government agency, would be authorized, in its discretion, to establish a private corporation to provide competitive services, currently accounting for only about 10 percent of Postal Service revenues. The corporation could venture into nontraditional services and engage in joint ventures with private companies. Although the private corporation would be 100 percent owned by the Postal Service, it could establish subsidiaries and sell shares to be sold to the public.[33] Despite the limited nature of the reforms by international standards, congressional approval is uncertain.

---

[31]In 1994, after two years of study and public debate, the Conservative government proposed reductions in the monopoly and privatization of 51 percent of the U.K. Post Office. Although supported by the Post Office, the proposal was narrowly defeated by opposition from postal unions and (apparently unfounded) concerns over the future of rural service. More recently, the U.K. Post Office's calls for reform have become increasingly urgent: "The forces of globalization are rendering obsolete the idea of a national postal market." Tim Walsh, director of International Affairs and Business Strategy, "The Governance of International Postal Networks in a Changing Market Place," *U.K. Royal Mail* (September 16, 1997).

[32]Examples include Argentina, Chile, Singapore, South Africa, and Tanzania. See generally, K. Ranganathan, *Redirecting the Post: International Postal Sector* (Washington: The World Bank, 1996).

[33]H.R. 22, the Postal Modernization Act of 1998, introduced in the 105th Congress by Rep. John McHugh (R-N.Y.), chairman of the House Postal Service Subcommittee. Just before the 105th Congress adjourned in October 1998, the subcommittee reported favorably on H.R. 22. The bill still awaits a vote of the full Committee on Government Reform.

Other developed countries in which prospects for major postal reform appear dim are France, Canada, and Japan. France led opposition to postal reforms proposed by the European Commission in the *Green Paper*. In 1997, a Senate committee reiterated French skepticism over privatization and demonopolization.[34] In Canada, in 1996, a review commission challenged the tenets of the international postal reform movement; it sharply criticized Canada Post's forays into nontraditional businesses and urged congcentration on the delivery of letters while they lasted and dissolution of the post office thereafter.[35] The recommendations were rejected by the Canadian government, but a new vision for the Canadian postal sector has not emerged. In Japan, the Ministry of Posts and Telecommunications has vigorously and successfully opposed fundamental postal reform.

The ultimate challenge of the postal reform movement will be to engender a sufficient consensus among countries to permit reform of the global legal framework. The worldwide organization of postal administrations is the Universal Postal Union, founded in 1874. The UPU meets once every five years in a general congress to revise the Universal Postal Convention, the convention regulating international postal services.

In August 1999, the UPU convened its 22nd congress in Beijing, China. Although the United States, led by the Department of State, as well as the Netherlands, Australia, and others offered reform proposals, the Beijing congress essentially rejected all efforts to move toward a more open, commercially neutral legal framework for the exchange of documents and parcels.[36] The anti-reform effort was led by Canada, France, and Japan, countries whose delegations were dominated by their post offices. The only glimmer of hope emerging from the Beijing congress was a decision to establish a "High Level Group" to study the future of the UPU. Unless the High Level Group

---

[34]Senator G. Larcher, *Sauver La Poste: Devoir Politique, Impératif Economique*, Senate Rept. No. 42, Paris, 1997.

[35]Canada Post Mandate Review Commission, *The Future of Canada Post Corporation*, Ottawa, 1996.

[36]Private operators asked the Department of State to develop a formal Statement of Position on key UPU policy issues by means of a public rulemaking. See Air Courier Conference of America, "Petition for a Rulemaking to Develop a Statement of Position of the United States Towards the Universal Postal Union," Kensington, Md., November 18, 1998.

acts with speed and boldness (and persuades the UPU to do likewise), the postal reform movement might leave the UPU behind as an unsalvageable relic of the past. Meanwhile, in 2000, the World Trade Organization is scheduled to initiate a new round of service liberalization negotiations in the context of the General Agreement on Trade in Services. Officials in and out of the WTO have suggested that postal and express services will be on the agenda. In one way or another, a new global framework for international delivery services appears inevitable, whether developed through UPU reform, WTO intervention, or a wholly new legal mechanism.

13. A Competitor's View

Frederick W. Smith

My perspective assumes that the Cato Institute is one of the few institutions that seem to have learned some lessons from history. It also assumes that people have not changed much in recorded time and that there are certain eternal truths about human nature. These assumptions apply to the subject we are here to discuss today: competing with the Postal Service.

The first "postal services" were established by the Romans. They understood the importance of rapid communications to preserve the far-flung organization of a vast empire. In fact, the Roman road system was essentially built to carry those communications, most of them military or state business. The infrastructure for that communication system heralded a modern type of market economy for the Roman Empire.

Subsequently, people marveled at the prowess of Genghis Khan in assembling his trans-Asiatic empire. However, few people recall the exquisite communications or post system he established for the purpose of controlling that vast empire, just as the Romans before him had done.

A similar pattern was reproduced with the emergence of modern society in the late Middle Ages. Modern postal systems had their inception in England during the reign of Charles I, who desired not only to have good communications but also to extort substantial taxes from the people who wanted to communicate with one another. This miscalculated overreach of authority literally cost him his life; he was beheaded.

Frederick W. Smith is founder, chairman, and CEO of FDX Corporation, parent company of Federal Express, and a member of the Cato Institute's Board of Directors.

I am sorry to report that in the recent past the U.S. Postal Service has exhibited the same lack of judgment that proved so costly to Charles I by overextending its authority beyond that which was intended by Congress when in 1871 it gave the Post Office a monopoly on the transportation of letters in this country. Prior to that time, the movement of mail was mostly a private endeavor. However, as the country moved in the post–Civil War era toward achieving its "manifest destiny," it became extremely important to establish a system of communications capable of connecting all the points of the growing domestic economy. I am confident that the lawmakers who enacted the 1871 postal monopoly law clearly understood the meaning of the word "letter," a term whose common usage had long been established.

Most physical items in the 1870s were relatively large and bulky and were transported by private transportation companies. It is noteworthy that they continued to provide that service even after the Post Office was given its monopoly on first-class letters. Many famous names with which we are familiar today, among them Wells Fargo and American Express, were in the business of transporting these physical items from one point to another. However, in the early years of the 20th century the distinction between the movement of things and letters began to blur. We started sending through the mail items that did not conform to Congress's understanding of the commonsense definition of the word "letter" under the 1871 postal monopoly law. I assume this development was directly related to the creation of the Sears Roebuck catalog. I read recently that the number of catalogs delivered in this country grew, in a relatively short period of time, from a yearly average of 6.5 billion in 1908 to approximately 13 billion in 1925.

Moreover, commodities, such as clothes, farm implements, and household items, began to be smaller and have more value. In addition, these commodities were no longer produced locally and thus had to be moved from one point to another. The increase in long-distance commerce generated by these new circumstances in turn produced an increase in the flow of commercial papers like waybills and printed advertisements. Correspondingly, the Post Office unilaterally added to its "letter" monopoly the movement of "commercial papers" and "advertisements" even though Congress did not explicitly or implicitly intend for the Post Office to have a monopoly on carrying these items. Thus, the Post Office's heavy-handed expansion of its monopoly from letters to other types of documents was accomplished through very aggressive legal steps. It continued this practice following the Postal Reorganization Act of 1970, which, inter alia, redesignated the Post Office as the U.S. Postal Service (USPS) in 1971.

Postal Service Imperialism

In one famous incident in the 1970s, the USPS responded in the affirmative to the question, "Is a political bumper sticker a letter and thus subject to the postal monopoly?" The postal official who responded to the query did concede, however, that if the bumper sticker were affixed to a bumper he would not consider it a "letter." This anecdote exemplifies the extent to which the USPS tried to overreach its monopoly authority. For many years, the USPS attempted to classify as "letters" and hence subject to its monopoly various types of items not commonly considered as such.

United Parcel Service's (UPS's) emergence as a transport delivery company in the early part of this century eventually posed a challenge to the USPS's carriage of lightweight parcels. After World War II, UPS flourished as a department store delivery company. UPS did a marvelous job of developing over a number of decades an efficient nationwide parcel delivery system that was so effective in dealing with Washington on postal rate and other relevant matters that it actually had a de facto quasi-monopoly on the movement of lightweight parcels in the United States. UPS's effectiveness along with other practical considerations, which are addressed below, compelled the Postal Service to rethink its participation in the movement of commodities and eventually to exit the parcel market.

The Postal Service discovered in the course of its daily operations that the equipment, the sorting facilities, the pickup and delivery vehicles—among other things—that function so well for the transportation of letters did not so easily accommodate the movement of bigger parcels and commodities. This difficulty is perceivable in the structure of the small postal jeep vehicles, which are specifically designed to allow the driver, who sits on the right side, to insert in post boxes lightweight publications and letters without having to leave his seat.

The Emergence of Express Mail Services

A few years ago a number of circumstances forced the USPS to re-think its expansionist strategy, which sought to encompass various items beyond its congressional mandate for a letter monopoly. In the early to mid-1970s the USPS became the subject of scathing criticism from postal customers whose very urgent parcels it failed to deliver in a timely manner. This significant shortcoming was publicized by the financial services industry and served to highlight the first breach in the USPS's very broad definition of "letters," which was set out in a series of postal monopoly regulations promulgated by the Postal Service and not by Congress.

The USPS counterpoised this attack by excluding from its monopoly very urgent communications, which it classified as "letters" although most of them were not "letters" at all. They were bond rate sheets, abstracts, manuscripts, and all sorts of other documents whose late delivery had an adverse impact on the business of customers. The nature of those items made it necessary that they be delivered "absolutely, positively overnight," to borrow a phrase coined for FedEx's incipient transportation service, which was fast and reliable. Hence, the emergence of the private express mail business was a rational response to market demands. Moreover, it emanated from the necessity to counterbalance the USPS's inefficiency by facilitating the movement of urgent communications, which the USPS duly recognized had to be excluded from postal monopoly regulations.

Notwithstanding its acknowledgment, the Postal Service attempted to carve for itself a niche in the market for an express mail service. However, it found itself unable to compete with the service features, the reliability, and the performance standards initiated by FedEx whose innovations were later emulated by UPS and Airborne. The USPS's unsuccessful foray into the express mail market is best illustrated by its declining market share, which has gone from about 45 percent of a very small market in the mid-1970s to around 6 percent today. In contrast, FedEx has a comparative share of 50 percent of that particular segment of the overnight market. The rest is divided primarily between UPS and Airborne. The express mail portion of FedEx's business actually accounts for a relatively small part of FedEx's overall revenues and an even smaller part of FDX's,

FedEx's parent company, revenues. Nevertheless, it is an extremely important segment of our business.

In the years that followed its rout from the express mail market, the Postal Service was content to focus mainly on the movement of invoices, letters, magazines, catalogs, and similar items. However, in the past decade or so it began to face a business problem with which many private companies have had to contend on numerous occasions: technological obsolescence. Letters and all the "things" that the Postal Service had subsequently categorized as such, which constituted the foundation of its monopoly, were now being diverted to an entirely different means of communication: electronic transmission. The Postal Service responded to this new innovative assault by diverting the revenue it derived from its monopoly on letters and their first cousins, publications and printed matter, and using the profits to reenter a business that was being handled successfully by the private sector.

Yet, its retreat from the overnight express mail business did not completely deter the USPS from exploring a new venture in this market. It developed a "quasi-express" product cleverly positioned between mail, which is considered slow and not very modern, and express, which is fast and provides instantaneous proof of delivery to customers. This new product was branded Priority Mail and it has, in essence, supplanted parcel post as the Postal Service's packaged-goods transport endeavor.

The problem with the USPS's vain attempts to compete in the express mail market is that there is not a shred of evidence that its entry into the field serves any public interests. There are, to be sure, important interests worthy of consideration, primarily those of postal workers and the postal family. However, a convincing argument has yet to be made to show that the public interest requires the Postal Service to use its monopoly on the movement of letters to gain an advantage in a service that can be and is being provided more efficiently by private enterprise. Moreover, it is noteworthy that these private companies, with which the USPS seeks to compete, pay taxes while the USPS does not; purchase license plates for vehicles, which the USPS does not; and, unlike the USPS, must comply with zoning restrictions and pay fees and other charges; are subject to customs laws; and are constrained by a host of government-imposed burdens.

False Advertisement?

It is not only vexing that the USPS takes the position not only that it can provide a competitive service like Priority Mail under the foregoing conditions but that it can also advertise it to the public without being subject to the same rules that govern private-sector advertising. This abuse of governmental privilege prompted Federal Express to file a lawsuit against the Postal Service for its Priority Mail advertisements because they were false and misleading. If a private enterprise like FedEx sought to imitate the USPS's advertising practice, our company would undoubtedly be found liable for fraud. The Postal Service defended itself against our lawsuit by stating essentially the following: "We're the Postal Service and we don't have to obey those rules." The "rules" to which the USPS made reference are provided under the Lanham Act, a federal law that prohibits deceptive competitive trade practices.

A recent *Consumer Reports* study published last year during peak season, the time it is most difficult for us to maintain the highest possible service levels for our customers, supports our contention that the Priority Mail advertisements are false and misleading under the Lanham Act. *Consumer Reports* found that FedEx's overnight delivery service was reliable over approximately 97 percent of the time. Our very good and able competitor, UPS, had 94 percent overnight reliability. The USPS's express mail overnight product, according to *Consumer Reports*, was 65 percent reliable. In the area of second-day delivery service, FedEx again led the pack with a reliability success rate of 97 percent, followed by UPS, which had a 90 percent rate. In contrast, the USPS, which spends hundreds of millions of dollars a year advertising Priority Mail as a two- to three-day (the latter in very small print) product, had a reliability success rate of 60 percent for the two-day service.

I want to reiterate my last statement to underscore FedEx's point about USPS's false advertising practices: Express Mail sent "overnight" via the USPS was *not* delivered overnight 35 percent of the time, and the USPS's Priority Mail (two- to three-day service) was delivered as promised 60 percent of the time. The USPS states in defense of its appalling performance that its Priority Mail service is provided with the added premium (i.e., free of charge) of Saturday de-

184

livery, a service which private transportation companies provide at extra cost. Yet, anyone who goes to the post office and asks for Priority Mail service with the Saturday delivery feature will be told by the postal clerk that the USPS does *not* guarantee that feature.

In a nutshell, the problem as I see it is this: despite vast differences between the Postal Service's products and those of private express companies, the Postal Service advertises its products as comparable to ours. Therefore, in essence, the USPS's advertising claim for such products is, to put it kindly, an incredible overreach. I would not go so far as to characterize this overreach as being as great as that exhibited by Charles I, but it is perhaps not far behind.

Legislative Reform

Now, let us consider the specific circumstances of our subject: we have a very large and distinguished public institution; it is the best in the world; it is a great value; it built this country; and it has an impressive history. I make this characterization sincerely. I like the people who work for our Postal Service. However, there are many things in American life that have had a great history, for example the cavalry. Yet, we do not do cavalry charges anymore. We must recognize that there are many institutions that long ago passed into history. Therefore, the question that the United States needs to ask itself in 1999 is as follows: should this hallowed institution be allowed to diversify into new areas and provide services that taxpaying private enterprises provide more reliably and efficiently? I believe the answer to this question is no.

This is not to say that I do not understand quite clearly the political reality and the important private interests represented by the postal workers and their families. I also understand people's interest in subsidized universal mail service, a relevant fact in the remote areas of the United States. Yet, it would be entirely reasonable to say that Congress should keep the USPS from encroaching upon competitive sectors like overnight and express mail services. Federal Express would endorse this position if we thought it were politically feasible.

However, since it is not, we support the McHugh bill (H.R. 22 in the 106th Congress) because it is a step in the right direction. It aims to separate the commercial business of the USPS, which should not be supported under any rationale by taxpayer or mailer subsidization, by moving it toward the time it should be handled on a purely commercial basis, probably by a privatized USPS, Inc. The McHugh bill would give the Postal Service time to adjust, time to become commercially more responsible. For example, it would allow the USPS to accept that it is subject to the same advertising laws as the rest of the express transportation industry. It would also begin the process of leveling the playing field. This last consideration is most important and necessary because no justification exists for the unfair advantage the USPS has been allowed to enjoy in the past few years: massive diversification without any rules to control its use of public privileges. I am also pleased to report that we applaud a recent law that shifts the representation of the United States in the Universal Postal Union from the USPS, which competes in areas where the private sector performs quite adequately, to the State Department, which has no self-interest to safeguard and thus is better able to consider the broader interests of all concerned parties in the UPU.

In closing, I would like to stress that at Federal Express we do not regard the Postal Service as an enemy. The problem I have described is not one of life, liberty, or the pursuit of happiness. Rather, it is a question of the transfer, backed by the full force of government, of rents from one sector of the economy to another. The following comparison illustrates my point: FedEx operates one flight a day to China, where there are all sorts of public institutions that engage in private business. If we follow the example of the Postal Service, why would it be impossible to contemplate a scenario wherein the Army would carry the freight of our country to China? The Army has a marvelous fleet of trucks and many skilled truck drivers. Given that it costs the taxpayer and the country a great deal to support the Army, consider how much money we could save if we were to expand the job responsibility of the Army to include the trucking business, thereby allowing us to cross-subsidize the purchase of a few extra Tomahawk missiles.

Far from being an outrageous fantasy, the foregoing illustration underscores the sophistry that underpins the Postal Service's justification for cross-subsidizing universal mail service to remote Inuit villages in Alaska. The notion that cross-subsidization can be useful in that way is a fallacy. The few examples we have in the postal area have shown exactly the opposite of their intended effects. Canada Post was allowed to acquire a private express delivery company and before long its monopoly rents were subsidizing the competitor in the commercial sector, not vice versa.

As I conclude my remarks on the Postal Service and postal reform, I hope I have made it clear that my point is not to disparage the Postal Service, which I believe is wonderful, has a marvelous historical record, and employs wonderful people. Rather, it is that I believe what the USPS is attempting to do simply does not correspond with the values of the United States of America and is not in the best interest of the citizens of this country.

PART IV

PROPOSED REFORMS

14. Congressional Plans for Postal Modernization

Robert Taub

After an 18-month review of postal policy, congressional action on postal reform initially burst forth in June 1996 when Rep. John McHugh (R-N.Y.), the chairman of the House Postal Service Subcommittee, introduced the first comprehensive proposal to modernize our nation's postal laws since 1970. Following five extensive hearings in which the subcommittee received testimony from more than 40 witnesses, Rep. McHugh proposed a substantial revision to his bill, H.R. 22, in December 1997, in the form of a lengthy paper that provided a detailed description of the way he planned to modify it. In late February 1998, Rep. McHugh asked interested persons to provide written comments on his proposed revision by April, and through that summer he drew up a new version of H.R. 22, with updated legislative language based on the public comments received. The new bill was presented to the public on September 2, and on September 24, 1998, the Subcommittee on the Postal Service agreed to approve H.R. 22 and send it forward in the legislative process.

Rep. McHugh's plan for revising H.R. 22 has not pleased everyone. In early 1998, one postal union took out an advertisement in major newspapers that proclaimed, "Our Postal Service isn't broken. The last thing we need is for Congress to 'fix' it!" Indeed, the subcommittee's review of postal policy has been going on for so long—nearly five years—that now that we finally have a proposed answer, some people seem to have forgotten the question.

In describing Rep. McHugh's reform, therefore, it seems a good idea to begin with a brief review of the developments that prompted

Robert Taub is the staff director of the U.S. House of Representatives Committee on Government Reform, Subcommittee on the Postal Service. The views expressed here are his alone.

congressional interest in postal reform. Then I shall summarize Rep. McHugh's proposals to improve the postal system, and last, I shall discuss what happens next.

Why Postal Reform?

John McHugh took over the chairmanship of the House Postal Service Subcommittee in January 1995. Looking back, it seems that one can distinguish four factors that led him to his current plan for reforming the postal system.

The first and most important factor was certainly the U.S. Postal Service's (USPS) repeated calls for reform of the regulatory system. Postmasters General have been making that demand, supported by weighty consultants' studies, ever since the Postal Service Commission failed to recommend the proposal for a 30-cent stamp in 1991. The Postal Service's case for reform, however, goes far beyond anger at regulatory interference. As then–Postmaster General Marvin Runyon put it in 1996:

> The postal world is no longer an unchanging fixture of the American scene, and significant adjustments in the ratemaking process will be needed in the coming years to allow the Postal Service to respond to the emergence of more intense competition across many of its products lines. Such reform is crucial to the long-term interests of the Postal Service, its customers, its employees, and the general public.

A marked decline in the growth rate of first-class mail over the past decade has amply underscored that point. Indeed, the Postal Service has stated that by the year 2000, some 38 billion business-to-business transactions that are normally sent through the mail will go into electronic transmissions. Today, when a Postmaster General points to the rise of e-mail, fax, the Internet, and private express companies, few challenge his assessment that "The postal world is no longer an unchanging fixture." To adapt to new times, the current Postmaster General, William Henderson, has joined his predecessor in calling for less regulation, more commercial freedom, more control over labor costs, and clear authority to offer new products.

A second development motivating postal reform has been a series of economic studies. They suggest that the United States may not be getting a good deal for its postal dollar. While U.S. postage rates are low by international standards, the postal system possibly could be doing much better. According to some of the economic studies, if the Postal Service operated at private-sector levels of efficiency, postage rates could probably fall 15 percent or more. High postage rates are protected by the postal monopoly. They lie outside the control of the Postal Rate Commission, as the PRC regulates only fairness between rates, not the overall level of postage rates. Indeed, as was the case in 1998, it is legally possible for the Postal Service to insist upon a rate increase that outpaces inflation even while it is earning large profits. Other economic studies indicate that the cost of sustaining universal service may not necessitate significantly higher postage rates for most mail, as was once believed. Various studies suggest that universal service costs account for less than 1 percent of postage rates. The high postage rates that are made possible by the postal monopoly pay for various types of inefficiency that mailers have consistently decried, but not universal service. In short, we may have universal postal service in the United States despite the postal monopoly, not because of it.

Complaints from captive customers and private competitors also played a role in Rep. McHugh's deliberations. They have argued for many years that it is unfair for the Postal Service to compete with private companies while ignoring laws that private companies must obey and loading overhead costs on monopoly customers. Whereas the previous Postmaster General argued for more competitive freedom while retaining all the Postal Service's special legal privileges, some competitors and members of Congress have argued passionately that the Postal Service should be barred from competitive markets altogether. Rep. McHugh, however, has chosen a more moderate course: to allow the Postal Service to compete in all markets, provided it does so on the same terms and conditions as are faced by private companies.

A final ingredient in Rep. McHugh's thinking has been the wave of postal reforms in other developed countries. Others have gone before us in tackling the problem of how to modernize the postal system in light of changing technologies. Germany, Sweden, New Zealand, and Finland have enacted laws to abolish their postal monopolies and force their post offices to become more efficient and commercial. Australia is not far behind. The Dutch post office is two-thirds privatized and has embarked on all sorts of new ventures.

Indeed, the European Union recently decided to limit all European postal monopolies—even in countries with inefficient systems like

France and Italy—to services priced at five times the basic stamp price or less, or to transporting items weighing 350 grams or less (12.5 ounces). Those countries have adopted postal reform laws because of the same technological and commercial pressures facing the USPS. They have done so despite the same types of political opposition that Rep. McHugh faces. And they have done so with the same commitment to preserving universal postal service in their countries that one would expect to see in this country. Americans have taught other countries a lot about regulatory reform in many industries; in the postal area, we have something to learn from others.

Where's the Beef?

So how does Rep. McHugh propose to improve the situation? John McHugh, a moderate Republican, has a background in state and local government. He has good relations with labor unions. He comes from a rural district in New York State along the Canadian border. As one would expect from his background, Rep. McHugh is looking for a postal reform strategy that will positively improve the system without threatening the future of the Postal Service, jeopardizing postal service to small towns, or disrupting the reasonable expectations of postal employees. His approach to reform is to emphasize two goals. First he wants to give the Postal Service more freedom to manage its business and compete in competitive markets. And second, at the same time, he wants to strengthen and clarify rules that protect the public interest.

To meet those twin goals, Rep. McHugh would adopt different rules for noncompetitive and competitive products. In both areas, he would give the Postal Service more commercial flexibility than it has today. In the noncompetitive area, his proposal is relatively longer on rules to protect the public interest and shorter on commercial flexibility; in the competitive area, there is extensive commercial flexibility and only a few basic rules, as competition is viewed as the primary protector of the public interest.

The dividing line between noncompetitive and competitive products is important to understanding the McHugh proposal. According to the proposal, a "noncompetitive product" is one for which the Postal Service can raise prices and not lose business to others offering similar services. Even products outside the postal monopoly can be considered noncompetitive if a mailer has no choice other than the Postal Service. That is the same test that the Federal Communications Commission used in deciding whether or not to subject AT&T to strict regulation in a given market. Over time, as genuine competition developed, the FCC gradually deregulated AT&T's services. The McHugh proposal envisions the same mechanism in postal services. If and when effective competition develops, the Postal Rate Commission—renamed the Postal Regulatory Commission under the bill—can transfer products from the noncompetitive to the competitive category.

Under that approach, the vast majority of Postal Service revenues—about 93 percent—are today earned from noncompetitive markets. According to many mailers, that is a bit too much. Indeed, according to a 1995 Harris survey (done for the Mailers Council) almost 80 percent of business executives believe more competition would result in better postal service. Therefore, taking a page from international reforms, Rep. McHugh proposes to shift the dividing line between noncompetitive and competitive products by reducing the postal monopoly for the carriage of "letters" if the price of service is more than six times the amount charged for the first ounce of the basic first-class stamp, or for any letter weighing more than 12.5 ounces. For example, with a first-class stamp price at 33 cents, the bright line for the monopoly will be letters priced less than $1.98. As a practical matter, a $1.98 limit on the monopoly moves two-pound and under Priority Mail outside the monopoly. The McHugh plan also would classify all Priority Mail as a "competitive product" immediately, since the Postal Service already uses the entire product to compete head-to-head in the competitive two-day or more marketplace. Competition from private carriers also is likely to develop fairly quickly. The result is that, under the McHugh plan, about 89 percent of Postal Service revenues would be derived from noncompetitive products and about 11 percent from competitive products.

For noncompetitive products, Rep. McHugh proposes several changes that, he believes, will streamline and improve the regulatory scheme. First, he eliminates the requirement that the Postal Service and mailers must slog through a long rate case before every change in rates. Instead, every five years, the Postal Regulatory Commission will establish a "price cap" for rate increases at the rate of inflation, measured by the Consumer Price Index, minus an allowance for productivity increases. Each year the Postal Service can increase rates for some or all products up to the price cap by giving 45 days' notice. In that way, in an approach favored by some mailers, the Postal Service will be able to schedule small annual rate increases for some products instead of larger increases every three or four years. All mailers will be assured that no rate can exceed this "CPI-X" formula.

Also, for the first time, the price cap will limit the authority of the Postal Service to raise rates whenever it feels the need for more money. Furthermore, the McHugh plan limits the ability of the Postal Service to charge noncompetitive mailers for losses and overhead costs run up in competitive markets. Under the McHugh approach, competitive products collectively must pay their fair share of overhead costs and repay past losses. At the end of each year, the Postal Regulatory Commission would "audit" the Postal Service's accounts to ensure it complies with the rules.

The McHugh proposal also would, for the first time, ask the Postal Regulatory Commission to monitor and report service levels achieved by noncompetitive products, although the Postal Service itself would continue to set the service standards. Another provision of the bill looks beyond the review process and requires the Postal Service to conduct a broad investigation into appropriate standards for universal service and to report its recommendations to Congress.

The McHugh proposal would make several improvements in the legal framework for competitive products as well. Not only will the Postal Service be able to make changes in the rates and classes for competitive products without a rate case before the Postal Regulatory Commission, it also will be able to change rates as often as it likes without advance notice. Nor will the Postal Service have any restrictions on discounts. Indeed, the Postal Service will face only two restrictions in pricing competitive products. First, the price for each product must cover its costs. Second, the revenues from all competitive products collectively must make the same proportional contribution to overhead as noncompetitive and competitive products combined. In other words, like a private company, the Postal Service may price some products more aggressively than others, but it has to pay for the practice by raising prices a little on other competitive products. It cannot simply price all competitive products aggressively and load the overhead on users of noncompetitive products. Also like a private company, the Postal Service will be allowed to finance competitive ventures without oversight by the Treasury Department, a long-time goal of the Postal Service, and at the same time it will be subject to the same antitrust and business laws to which private firms are subject. As with noncompetitive products, the Postal Regulatory Commission will audit the Postal Service's books at the end of the year to ensure that the Postal Service obeyed the rules in pricing competitive products.

Another important area that the McHugh proposal addresses is the Postal Service's authority to introduce new products. Under the subcommittee-approved version of H.R. 22, the Postal Service will be allowed to conduct "market tests" for new products for up to three years without meeting the pricing requirements of the act. That freedom applies to both noncompetitive and competitive products.

In addition, for the first time, the Postal Service will have clear statutory authority to go beyond the traditional postal business. The Postal Service will be permitted to engage in any nonpostal business or any joint venture that it deems appropriate, if it does so by means of a new private law corporation. Funding for the private law corporation is limited to money earned from competitive products. In adopting the provision, Rep. McHugh has addressed head-on the issue of the Postal Service's broadening of its mission under questionable statutory authority to engage in nonpostal activities and businesses, such as electronic commerce services. While rejecting the argument that the Postal Service should be confined to its traditional business and wither as demand for that business declines, Rep. McHugh's proposed structure for nonpostal activities prevents the USPS from leveraging its government status and $60 billion revenue stream as it does today. The proposal is adapted from the organizational provisions of Conrail, COMSAT, and the U.S. Enrichment Corporation.

Finally, Rep. McHugh proposes to bring international postal services within the same legal framework as domestic services. Most international mail would be considered "competitive products" and therefore subject to little regulation. International single-piece letters and parcels would be considered noncompetitive. Consistent with a recent statutory change, the job of negotiating international treaties affecting postal and delivery services has already been taken from the Postal Service and assigned to the Secretary of State. Under the McHugh proposal the Postal Service would be free to negotiate international commercial agreements without presidential consent, as presently required.

What Happens Next?

It seems that a postal modernization bill is inevitable in the next five years or so. Carriage of letters is the core of the Postal Service's business, and long-term decline appears certain. That means that the United States, like other developed countries, must decide whether to phase down the Postal Service or refocus its core business on competitive products. There are only two or three legislative options for refocusing the business of the Postal Service. One is to go cold turkey, abolish the postal monopoly, and bar the Postal Service from competitive markets, winding the Postal Service down as its traditional business declines. That is an approach advanced by some in Congress. Another is to operate the Postal Service as a hybrid, part public service and part competitive enterprise, allowing the Postal Service an opportunity to achieve private-sector efficiency gradually or prove that it cannot do so. This is the option chosen by Rep. McHugh and approved in a bipartisan manner by the Postal Subcommittee. Until very recently, the Postal Service had been, in effect, making a fait accompli third option: competing more and more with the private sector while retaining special legal privileges. It is doubtful that any Congress would accept such an approach after more than 20 years of deregulating America's infrastructure industries.

Whatever postal reform path is chosen, it seems likely that it will take some time for the Postal Service to adapt. The McHugh plan, if finally enacted, would set in motion a series of reforms that would probably not be fully implemented until some time in 2007 or later, the end of the first five-year price-cap rate cycle. Those who support amendments or alternatives to the McHugh plan must keep such time frames in mind. Reasoned and gradual change is the friend of all who wish to see a healthy and efficient postal system in the next century.

15. The United States' Postal Contradiction

Murray Comarow

On May 15, 1998, William J. Henderson became the 71st Postmaster General of the United States. A postal employee for 26 years, and the son of a lifelong postal employee, he bosses 823,918 clerks, carriers, and others who deliver 196 billion pieces of mail a year to 144 million businesses and households. That is more deliveries in a week than the combined United Parcel Service (UPS) and Federal Express (FedEx) deliveries in a year. Henderson took command at a propitious moment: the one-cent rate increase of January 10, 1999, is the first since 1994, the books show a profit, and service is generally good. Postal performance garners an 89 percent public approval rating, more than any other government agency, more than most businesses, and miles ahead of the people's sour view of Congress or the press.

That is not a bad legacy left to him by his predecessor, Marvin T. Runyon. In fact it is so good that we can speculate what would happen if Congress authorized the U.S. Postal Service to sell shares to investors. In this scenario, Postmaster General Henderson meets with Wall Street securities analysts to tout the financial health of his organization, citing its profitability, good service, and high public rating. On its face, an attractive opportunity.

USPS Structure

But not so fast. The Postal Service is a government entity, not "quasi-government" or "semi-private" as labeled by some pundits.

Murray Comarow is a Washington lawyer and Distinguished Adjunct Professor (emeritus) at American University, and was executive director of the President's Commission on Postal Organization and Senior Assistant Postmaster General.

It functions under contradictory and obscure statutory mandates that pose daunting and perhaps insoluble management challenges. The law requires the Postal Service to be efficient and businesslike. While it is not a business, the law requires that it behave like one.

To obey those mandates, a real business would need to be rationally organized, with a fair measure of control over its prices, wages, and facilities. In fact, the Postal Service's structure is irrational, and its managers have limited control over prices, wages, and facilities. To run the Postal Service, the President appoints nine Governors, subject to Senate confirmation. They select the Postmaster General and his deputy, and are charged by law to direct the "exercise of the power of the Postal Service." But to decide how much stamps should cost, a central revenue responsibility of its "business," the President appoints five other officials, who must also be confirmed by the Senate. They constitute the Postal Rate Commission, another government agency entirely independent of the Postal Service, and staffed by more than 50 lawyers, economists, and others.

When the Postal Service wants a rate increase, the PRC must hold hearings that take up to 10 months, involve as many as a hundred parties, and result in "recommended" rates being passed on to the Governors. The catch is that the nine Governors can only reverse the PRC if they are unanimous, a rare occurrence, and then only if they conclude that the recommended rates are insufficient to cover expenses.

The USPS wage regime also contradicts Congress' efficiency mandate. In 1970, the Nixon administration acted on Lyndon B. Johnson's initiative to reform the old Post Office Department, a patronage-saturated, money-losing operation that survived because Congress bailed it out year after year. Few taxpayers knew that their dollars made up the difference between postal revenues and postal costs. An 8-cent stamp, for example, concealed a 20 percent subsidy. If customers paid the full price of the mail, the real cost of that stamp would have been 10 cents.

In the pre-1970 Post Office, about 60,000 patronage jobs, mostly postmasters and rural carriers, were available to the political party faithful. Thousands more jobs were politically chosen, less openly. Decisions about construction and equipment contracts and locations of facilities were steeped in politics. Wages were set by Congress, with raises often coming just before election day.

The postal unions, fearful of losing their congressional ties, fought the Nixon-Johnson reform effort. Two actions bought them off. First, within a few years of the reform they received two pay raises totaling 14 percent. And second, to the proposed postal reform was added a provision authorizing independent arbitrators to set wages if collective bargaining failed. This second action must be clearly understood. Since the founding of the Republic, wages for federal employees have been set by the President and the agencies under congressional guidelines. In the case of the Postal Service alone, if management and labor do not agree, the matter goes to an arbitrator. Technically there are three arbitrators, but two are chosen by the parties, and thus the one "neutral" arbitrator actually decides cases. There is no appeal of the arbitrator's award.

Consider the effect: In 1968 the inefficient and highly subsidized Post Office Department spent 80 percent of its revenues on labor. Today, after tens of billions of dollars invested in state-of-the-art technology, supposedly to bring down costs as well as handle mail more efficiently, the ratio of labor costs to revenue still hovers at nearly 80 percent. Starting pay for a mail processor is $12.87 an hour; for a carrier it is $13.61. Fringe benefits add another 40 percent to costs. The average cost per worker runs about $50,000 a year, including retirement and health benefits. How that situation came about, from the customer's perspective, is not an inspiring saga.

In the early 1970s, with postal unions threatening unlawful strikes, frightened mailers and postal officials caved in to union demands and political pressure. In particular, they distorted or ignored the meaning of a key phrase in the Postal Reorganization Act of 1970, that postal workers should be paid "comparable to the rates and types of compensation paid in the private sector." But there were no really comparable private-sector jobs, claimed the unions. That claim might have surprised any number of companies whose clerks sort and distribute letters and packages.

Hard pressed, postal managers pegged postal wages to levels in highly unionized industries with little resemblance to postal operations, and signed off on no-layoff and generous cost-of-living concessions to boot. And so collective bargaining, with unions rattling the "no contract, no work" saber, no countervailing pressure from mailers, and an arbitrator waiting in the wings, resulted in "negotiated" contracts in 1971, 1973, 1975, 1978, and 1981. Since that time, and especially since President Reagan fired unionized air traffic controllers for their unlawful 1981 strike, unions have generally relied on arbitrators to get much of what they want. (An outstanding exception has been the National Rural Letter Carriers Association.) In December 1998, Henderson signed an agreement with the clerks union—with more than 300,000 members—that protected current outsourcing contracts but that barred further outsourcing without extensive consultation.

Bargaining and Arbitration

The ability of unions to push up wages stems in large part from the nature of arbitration, a process that undermines collective bargaining. Simply reaching agreements with management can subject union leaders to charges of "sell-out" from their rivals who aspire to leadership positions and who ask, "Why not take the next step?" Indeed, why not? Arbitrators rarely cut back on what management already offered. Bargaining with one eye on arbitration has another effect: It tempts both parties to take extreme positions, on the theory that the arbitrator will split the difference. (That is not always the case, but the perception is there.)

Binding arbitration covers more than wages. Ever see postal employees chatting it up in back of the counters when there are long lines of customers? They may well be supervisors who would like to pitch in to help customers but who cannot; the union contract will not let them. When managers tried to save costs by changing the way city carriers prepared their mail before delivery, the union protested. The issue went to an arbitrator who ruled in the union's favor. Thousands of grievances filed by postal unions are decided by arbitrators, or worse, settled by managers with strong cases who want to avoid being attacked as the bad guys.

The situation may get worse. In an August 28, 1998, interview with the *Federal Times*, Henderson said that "the Postal Service needs to hold managers accountable for losing grievances." Managers already know how not to lose grievances: Simply cave in.

Henderson is well aware of the impact of binding arbitration on wages and working conditions, as well as grievances. In a remarkable interview with National Newspaper Association leaders on July 7, 1998, he said,

> I think that binding arbitration doesn't allow management and the unions to be true, because you don't have to work out your problems. It's like siblings fighting—you don't have to solve it. I could go to my mother or father and they'll make a decision. Binding arbitration keeps you in that sibling rivalry. Because there are no consequences to it, there's no fallout from it. There's no strike, there's no blackout. There's none of that. So you end up squabbling and then going off saying, "Well, Mama made that decision. And that's it." That's OK when you're mediocre in your performance. But when you get to be more competitive that's no longer appropriate. You've got to fix it.

The first Postmaster General since postal reform in 1970 to confront this smoldering issue, he will receive little support. The Clinton administration and Republican and Democratic members alike of Congress actively seek union funds and votes. Shortly after Henderson's appointment, Rep. John M. McHugh's (R-N.Y.) Postal Service Subcommittee held oversight hearings, including another look at the sheer volume of grievances. One member after another, Rep. Benjamin A. Gilman (R-N.Y.) in particular, held management responsible. "How could you let things get so bad?" was the theme from both parties.

I thought Henderson, an uncommonly articulate and quick-thinking man, might say something like, "Mr. Chairman, we take our share of the blame. But it takes two to tango, and even some of our best managers have a high level of grievances because some union reps have their own agendas." No such response came, only promises to do better. He might also have pointed out that union representatives in grievance proceedings are on full pay, and some are paid a healthy per diem, in addition, out of union funds. Not exactly an incentive to settle. Rep. McHugh's H.R. 22 proposes a study of labor relations, but the arbitration issue would not be addressed by that study.

Even the mildest reform measures are likely to experience heavy weather. Rep. Henry Waxman (D-Calif.) told the National Association of Letter Carriers convention on July 17, 1998, that he opposes legislative reform: "We don't think the postal system is broken, and we don't need any drastic changes." Rep. Waxman is the top Democrat on the Governmental Reform Committee, which passes on reform measures. The union's president, Vince Sombrotto, promised to influence the 1998 elections "like we have never been involved before." Citing postal profits, Sombrotto said, "We want our share." American Postal Workers Union President Moe Biller chants his mantra, "Show me the money."

On September 21, 1998, Rep. Gilman (R-N.Y.) offered this amendment to H.R. 22:

> It is the sense of the Congress that nothing in this section should restrict, expand, or otherwise affect any of the rights, privileges, or benefits of either employees of the United States Postal Service, or labor organizations representing employees of the United States Postal Service, under chapter 12 of this title, the National Labor Relations Act, any handbook or manual affecting employee labor relations within the United States Postal Service, or any collective bargaining agreement.

It would take a lot of hard research to find a more deferential provision.

Costly Post Offices

At this point, our hypothetical security analysts are glancing at their watches, but they ask more questions and learn that this "business," as some postal officials call it, directed by Congress to be efficient, suffers from still more constraints.

Most small post offices lose money. Many could be replaced by "contract postal units" in local stores that are open during commercial hours, rather than 9:00 a.m. to 5:00 p.m. There are 6,050 such units in the United States, including 20 in the Washington, D.C., area. The 1970 postal reform law, however, erects a high barrier: "No small post office shall be closed solely for operating at a deficit. . . ." As a result, only a relative handful have been closed, usually after a two- or three-year procedure, and only after satisfying the PRC—another government agency, remember?—that procedures were meticulously followed and that the closing did not result from a deficit.

The Drug City Pharmacy in Dundalk, Maryland, has had a Contract Postal Unit since 1977. Its average yearly revenue is more than $320,000. The Postal Service pays the owner, Harry Lichtman, $15,960 a year. It is a good deal for the Postal Service. No facility to build or lease, and a need to pay only modest compensation. What is in it for Lichtman? Traffic, the engine that drives retail businesses. His CPU does not take bulk mail or set meters, but it handles everything else his customers need: stamps, parcels, money orders, and the like.

Pointing this out enrages the 28,000 postmasters, whose associations (they are offended if you call them unions, although their behavior is scarcely distinguishable) swing into action. The National Association of Postmasters and the National League of Postmasters are longtime rivals, but on this point they are united. They also bargain hard for more money, restoration of cost-of-living allowances, paid convention leave, and more.

In any event, closing small post offices is a dead or at least a moribund issue. Neither Henderson nor his predecessor has shown any taste for taking on the politically powerful postmasters. Both said that they have no plans to close unprofitable post offices. In fact, I myself do not advocate wholesale closure of small post offices; their value cannot be entirely measured by economic yardsticks. But case-by-case conversions to contract operations that give better service at lower costs should not be entirely taken off the table.

Benefits for Nonprofits

Postal reform also is stifled by political pressures to protect nonprofit organizations, more accurately termed the nonprofit industry, that receive special rates under the postal code. Represented by both the Alliance of Nonprofit Mailers and the National Federation of Nonprofits, their clients get their money's worth. Effective January 10, 1999, a few hundred sales letters from your local hardware store will cost 13 cents each. Similar letters from a nonprofit soliciting money will cost 7 2/10 cents each. That is because the Postal Service is permitted to charge nonprofits only half of the "institutional costs" that normal businesses are charged.

Because the law requires the Postal Service to be self-supporting, the result is that private businesses and personal mail subsidize the nonprofits. Congress is free to make that decision. It should implement it, however, by appropriating funds to the Postal Service—or directly to the favored nonprofits—rather than take it out of the hides of the rest of us.

Possible Reforms

The 1970 postal reform statute was a huge leap forward. It abolished patronage, forced the Postal Service to live on its income rather than on taxpayer subsidies, and permitted good men and women—especially women—to get the good jobs that had been cherry-picked by politicians. But a quarter century's experience reveals the need for change.

Most important is to deal with control over prices and wages. The PRC is a unique anomaly: a small bureaucracy layered on a big bureaucracy, with virtual control over prices and other functions. Neither the Postal Reform Commission nor the Senate or House reform bills three decades ago envisaged it. It was a last-minute, ill-conceived insertion by Sen. Gail McGee (D-Wy.), chairman of the Post Office and Civil Service Committee, and should be abolished. Full due process hearings should be conducted by a panel of three expert administrative law judges (detailed from other agencies) to protect the interests of all parties. Their decision should be subject to review by the Governors, as in the case of decisions by other rate-ssetting agencies, and the federal courts.

The usual objection to eliminating the PRC is that monopolies should be regulated. After all, the argument goes, corporate monopolies such as utilities are regulated by federal or state agencies. Although superficially appealing, that line of reasoning ignores the differences between private and government monopolies.

In the case of a corporate monopoly, shareholders look to management to maximize profits. In the case of the postal monopoly, there are no "profits" in that sense; the law requires that the Postal Service break even and that rates be set equitably and in the public interest. There are no similar guidelines on UPS or FedEx, which set their rates, as they should, based on corporate self-interest.

Wages should also be set by the Governors after collective bargaining and nonbinding mediation. The mediator's recommendation should be advisory to the Governors, who have the duty to balance "comparable" wages with service and budget needs.

The statute should also be amended, as the McHugh bill provides, to require appointment of Governors who have had experience in running large enterprises. The first Governors appointed by President Nixon were such a group, but most later appointees, however public-spirited and distinguished in their fields, lacked the background necessary to direct the activities of a huge, complex organization.

It is time, as well, for Congress to reconsider the question of part-time Governors. That they more than earn their pay is beyond dispute. Most Governors invest far more time and energy than their $30,000 annual pay covers. Their responsibilities are so complex as to justify substituting nine part-timers with five full-timers, who would appoint the Postmaster General, as today. That arrangement would continue to insulate the Postal Service in some measure from political pressures.

Legislative reform is essential if the Postal Service is to survive, but the reforms presently contemplated, some of which have value, are marginal, not fundamental. There is no present crisis, but every postal official and knowledgeable mailer knows that the economic trends are grim. The highly profitable "correspondence and transactions" category of mail (bills, bill payments, bank statements, letters) is threatened by new technology and changing business practices. That category represents 59 percent of postal revenue, and the Postal Service's share of the market is declining. The same is true of package services, international mail, and special services. Only advertising mail and periodicals are stable, but the marketplace is changing rapidly.

Lobbying by competitors such as UPS, FedEx, and newspaper associations is increasingly intense and effective, partly as a result of the Postal Service's inept handling of its relations with Congress before Henderson's regime. UPS president James Kelly has stepped up his public relations and legal assaults on the Postal Service, arguing that it does not compete fairly because it does not pay taxes and is exempt from parking restrictions and the like. Kelly demands a level playing field, but neglects to mention that the Postal Service carries a mandatory public service burden: to provide universal service at uniform prices that largely flow from arbitrators' wage decisions. Some observers unkindly speculate that the UPS assault may be partly calculated, in the spirit of "Wag the Dog," to draw attention away from the continuing effects of its own ineptly handled 1997 strike.

The question that Congress and the administration should face is not what is best for the Postal Service. It is what kind of Postal Service, if any, is best for the nation. The options range from privatization à la the Cato Institute's libertarian philosophy, to return to direct political control. Neither of those extremes nor any other fundamental reform is on the table. The key features of Rep. McHugh's bill involve price caps, productivity offsets, and financial incentives to encourage employees to be more efficient.

Another wrinkle in the McHugh bill would divide postal functions between competitive and noncompetitive activities and require equivalent revenue contribution between them, a proposal that ignores market realities. The former would be run like a private company that would be subject to taxation and state and local regulation. Incredibly, there are no limits on the activities that company could undertake. Bifurcating the Postal Service in that way would create a whole new array of intractable management problems. In any event, the bill evades the root causes that may either erode the Postal Service or require the huge taxpayer subsidies that kept it afloat until 1971. I am reminded of the late Eric Sevareid's dictum that "the major cause of problems is solutions."

Reform from Where?

The securities analysts have stopped looking at their watches and are edging toward the door, thinking, "Why is this guy wasting our time? The Postal Service is sliding toward oblivion, it cannot control its costs, it cannot set prices, it cannot close unprofitable offices, its business customers subsidize its nonprofit customers. Forgetaboudit."

They are right, and there is no major player or group of players in the postal arena able and willing to tackle the pathologies. Consider the following:

- The Clinton administration enjoys massive union support and is not about to jeopardize it.
- Republicans likewise court union votes and money; in the past 10 years, more than one-third of union members voted Republican in congressional races.
- The fractious mailing community is a whirlpool of contentious interests—first-class mailers, advertisers, cataloguers, parcel shippers, and nonprofits cannot seem to set aside their conflicting goals and unite even on cost control, which should be an

overarching issue. (Full disclosure: A major advertising mailer is a client.)
* The Postal Service itself does not have the stomach for a full-court press. I asked former Postmaster General Marvin Runyon on several occasions why he did not propose genuine legislative solutions; he said that any such proposals would be Dead on Arrival.

He may have been right, but he was wrong, nevertheless, not to lay the facts before the Congress. The Postal Service deserves much credit for good performance with one hand tied behind its back, but it can stay in business only by holding down labor costs, or by contracting out large chunks of its operations, and by finding large new sources of revenue (never mind the coffee cups and T-shirts). It has already outsourced its Priority Mail system to Emery Worldwide Airlines; it signed a $1.4 billion dollar contract in 1997. Emery is doing what postal clerks and mail handlers once did: processing the mail, but at lower cost. The clerks' union wants that contract terminated and aims to block future outsourcing. The city and rural carriers unions take the same position against outsourcing.

When Henderson took the helm, he promised to focus on public policy, people, and performance. A major public policy issue is the monopoly on first-class mail, and its traditional offspring, the sanctity of residential mailboxes. On August 31, 1998, at the annual Postal Forum, Henderson predicted that the Postal Service will not be able to maintain its letter monopoly indefinitely, nor will Congress continue to block private delivery to mailboxes. His prediction hung in the air; no message was delivered as to the pros and cons of the monopoly and the mailbox restriction. If the monopoly is eliminated, will Congress free the Postal Service from its universal service mandate, or from price regulation? Not a chance.

On the same occasion Henderson said that the Postal Service "needs to be deregulated and commercialized." As the latest version of H.R. 22 would in fact strengthen PRC regulation, will he resist those provisions? In the September-October 1998 issue of *Mailing Systems Technology*, Bill McCart wrote,

> Without [monopoly] protection, private companies will pick off the high-volume markets and offer service at well below USPS rates. Private companies will be able to do this and still make a profit, because they can decline to serve . . . any area that isn't profitable. If it wants to

continue providing universal service, the USPS would have to scrap its current rate structure. That means the end of all one-price-anywhere-in-the-country rates, especially first-class mail. . . . You might pay, in today's dollars, 15 cents to send a letter within your city, but 98 cents to mail it to a rural area on the other side of the country. (p. 8)

This is not necessarily all bad. What is bad is to permit the Postal Service to slide into such a situation without prior analysis. A careful examination will not occur unless the Postal Service itself faces the basic contradictions embedded in the present law and proposes clear and bold steps to deal with them.

Some will argue that Postal Service proposals to eliminate arbitration, reduce the power of the PRC, and the like would be Dead on Arrival, as Marvin Runyon said. That may prove to be the case, given what is described as "political realities," but not necessarily. The DOA prophets are often wrong. In 1967, postal reform was also thought to be DOA by the chattering class. The same is true of the creation of the Department of Defense and a separate Air Force: Few believed that the West Point-Naval Academy lobbies could be defeated. The same is true of the Environmental Protection Agency, established in the Nixon administration, in the face of powerful Democratic committee chairmen eager to preserve their turfs: Health Education and Welfare—air pollution, Interior—water pollution, and the like.

Congress has been kind to postal competitors. In October 1998, acceding to corporate lobbying, it took from the USPS and put into the hands of the State Department the power to negotiate international mail agreements. Nor will the Postal Service represent the United States at the Universal Postal Union. A State Department official told me privately that State did not seek those responsibilities. Even more remarkably, there were no congressional hearings. It is possibly relevant that for 1997 and the first half of 1998, UPS was number one in corporate political action committees ($1,766,976). FedEx was third ($1,352,296).

Other competitors include Parcel Express; Mail Boxes, Etc.; and the Coalition Against Unfair Competition, which claims to represent about 10,000 businesses. Yet another coalition, the Main Street Coalition for Postal Fairness, says it represents mailers responsible for 40 percent of mail volume. All lobby against misuse of monopoly power and deplore postal plans to offer fund transfers, copy service, and the like. The conference report on the notorious 3,823-page 1999 Omnibus Budget bill, passed three hours after it was moved for adoption, requires the Postal Service to delay any new competition or nonpostal services until it reports to Congress, a clear shot across its bow and another victory for the lobbyists.

The organizing principle of postal reform in 1970 was to provide a public service in a businesslike way. That mandated a reasonable degree of insulation from politics. Powerful symbols of that guiding principle were removal of the Postmaster General from the Cabinet, abolition of patronage, and reliance on customers, not taxpayers, for revenue.

Starting with binding arbitration and the PRC, the Congress has undermined that principle. Bit by bit, it has further weakened it, and in the next legislative session, it may recreate an unmanageable institution, affording its competitors and critics an excuse to return it to a politically driven agency, or to privatize it.

That may be welcomed by some of the players in this game, but it could be bad news for the millions of individuals and businesses who rely on the mail. The Postmaster General understands that situation, but understanding is not enough. Diagnosing the legislative pathologies of our society is appropriate for academics and the prime-time talking heads. Leaders search for ways to translate insights into political action.

In the present climate, especially with Republicans still struggling with the 1998 election results, that will be extremely difficult. It will require mobilizing support from the more far-sighted mailers, and perhaps even one or two associations or unions who see reform as responsive to their own concerns. A blue-ribbon presidential commission would probably be the most effective approach, but do not hold your breath.

Other possibilities include an all-encompassing study by a highly credible group, perhaps a joint American Enterprise Institute–Brookings Institution effort. That study might draw on former Postmasters General, Governors, and PRC chairmen, as well as the usual suspects. But the game cannot begin before the kickoff, and that is up to William J. Henderson.

16. A Free Market Critique of Postal Reform

Douglas K. Adie

The Post Office was set up to facilitate communications when America was a frontier and horses carrying messages constituted the national communications network.[1] Today private firms and individuals send messages via telephones, cell phones, faxes, cable, computers, television, e-mail, and private package delivery and overnight express services. Private banks wire funds instantaneously anywhere in the country and the world, and stocks are bought and sold online. Communicating is no longer a problem. But the U.S. Post Office (USPS) has not changed sufficiently in light of the communications and information revolution.

In 1970 the Post Office was reorganized. The new USPS eliminated much of the political patronage and partisan politics that often determined who received appointments and promotions. But reorganization has not yielded efficiency. For example, after 30 years the Postal Service still spends some 80 percent of its total revenues on labor, as it did before reorganization.

To meet future challenges the Postal Service could consider contracting out for more of its labor-intensive services and other cost-cutting measures. But such actions usually yield marginal results[2] and inevitably run into union opposition. In fact most efficiency gains, from the use of new technology or contracting out, simply re-

Douglas K. Adie is a professor in the Department of Economics, Ohio University in Athens, Ohio, and author of *Monopoly Mail*, published by the Cato Institute. Although he is grateful to his colleagues at Ohio University for their suggestions, the opinions expressed are his alone.
[1]See Peter J. Ferrara, "Postal Service Problems: The Need to Free the Mails: in *The Last Monopoly*," ed. Edward L. Hudgins (Washington D.C.: Cato Institute, 1996), p. 26.
[2]Douglas Adie, *Monopoly Mail: Privatizing the United States Postal Service* (New Brunswick, N.J.: Transaction, 1988), pp. 79–81.

sult in higher salaries and benefits or reduced workloads for the remaining workers. In addition, contracting out creates new interest groups that support the status quo against substantive reform. Private contractors and suppliers such as airlines or independent truckers, with whom the Postal Service might contract, will oppose privatization to protect their arrangements with the USPS. It seems that the only remedy for future declining revenues is for the Postal Service to continue to seek new sources of revenue by offering new services.

A legislative reform that takes account of this strategy is H.R. 22, which was first introduced in the House of Representatives by Rep. John McHugh (R-N.Y.) in 1996. That approach attempts to separate the Postal Service's monopoly functions (i.e., first- and third-class mail delivery, which face no competition) from the competitive functions that face private-sector suppliers. Under H.R. 22 the Postal Service would be allowed to introduce new services but those services would be subject to most of the same taxes and regulations that private competitors face. Although the approach might seem promising in principle, a look at the details suggests it would create even greater problems, including an unfair advantage against competitors.

The Firewall

H.R. 22 would create within the Postal Service separate entities for competitive and noncompetitive services. New services could be introduced through a private law corporation. Under that arrangement the Postal Service could engage in partnerships or joint ventures with private firms. Within three years those services would have to pay their own way or request an extension of support. Further, after an incubation period the competitive operations are supposed to contribute to the overhead costs of the Postal Service.

Crucial to such an arrangement, however, are the "firewalls" that separate the Postal Service's competitive and noncompetitive functions. Firewalls sometimes are employed by private businesses. Bank holding companies, for example, under federal law have had to keep their insurance, brokerage, investment banking, and regular banking functions separate. Even the trading department of an investment bank is not permitted to communicate with the mergers and acquisitions department for fear that the former might discover which companies the latter is acquiring, and trade on that information to the detriment of their customers and market integrity. Also the Glass-Steagall Act, which was recently repealed, did not even allow brokerage and investment banking functions within the same four walls of a bank, lest the important function of a bank related to the provision of money to the economy be confused by the bank's need for capital to finance a lucrative corporate reorganization.

The most effective form of firewall in the private sector is physical separation, as Glass-Steagall had required. Each company or division will have separate personnel, offices, equipment, capital, and accounts devoted solely to its particular tasks. In other words, an effective firewall requires internal reorganization of resources, not just reorganization on paper. General Motors provides an example of an effective firewall. Each division—Buick, Cadillac, Chevy, Oldsmobile, and Pontiac—has separate plants, employees, products, and revenues. GM has a strong financial incentive to maintain such an arrangement. Separating production of different automobile models into different divisions enables GM's management and, ultimately, its owners, to monitor costs, revenues, performance, and profits for each division. Such information helps GM to reward or punish the divisions that do well or poorly, making the entire company more efficient and profitable.

Under H.R. 22 the Postal Service would be divided more on paper than in reality. The same buildings, equipment, trucks, and personnel likely would do double or triple duty as they do now, facilitating both competitive and noncompetitive services. Such an arrangement raises serious problems concerning the way revenue from the different postal functions would be allocated to cover fixed costs. In theory it would be done on the proportion of revenue generated by the different postal services. But such an approach leaves a lot of room for creative accounting and cross-subsidization. In the first instance, an accounting separation alone would be extremely difficult to accomplish. For example, is it realistic to expect that every worker can be closely monitored to determine how many minutes are spent on functions for different services? USPS officials themselves protest that the accounting necessary to maintain even that paper firewall between various functions is unworkable. Another problem is that the "profits" generated by competitive activities are to be used to fund or expand such services as well as to pay bonuses to managers and workers. Such a provision creates incentives for the competitive functions to foist as much of their costs on the noncompetitive activities as possible so that the competitive functions will contribute less to overhead costs and show higher profits out of which bonuses can be paid.

Under H.R. 22 a Postal Regulatory Commission (a reorganized Postal Rate Commission [PRC]) would monitor the activities and accounts of the Postal Service in an attempt to maintain the integrity of the firewalls. From one perspective that would be a good thing. The new PRC perhaps could bring to light inefficiencies in the Postal Service, problems that currently are glossed over. But the Postal Service itself will have an incentive to obfuscate if not outright misstate information. Ultimately, paper firewalls will burn. They will not be able to record accurately the expenses of the competitive and noncompetitive postal services, and thus will be unable to allocate costs appropriately.

Innovation and New Products

Under H.R. 22 the Postal Service would be allowed to introduce new experimental services that would have a three-year grace period in which to become profitable. That period could be extended if it has not achieved its goal but can show prospects. It could even enter into partnerships with other companies to offer such services. But the Postal Service has a poor record of innovation. That raises the question of what happens if a new, competitive USPS enterprise fails? Will the taxpayers be stuck with the bill?

In the past when the Postal Service employed new technology such as the letter-sorting machines, the efficiency gains did not reach customers in the form of lower postage rates, or the public as a dividend on its investment. Instead, such gains were squandered to cover the costs of other inefficiencies, including wage increases for existing employees, featherbedding, increased employment, and even graft.[3]

So can the Postal Service meet the challenge of offering innovative services? The record suggests not. For example, the Postal Service's

[3]For a discussion of this thesis, see Adie, footnote 27, pp. 165–66.

package volume fell by more than 50 percent between 1959 and 1979.[4] Perhaps part of the explanation was that the government carrier damaged half the packages marked "fragile."[5] Certainly part of the explanation was the emergence of private package carriers like United Parcel Service. To meet the challenge, instead of addressing quality problems head-on, the Postal Service between 1971 and 1976 created a National Bulk Mail System with 21 major and 12 auxiliary regional bulk mail facilities, at a cost of nearly $1.5 billion. Each center occupies a strategic location and processes all bulk mail—including parcels, circulars, advertisements, and magazines—passing through its area with elaborate and expensive machinery. Despite the expenditure on that network, the bulk mail network, the USPS did not recapture its parcel post business; UPS still carries some 90 percent of all parcels.

The Postal Service in 1982 introduced E-COM. That system allowed customers to walk into one of 25 post offices, have a postal employee e-mail a message to someone via one of the other 25 post offices, with mail carriers able to deliver the message the next day or even the same day to the recipient. Unfortunately it could still take two days or more to deliver the message. Rep. Glenn English (D-Ak.) chairman of the Government Operations Committee, concluded that E-COM "certainly looks like a turkey and it gobbles like a turkey."[6] For each E-COM message the Postal Service charged its customer only $0.26 during the first year of the system's operation, while the actual cost was $5.25. By the time the system was terminated in 1985 it was still being subsidized by more than $1.00 per letter.[7] The Postal Service set up a similar system in 1979, INTELPOST, an electronic mail service to send instantaneous facsimile copies between continents. The USPS grossly overestimated the size of the market for this service. The USPS' provision of the ser-

---

[4]*Report of the Commission on Postal Service*, Vol. 1 (Washington, D.C.: Government Printing Office, April, 1977)

[5]U.S. General Accounting office, "Observations and Questions on the Development of the National Bulk Mail System," (Washington: General Accounting Office, 1974), p. 18. Also see John T. Terney, *Postal Reorganization: Managing the Public's Business* (Boston: Auburn House, 1981), pp. 59–60.

[6]*Washington Post*, December 4, 1983, quoted by James Bovard in "The Last Dinosaur: The U.S. Postal Service," Cato Institute Policy Analysis no. 47, February 12, 1985, p. 7.

[7]"Postal Service May Close Its Electronic Mail Service," *Wall Street Journal*, June 7, 1985, p. 14.

vice was unreliable, consumers did not purchase it, and the venture failed, too, in 1984.[8]

Under H.R. 22 the Postal Service is supposed to meet the costs of producing any new service within three years. But a serious problem would arise if the new services fail, as many no doubt will. When a private firm fails, the owners lose their investment, workers and managers lose jobs, and assets of the company are sold off to cover debts. But what will happen if a service offered by one of the Postal Service's new divisions continues to lose money? That division would not be able to make its contribution to overhead costs, meaning that revenues from the noncompetitive postal services will have to make up the difference.

Further, running an operation for three years that in the end does not break even means incurring a lot of debts. If the noncompetitive part of the Postal Service covers initial investment costs, that would mean that the Postal Service, that is, customers or taxpayers, would have to absorb the losses. If a division offering a new competitive service borrows from the private sector and, in effect, goes bankrupt, how will those costs be covered? Normally in the private sector the creditors would seize assets. But would that be allowed or possible with public assets? Could Postal Service equipment, trucks, or buildings be sold to cover debts? When the same facilities are used for competitive and noncompetitive services, it would be difficult.

What would happen if a competitive division were in a joint venture with a private firm? We see that even without legislation, the Postal Service is engaging in such ventures. For example, it has begun a partnership with Seattle-based Airborne Freight Corp., the third largest express-delivery company.[9] The Postal Service has given Airborne a 60 percent discount on postal rates for the delivery of its packages to residential addresses. Airborne will presort packages and transport them to the local post office closest to the delivery address; then local mail carriers will deliver the packages on their regular routes. The USPS also is planning to offer a joint two-day service to Europe in conjunction with DHL of Brussels.

[8]"INTELPOST: A Postal Service Failure in International Electronic Mail" (Washington, D.C.: U.S. House of Representatives Government Operations Committee, April 11, 1984), p. 9.

[9]See "U.S. Post Office Plans to Deliver For Airborne," *Wall Street Journal*, Vol. 21, No. 1, June 3, 1999, p. A28.

Although not part of current legislative reform proposals, USPS divisions offering competitive services might be allowed to sell stock to raise capital. Such a situation, some would argue, would inject private market incentives into such divisions. After all, shareholders would put pressure on competitive service divisions to operate in the most efficient manner and would help make certain that all profits are not eaten up by management bonuses and pay increases. (Such pressure certainly would be diluted, as the government likely would retain majority shares in such operations.)

But in the case either of joint partnerships or of shareholders, if a USPS competitive division could not meet its costs, the same problems would occur as with a division with no private-sector participation. Worse still, the private parties would be a constituency that would pressure the government for a bailout, either from USPS revenues or through a special appropriation.

Rate Setting

Another problem with H.R. 22 concerns the new rate-setting process it would establish for postal services. In a competitive market system, prices are established by supply and demand. When there are no barriers to entry, new firms will enter if the prices charged for goods or services by an existing firm are too high. As new firms enter, the supply increases and drives down prices to the average firm's break-even point, where price equals average cost equals marginal cost. That is also the lowest average cost and the most efficient production point where resources are being used in their highest valued way. The price is optimal for consumers and any deviation from this price is suboptimal.

The Postal Service, as a government monopoly, faces no competition for first- and third-class mail delivery. Thus it has an incentive to choose "profit-maximizing" prices for the same service, and even to discriminate in pricing, charging different customers different rates. Mailers of advertisements for local stores might be able to place more ads or circulars in local newspapers if postal rates are too high; that is, the mailers have a high price elasticity. The Postal Service might charge them lower rates because they have alternatives to the mail. Higher rates might mean that the USPS would lose substantial business. Citizens with fewer alternatives, that is, with a

217

lower price elasticity, who have few cost-effective ways to pay monthly bills other than through the mail, could be charged higher prices. To deter such profit-maximizing behavior in the absence of market competition, the PRC currently must approve the rates that the Postal Service can charge. When the USPS wants to change rates or introduce new services, it must apply to the PRC. After a lengthy process the PRC makes recommendations that the Postal Service can accept, modify, or reject, but only with the unanimous consent of the Postal Service Board of Governors.

H.R. 22 changes the way rates are set. Specifically, it would require the new Postal Regulatory Commission to establish a five-year "price cap" for rate increases at the rate of inflation (that is, Consumer Price Index) minus an allowance for productivity. Rate caps would apply to a bundle of services but not to any specific service. Under H.R. 22 the Postal Service would be free to practice price discrimination between different customers as long as it did not violate the rate cap on its bundle. The complexities of the new approach would provide many opportunities for the USPS to manipulate rates to maximize profits rather than run its operations more efficiently.

The Postal Service no doubt would justify, for example, giving large mailers significant price discounts, based on the lower costs of processing large volumes of mail. Yet the Postal Service officials have at times claimed that most of its costs are fixed rather than variable, and that the infrastructure for collection, sorting, transport, and delivery all operate at about the same cost whether the volume of mail is large or small. If that is true, there is little savings from processing a few large rather than a lot of small orders. In other words, the Postal Service's schedule of prices for the same service enables it to maximize profits rather than increase efficiency.

H.R. 22 does establish some small checks on such pricing policies. First, the price charged for each entire competitive product must cover at least its variable costs. But determining such costs when numerous products use the same infrastructure is problematic. Second, revenues for all competitive products taken together are supposed to make the same proportional contribution to the overhead of the infrastructure of all products taken together. But not only is such a determination itself problematic; it also must be made after the fact. Only after extensive accounting and audits is there even a hope of finding that proportion. Even the H.R. 22 regime seems to recognize those problems since it allows for use of a fudge factor, the so-called Z-factor, to be used in the computations of rates. Further, H.R. 22 contains no mechanism to force compliance with this payment system.

Other Problems

The reforms proposed in H.R. 22 contain other problems. One concerns the issue of "residual claimants." Private firms are owned by stockholders or shareholders who receive dividends when the firm makes a profit. Left to their own devices, workers and managers would consume all profits as higher salaries and bonuses. Thus owners, who are separate from management, monitor and check managers. They elect the board of directors, which hires, fires, and uses stock options to give managers an incentive to preserve the residual profits for themselves. If owners cannot hold profligate management in check, the company will not produce profits, share prices will fall, and perhaps corporate raiders will buy a controlling interest in the company and make the changes in management necessary to restore profits.

Public enterprises like the Postal Service, however, have no residual claimants and no discipline from the capital market. Under H.R. 22, profits from competitive services would be paid to Postal Service workers and managers, not as wages and salaries but as a bonus at the end of the year. That approach is meant to give management and workers an incentive to be productive. But in fact it would give Postal Service employees an incentive to convert or use USPS assets, including some 40,000 USPS properties nationwide, to produce profits that they would consume as bonuses, unchecked by owners that would look out for the efficiency of postal operations. Under H.R. 22 the new Postal Regulatory Commission could prevent the dispersal of up to one-half of the profits as bonuses if performance goals and service standards are not met. But that means that even in situations of egregious abuse and inefficiency, Postal Service workers and managers would still receive one-half of the profits. Further, it is questionable whether the new commission would have the political fortitude to withhold any part of the profits.

Another problem with proposed postal reforms concerns how complaints about postal practices are resolved. Currently, when the

Postal Service wants to raise rates or begin a new activity or even make a significant change in how it operates, it must secure the approval of the PRC. Further, private competitors and other interested parties can bring complaints about unfair USPS practices to the PRC.

Currently, PRC rulings can be overturned only by the unanimous consent of the USPS Board of Governors. Under H.R. 22 most of those issues will not even come before the new PRC, and new PRC rulings on rate issues can be rejected or modified with only a two-thirds vote of the Postal Governors. That provision weakens an important protection for the private sector and postal customers.

Conclusion

Policymakers and USPS officials all seem to recognize that the U.S. Postal Service's days as a traditional government monopoly are numbered. The trend toward privatization is worldwide. Sweden and New Zealand already have repealed their postal services' monopoly status and sold company shares to the public. Germany will make an initial public offering of shares in Deutsche Post in the year 2000.

The dangers of holding onto inefficient and outdated monopolies is seen in the case of Guatemala. That country's government postal monopoly is so inefficient that private carriers for both domestic and international deliveries have sprung up and, while technically illegal, are tolerated by the government because without them Guatemala's mail would stop flowing. Private firms handle approximately 70 percent of Guatemala's mail. The government itself uses such carriers to send out telephone and water bills, court summons, municipal tax notifications, and other important papers.[10]

The question is not whether the USPS should be privatized, but when and how. The H.R. 22 approach pretends to move the USPS in the direction of privatization in open-ended steps with no clear vision. A better approach would be to radically privatize:[11] repeal the

[10]The information in this section comes from Carroll Rios de Rodriguez, "Pushing the Envelope: Guatemala's Private Delivery Services," *Regulation* (Winter 1998): 41–48.

[11]See Douglas K. Adie, "Breaking Up the Postal Monopoly," in *The Last Monopoly*, pp. 121–30, where I recommend abolishing the private express statutes, spinning off the parcel post and overnight mail business, then dividing the remainder into a support-services company and five regional delivery companies, which are all sold to the public.

monopoly and other special privileges; break up the Postal Service into private companies and sell them to private investors and employees. Then, and only then, should the Postal Service, as a private company, be allowed to introduce new services and enter new lines of business, on a completely fair and equal basis with all private competitors.

Index

Cato Institute

Founded in 1977, the Cato Institute is a public policy research foundation dedicated to broadening the parameters of policy debate to allow consideration of more options that are consistent with the traditional American principles of limited government, individual liberty, and peace. To that end, the Institute strives to achieve greater involvement of the intelligent, concerned lay public in questions of policy and the proper role of government.

The Institute is named for *Cato's Letters*, libertarian pamphlets that were widely read in the American Colonies in the early 18th century and played a major role in laying the philosophical foundation for the American Revolution.

Despite the achievement of the nation's Founders, today virtually no aspect of life is free from government encroachment. A pervasive intolerance for individual rights is shown by government's arbitrary intrusions into private economic transactions and its disregard for civil liberties.

To counter that trend, the Cato Institute undertakes an extensive publications program that addresses the complete spectrum of policy issues. Books, monographs, and shorter studies are commissioned to examine the federal budget, Social Security, regulation, military spending, international trade, and myriad other issues. Major policy conferences are held throughout the year, from which papers are published thrice yearly in the *Cato Journal*. The Institute also publishes the quarterly magazine *Regulation*.

In order to maintain its independence, the Cato Institute accepts no government funding. Contributions are received from foundations, corporations, and individuals, and other revenue is generated from the sale of publications. The Institute is a nonprofit, tax-exempt, educational foundation under Section 501(c)3 of the Internal Revenue Code.

CATO INSTITUTE
1000 Massachusetts Ave., N.W.
Washington, D.C. 20001

DATE DUE